AGAINST THE TIDE

*Women Reformers
in American Society*

Edited by **Paul A. Cimbala**
and **Randall M. Miller**

PRAEGER

Westport, Connecticut
London

Library of Congress Cataloging-in-Publication Data

Against the tide : women reformers in American society / edited by
  Paul A. Cimbala and Randall M. Miller.
    p.   cm.
  Includes bibliographical references and index.
  ISBN 0–275–95806–X (alk. paper)
   1. Women social reformers—United States—Biography. I. Cimbala,
Paul A. (Paul Alan), 1951– . II. Miller, Randall M.
HQ1412.A343   1997
303.48'4'092273–dc21   96–47662

British Library Cataloguing in Publication Data is available.

An expanded, hardcover edition of *Against the Tide: Women Reformers in American
Society* is available under the title *American Reform and Reformers:
A Biographical Dictionary* from the Greenwood Press imprint of Greenwood
Publishing Group, Inc. (ISBN: 0–313–28839–9).

Library of Congress Catalog Card Number: 96–47662
ISBN: 0–275–95806–X

First published in 1997

Praeger Publishers, 88 Post Road West, Westport, CT 06881
An imprint of Greenwood Publishing Group, Inc.

Printed in the United States of America

The paper used in this book complies with the
Permanent Paper Standard issued by the National
Information Standards Organization (Z39.48–1984).

10 9 8 7 6 5 4 3 2 1

Copyright Acknowledgment

Excerpts from Betty Friedan, *It Changed My Life*, reprinted by permission of Curtis Brown, Ltd.
Copyright 1963, 1964, 1966, 1970, 1971, 1972, 1973, 1974, 1975, 1976, 1985, 1991, by Betty
Friedan.

Contents

Preface

This collection of eleven essays derives directly from a larger work, *American Reform and Reformers* (1996), in which all but one of the contributions to *Against the Tide* originally appeared. This paperback edition focusing on women reformers includes an essay on black abolitionist Mary Ann Shadd Cary, written by Paul A. Cimbala expressly for this volume, and a revised introductory essay on the character of American reform and women's place in it. The essays are arranged in a rough chronological order, charting the development of American reform over time and the interplay of American women reformers across a spectrum of reform activity. The essays, thus, not only discuss women's roles in reform but also offer lenses to see reform through the eyes of different women.

In selecting the reformers and reforms represented in this collection, we made no attempt to be comprehensive. Women were (and are) invested in so many different reforms, their influence on the character of American reform was (and is) so pervasive, and reform has shot out in so many directions that any attempt to provide total coverage of women in reform or of American reform would be futile. Rather, by offering a series of case studies showing women in a variety of American reform movements, *Against the Tide* tries principally to mark the basic contours of American reform thought and action and to locate women within the American reform tradition. In so doing, it challenges the assumption that men's experience counts as *the* narrative for any historical event or movement.

Each essay stands on its own, with its own story and its own particular history of a woman reformer and a movement. None of the subjects was a minor figure, and none of the reforms was a fringe movement. Each essay also suggests how particular individuals worked out their own ideas. When read together, the essays show that American reform and American women intersected in countless complex ways and that neither men nor women have an exclusive claim to the American social conscience. The essays also remind us that women's social and political activism is no recent invention. From the first days of the republic through the end of the twentieth century, women have been organizers as well as advocates of social reform. All the women included in *Against the Tide* were both organizers and advocates for particular reforms. Each essay, then, discusses both the person and the movement.

The essays are about women reformers and American reform. They are not written as "women's history" per se, which is to say that they do not attempt to engage directly the historiographical issues roiling in that field. That said, it is useful to note that the essays might be comfortably situated in what historian Gerda Lerner has termed "the third stage" of women's history—namely, the effort to analyze how and why gender mattered in human experience. Rather than viewing their subjects in terms of "compensatory" or "contributory" history where the intent is primarily to identify women in history and catalog their contributions, the authors have tried to understand how and why these *American women reformers* engaged society as they did and how such engagement affected American institutions and life.

Finally, a word about the title. In America, reformers generally, and women especially, have swum against currents of public opinion and complacency and insisted that the American people and polity steer toward social justice. As such, reform has demanded strenuous, sustained effort to stay on course. The women represented in *Against the Tide* charted different routes to social reform, but they converged in their belief that making such journeys was necessary for the betterment of both self and society. And so it has proved to be.

In bringing together these essays into a paperback edition, we again thank all those people and institutions who made the parent volume, *American Reform and Reformers*, successful. That book and their efforts also made *Against the Tide* possible. Regarding the paperback edition, both Cynthia Harris and Alan Sturmer at the Greenwood Publishing Group encouraged and guided this project with intelligence and efficiency. Marion Roydhouse and Katherine A. S. Sibley improved the introductory essay by their incisive comments. In preparing the new material for this edition, we found congenial conditions and ready assistance, not to mention excellent resources on American reform, at the Canaday Library of Bryn Mawr College, the Magill Library of Haverford College, the Van Pelt Library at the University of Pennsylvania, the Drexel Library of Saint Joseph's University, and the Duane Library of Fordham University.

Introduction

RANDALL M. MILLER

This collection of essays focuses on important American women reformers and the reforms they most directly affected or led. Each chapter combines biography with historical analysis of a particular reform to establish the context and character of the movement each woman embodied or represented. The chronology of subjects treated runs from the early nineteenth century to the present. The experience of *American* reform dictates such an approach, for since the dawn of the republic, American reformers, women and men, have believed in America as a special, even divinely ordained, society capable of building a more perfect world. The germination of reforms over the past two centuries attests to the persistent power of this belief.

The idea of America as a regenerative force preceded, and in some ways even precipitated, the creation of an independent United States, but it emanated most powerfully from the American Revolution. The Revolution fostered both an obligation and an opportunity to reshape government, society, and even the human condition. Freed from the past, Americans could make their own future. Such liberty also made Americans self-conscious and critical of their republican experiment. Without a sense of purpose and without self-criticism, Americans believed, no nation could prosper and no people could properly govern themselves. American reformers from the late eighteenth century until today have used revolutionary rhetoric and invoked the Revolution's legacy to justify their calls for reform and renewal, though admittedly others have drawn on similar language and inheritance to contest the means and ends of various reforms. Although no consensus about the exact course of American reform emerged from the Revolution or after, an abiding sense of special purpose, of reform, has run through American history. Women, as these essays collectively suggest, have been central to that process.

Since the days of the Puritans, Americans have sought to reconcile individual responsibility and community demands. However much they have celebrated getting ahead and elevated self-made men to political and social pedestals, even ignoring the means by which such men acquired their wealth and power, Americans also have charged all people, women and men, with moral responsibilities to their communities. The Judeo-Christian core of American morality, especially the powerful Calvinist cast of early American religion and rules of public behavior, combined with the American Revolutionary sense of mission to invest the nation with a moral character and obligation. If America was the "new Israel," a redeemer nation, as countless sermons and speeches have echoed since the dawn of the republic, it must, reformers insisted, in fact build a just society, lest God visit His wrath on America as He did on the Israel of old. Indeed, during the nineteenth century God's judgment seemed imminent to America's largely Protestant intellectual and religious establishment, still imbued with a scriptural sense of time and worried about the commercial and industrial transformation of the nation. Then, too, many reformers believed that Americans needed to act while their institutions and society were still in a plastic state capable of being reformed. Before the mold was set, reform had to occur.

Until the age of the Enlightenment, religious fervor was the principal spur to popular social protest. During the nineteenth century, religion still inspired and guided much social reform, and women especially translated conscience into social concern. But liberalism and socialism also emerged by the late nineteenth century as potent new springs of social protest and campaigns for reform. While often including a vigorous political thrust aimed at remaking the state as the agent for improving the human condition, both liberalism and socialism shared the belief in the possibility of building the good society in this world rather than waiting for divine judgment. Now was the time to act. Moreover, adherents of liberalism and socialism also rejected the past as a model for what should stand as a proper social order.

The belief in the mutability of American society gained popular strength from the liberal tradition that harks back to the days of Jefferson and Jackson. Americans generally have believed in progress, as the prospects of improving their condition and creating a new society require that they do. Such beliefs have pointed Americans' civic and moral duties away from self-indulgence and toward a sense of collective responsibility for others. Reformers unvaryingly reminded Americans of those obligations.

Prosperity added to the moral obligation of the few to share their wealth in ways that would improve the lot of the many. In his "gospel of wealth," Andrew Carnegie summed up an attitude underlying much American belief when he argued that prosperity must bring about public good. Although Carnegie and many other Americans left the final responsibility for uplift with the individual rather than the society, as historian Daniel Boorstin observed in *Democracy and Its Discontents* (New York, 1974), one of the "great unifiers" holding a diverse people together is that the struggle for equality and justice "has been, in large part, the struggle of some Americans for the rights of *other* Americans,'' and the ''some'' often were ''haves'' reaching out to ''have nots.'' The activism of propertied whites in the antislavery and civil rights crusades or the concern of such ''patricians'' as Eleanor and Franklin Roosevelt for the downtrodden are but two examples of such outreach.

The sense of common purpose, from its various sources, has encouraged and shaped American reform for over two centuries. It has helped make possible the translation of sentiment into interest, the mobilizing of popular support to right moral and civic wrongs. It also has made American reform less radical than it might have been had the sources of reform and the reformers themselves come from desperation and alienation.

American reform has been almost wholly homegrown. While borrowing and adapting ideas and responding to ideological and philosophical impulses from abroad, American reformers largely have relied on native ideas, interests, and identities to make their case for particular reforms. Jane Addams, for example, visited Toynbee Hall in London and sat at the table of Tolstoy in Russia, but the settlement house movement she did so much to establish in the United States was adapted to American circumstances and needs and rooted in American institutions and language. Opponents of reform—from proslavery apologists who charged abolitionists with being agents of a British conspiracy during the 1840s and 1850s, to business leaders who claimed labor organizers were agents of European socialism and anarchism during the 1880s and 1890s, to segregationists who labeled civil rights activists as agents of Soviet communism during the 1950s—have depicted reformers as outsiders. By using the language of their native American culture and by being principally natives of that culture, however, American reformers have been able to counter claims that the changes they have proposed are ''un-American.'' The reformers' emphasis on persuasion rather than violence, and their interest in recruiting popular support, repeatedly have pulled reform close to the center of American consciousness and conscience. Because of their own faith in American democratic values and institutions, American reformers have operated openly rather than in secret societies. In the United States, which French observer Alexis de Tocqueville rightly characterized as a nation of joiners, reform succeeded by appealing to Americans' voluntarism, by enlisting people who wanted to combine to effect change. It was this very voluntarism that gave women an opportunity to join in, even to lead, efforts to remake society.

The chapters in *Against the Tide* focus on *reform* rather than radicalism—on the reshaping and redirecting of society rather than its uprooting. In emphasizing reform over radicalism—indeed, in distinguishing between the two—it is useful to recall Raymond Williams's *Keywords: A Vocabulary of Culture and Society* (New York, 1976) in which he observes that such terms as ''reform'' and ''radical'' are fluid and sometimes interchangeable, and that their meanings are grounded in particular historical contexts. However much American reformers might not deserve the label ''radical,'' many of them were regarded (and in several instances regarded themselves) as radicals in their own day and proposed substantial changes in social structure and the redistribution of power. This was often true of women, who generally have had to operate outside the normal channels of public power and whose insistence on being heard at all was itself a call to reorder society and polity. In fact, the lines separating reform from radicalism have remained blurred and porous, making clear distinctions between reformer and radical problematic. One generation's radical outcast might be embraced as another generation's reformer hero or heroine. The abolitionists, for example, were so transformed in Northerners' collective estimation from the 1830s through the Civil War.

Throughout American history, radical ideas have informed and inspired reform effort, and reforms have become radical. Antislavery, for example, moved from the cautious, gradual abolition strategies of the Quakers and the Revolutionary-era generation to the immediatism and moral certainty of the evangelicals and Garrisonian abolitionists. Internal tensions regarding direction and purpose within a "reform" movement might make it conservative and radical at the same time. Such was the case in antislavery when the failures of gradualism and moral suasion gave way to calls by some for accommodations with and entrance into the political world, and calls by others for self-purification and further removal from the corrupting influences of society and politics.

Still, reform and radicalism were (and are) not wholly synonymous. They have sought and had different outcomes. One of the striking common characteristics of American reform over time has been its combination of idealism and realism, with pragmatism often tempering visionary portraits of what American society ought to be. Reformers expected to change society by argument and action. Understanding American society and beliefs, adapting to political realities, and appealing to public conscience and self-interest forced reformers to consider the practical aspects of how to enlist popular support for their ideas and programs. Where true radicals were alienated from the larger American culture, which they considered as beyond redemption, reformers, women among them, commonly sought alliances with powerful elements and the public in a culture they hoped to redeem.

American reformers generally operated outside of government, but they expected their words and actions to affect public policy. Few prominent reformers have held national governmental office. Disfranchised until the twentieth century, women reformers often had no choice but to use extra-legal means of protest and to rely on moral suasion and lobbying rather than ballots to inform public policy. Such tactics worked best at the local or state levels, where women exercised real political influence even before they won the suffrage fight. Women and men reformers did have political ideas. And they fought for them.

Defining government's place in reform proved more difficult. During the nineteenth century many reformers, from temperance supporters to health advocates, emphasized individual self-control as the way to the improvement of self and society. In the words of Ralph Waldo Emerson and Margaret Fuller, among others, social amelioration began with self-regeneration. But during the twentieth century many reformers, from prohibitionists to environmentalists, have looked to government to regulate private as well as public behavior. The emphasis in reform shifted increasingly, if still incompletely, from internal to external control, and from voluntarism to public agency. The sheer numbers of people needing assistance in such matters as education, health, nutrition, employment, and equal access to public institutions and places made reformers look to agencies able to provide adequate resources and to cope with the size and complexity of social problems in the modern age. As government became more important in all aspects of social life and policy, more reformers focused attention on its structure, politics, and personnel. Some reformers, especially the Populists and Progressives and modern civil rights activists, made civic reform central to their overall programs for social and economic change. For many women reformers, civic reform meant equal access to government and power.

Despite the importance of government in reform thinking, the essays in *Against the Tide* emphasize social rather than civic reform. In part, this reflects a difference in style and strategy between men and women, though, admittedly, from the anti-saloon campaigns through Progressivism, women marched in the vanguard of the boot-out-the-bosses and clean-up-government crusades. In a larger sense, the emphasis on social reform fits the American reform pattern. Civic and social reform were never separate, but reformers tended to look to improvements in government as a means toward a more general social transformation rather than an end in itself. An undercurrent of distrust of government courses through American history, and even those reformers most insistent on using public policy have remained ambivalent about entrusting too much authority to government. Indeed, some modern reformers have charged that from Roosevelt's New Deal through Johnson's Great Society, government has blunted the thrust of reform, muting and even transmuting it in ways that reinforce rather than reorient American institutions. They have warned that conceding responsibility for reform to government rather than assuming it themselves has left Americans morally flaccid. From the 1960s on, in fact, one of the most powerful forces in American reform has been the effort to return moral and civic responsibility to the individual, making each person feel responsible for keeping the environment clean, deciding about abortion, coming out for civil rights, supervising school curriculum and programs, and more. In any case, reformers, not government, have initiated change; government has responded to and managed social changes proposed and demanded by those outside government. The essays in *Against the Tide* reflect that struggle between private and public controls that has marked American reform throughout its history.

One of the more significant developments in American life has been the growing specialization of people's skills, interests, and occupations. The complexity of modern life and the demands for efficiency often have discouraged a holistic approach to solving social problems. Social reform, too, has become specialized. Throughout much of the nineteenth century, one would find an interlocking directorate of American reformers; the same individuals engaged in a host of social reform efforts ranging from penal reform to antislavery to temperance, under the overarching assumption that all evils were interconnected and so required coordinated action to cleanse America. As late as the 1890s, Frances Willard linked temperance, anti-prostitution, public school reform, pacifism, and woman's suffrage in a "do everything" strategy to bring all of society under review. During the twentieth century, reformers tended to focus on a single issue, sometimes to the exclusion of all others. To be sure, a Jane Addams and a Dorothy Day, among others, moved outward from single concerns to a more embracing vision of change, and antiwar activists and feminists of the 1960s and 1970s framed their protests in global terms; nevertheless, specialization is one mark of modern American reform that distinguishes it from its nineteenth-century forebears.

American reform neither was nor is linear. Reforms crashed upon America in waves, each with, in the words of Ronald Walters in *American Reformers 1815–1860* (New York, 1978), "a decade or more of intense activity followed by periods of relative apathy about social problems." Intense reform activity erupted during the 1830s and 1840s, the late nineteenth and early twentieth centuries, the 1930s, and the 1960s but abated soon after each surge, generally when a war siphoned off and redirected reform energy to the nation's service. Each wave left residues of reform interest and strategy in the American consciousness that subsequent reformers picked up, and many reform movements long outlived their founders because of the institutions they built. Still, each reform surge has had its own character and focus. Each new reform generation wrote its own agenda, built its own institutions, fashioned its own instruments. The religious assumptions and drives of antebellum reform receded by the twentieth century as science advanced in public respect; reliance on self-control yielded to demands for governmental regulation; and so on.

No particular reformer personality type emerges from the collective biographies of American reform. Although some reformers came from reform family traditions and many held strong religious convictions, we can see no single factor that determined why they became reformers. The cultural context and even family background that pushed one person toward reform might have pulled another person away from it. Regarding context, it is significant that as early as the 1830s it was possible to make a career of reform. Increased literacy rates, technological advances that reduced the cost of printing, and transportation improvements that created a national market for ideas as well as goods allowed one to make a living writing books and editing a newspaper or journal. Reform became a profession, however low-paying and precarious. For women, especially, a life in reform promised a way to exercise public power by influencing public opinion and by building institutions. Yet the specific personality factors which inclined people to devote their lives to a cause remain unclear. It did of course matter that women reformers were women.

Women's impact on American reform has been profound. The sheer numbers of women who have enlisted in social reform activity over time gave them a political force rare among nations. Perhaps only Great Britain in the Western world had so many women engaged in reform movements during the nineteenth and early twentieth centuries. In the United States, women were in some sense expected to care about the morality and character of society. Whether as "Republican mothers" after the American Revolution nursing their children with patriotism and moral instruction; or as Progressives in the early twentieth century pushing for clean milk and Americanization programs for urban, immigrant children; or as "modern women" today demanding equal access to and respect in school and workplace for all—American women have had public responsibilities to keep the nation's conscience, if not more.

Women reformers did not struggle alone. The cross-pollination of reform activity, especially during the nineteenth century, led to groups of women and men reformers who shared common, and widespread, reform interests. The visibility of reform, first in the age of the penny press and later with muckraking journalism, meant that reformers would know of one another if they did not in fact know each other. For women, knowing about, as well as knowing, other women reformers gave them greater credibility and confidence as critics of American society. At the same time, because men, too, engaged in many similar reforms with women and in some cases even followed their lead, reform was not "devalued" as "women's work." A "feminization" of particular reforms, especially ones like the woman's suffrage movement that focused primarily on achieving rights or social justice for women, did occur, with an attendant public tendency to dismiss such reforms as "trivial," but the centrality and vitality of women in other reforms, such as Progressivism, temperance, pacifism, and civil rights, to name several, added to the energy and appeal of those reforms. Still, as the essays collectively suggest, women did not spend their reform energy everywhere. Some issues, such as educational reform, temperance, and anti-lynching, attracted them more powerfully than others.

For women in reform, the personal became political. Much discussion about power has been framed in terms of a dichotomy between the public and the private spheres. Recent work, especially by feminist scholars, has recast the narrative about power to suggest that no clear boundary separates public and private. By such redefinition, "political" activity historically was not just running for or holding office, or even voting; rather, circulating petitions, managing boycotts, sewing flags, organizing relief, defending morality, and so much more, all constituted "political" action and interest. More than anything else, voluntary associations allowed women to democratize the political order and to socialize themselves to civic duty. Also, as Sara Evans has written in *Born for Liberty: A History of Women in America* (1989), by creating "new public spaces—voluntary associations located *between* the public world of politics and work and the private intimacy of family—women made possible a new vision of active citizenship unlike the original vision based on the world of small farmers and artisans." Women remade politics. What emerges from such a perspective is the recognition that women's involvement in American political and public life was natural and varied, if also contested.

The terms of political engagement and public interest differed over time and according to place. During the nineteenth century, for example, urban middle-class Northern women had both more latitude and opportunity for collective reform action than did rural Southern women. Just getting together to meet was easier in a city with bells and clocktowers to mark the time. Even in the twentieth century, the telephone and automobile could not break down the social isolation within suburbia that inhibited women from organizing. In one sense, Betty Friedan, who lamented the loss of the "convenience" and ready contacts of city life when she moved to the suburbs, found in organizing women a way to restore social bonds necessary for social reformation. So, too, during the nineteenth century concerns over the human costs of rapid industrialization and urbanization were more immediate and real for Northern women than for Southern ones. Amid the jostling, noise, and smells of teeming river wards, it was not possible to escape the fact that the world of the New England village was passing away, its culture and leadership under assault. A new social order demanded social action—or so some women and men thought. Meanwhile, codes of honor in a patriarchal society rooted in racial slavery constrained the public roles of Southern white women. The Grimké sisters of South Carolina had to leave the Old South in order to criticize it.

Middle- and upper-class women who had domestic servants and leisure time had more advantage in organizing and sustaining reforms than did poor women forced to struggle each day just to feed and raise a family. A woman might forego marriage and family for a life of activism, and even find a "family" or community within reform, as did several women represented in this book; in doing so, they often challenged society's conventions about what a "true woman" really was and ought to do. Most women reformers came from backgrounds of at least modest wealth and had the education and resources to devote time to reform, but women activists came from all classes, colors, and conditions. Women's involvement in reforms raised questions about "woman's place" in American society.

Not surprisingly, opponents of particular reforms used women's presence in them to argue that the reform itself "corrupted" public morality and threatened social stability by taking women from their "proper sphere" in the home and thrusting them into the sordid world of politics and commerce. Sometimes, though, criticism of women as reformers came from within reform movements. Many antislavery men, for example, recoiled from the idea that women could address "mixed gatherings" of men and women. And in having to choose whether to link woman's suffrage to black suffrage after the Civil War, Radical Republicans hardly flinched when they put black voting ahead of bringing women to the ballot box. The radicalism of woman's suffrage, they argued, would bring down any support for black enfranchisement if the two causes were hitched together.

Whatever the concerns about women in public life, many Americans thought that women ought not, or could not, be indifferent to public morality. Indeed, during the nineteenth century, the assumption of woman's supposed innate moral superiority that argued for her confinement to the home to practice "domesticity, piety, and submissiveness" also argued for her role as the moral arbiter within the home and, by implication, for such a responsibility in society generally. Some women reformers followed that logic to claim public—and, thus, political—authority outside the home, in education, temperance, anti-prostitution, and a host of other reform concerns that persisted into the Progressive era. The argument for women's supposedly more highly developed moral sense echoes even today in political rhetoric. And it thus still cries out for women's engagement in American public life. Other women reformers rejected notions of woman's special moral gifts, warning that such an argument meant accepting perpetual inequality. They instead insisted on all the political rights due them as human beings in a democratic polity. They argued that women were political creatures by natural right and, as such, had the duty to understand and shape public life and institutions.

Women in reform also were political because they sought power to shape society, whatever the disavowals by some reformers that they had any "political" ambitions or goals. Many women reformers understood the difference between "influence" and "power" and moved toward acquiring the latter. During the antebellum period, for example, antislavery women held fairs that raised large sums of money that financed the publishing and lecturing activities of antislavery men; such fundraising gave women "influence" but not "power" within the movement, as they came to understand when men did not consult them over strategy or accept them as leaders. Indeed, the women's rights movement sprang directly from the frustrations of women reformers in the antislavery and temperance movements, where women's contributions were often limited by social conventions. Likewise, a spur to the modern women's rights movement came during the civil rights crusade when men would not let women sit in on strategy sessions. Such snubs caused women reformers to press for real power on their own terms.

They had the skills to do so. In what historian Eleanor Flexner termed the "century of struggle" to gain the ballot and the right to hold office, women demonstrated remarkable organizing and advocacy skills. Women acquired such skills by running women's clubs, lobbying for pensions for Civil War veterans and widows, or performing myriad behind-the-scenes tasks during political campaigns that kept women from the polls but profited from their petition drives, fundraising, and ballyhooing of candidates. In those and any number of other ways, women learned enough about politics and, more important, gained enough confidence in their own ideas and skills to get the vote and a measure of political respect. The ways that women reformers found allies, built coalitions, formed networks—all political skills—are explored in various degrees in the following chapters.

No single woman's voice emerged to speak *for* American women, or reform, and no consensus among women ever congealed regarding any single reform question—there were antisuffragists, too. Many factors in addition to gender influenced how (and if) women and men approached any reform issue. Examining a particular reform from differing perspectives, as reading the two essays on anti-lynching in this book allows us to do, points to the significance of race, place, and class in shaping a reform sensibility and strategy.

What any survey of American reform and women reformers reveals is both the persistence and vitality of the American reform tradition and the personal tenacity and social diversity of the reformers. Ralph Waldo Emerson once observed that in America, where the people are in a constant state of inventing and reinventing themselves, all Americans are reformers at certain times in their lives. Reform constitutes the marrow of American identity. The women discussed in *Against the Tide* spoke in their own ways to the ongoing struggle to define a just society in America, and sometimes had a different experience and expectations than male reformers. They each approached the issue as Americans and as women. In doing so, they all chose a life in and of reform. But from a historical perspective, they also represent particular case studies in the problem of identifying and interpreting American reform and women as reformers. As such, understanding their lives as reformers promises access into the soul of American culture.

NOTE

This introductory essay has been adapted from my "Introduction" to Randall M. Miller and Paul A. Cimbala, eds., *American Reform and Reformers: A Biographical Dictionary* (Greenwood, 1996).

Against the Tide

Catharine Beecher
and Domestic Relations

KATHLEEN C. BERKELEY

Four years before her death in 1878, Catharine Esther Beecher, who once had ranked among the "most famous women in America," decided to take stock of her life's accomplishments and present them, for the last time, to her public.[1] Her achievements had been legendary: founder of several institutes of higher education for women, including the once prestigious Hartford Female Seminary; the driving force behind the American Woman's Educational Association; and the author of close to thirty publications on such pressing social issues as educational reform, religion and ethics, slavery and abolition, the condition of women's health, dress, diet, calisthenics, the principles of domestic science, and the rights and duties of American women. With her place in the limelight increasingly usurped by the fame of her sister Harriet Beecher Stowe; the growing notoriety surrounding her brother Henry Ward Beecher; and the budding career as a woman's rights advocate of her half sister Isabella Beecher Hooker, she issued her carefully crafted autobiography as a reminder of her "integrity of purpose and her professional commitment to the cause of women."[2]

Fearful, perhaps, that Isabella's brand of feminism was gaining ground, Beecher wrote her memoir also as a call to arms. Several years before, in public lectures and in print, she had castigated the woman's movement for "uniting all the antagonisms that are warring on the family state" and had characterized the movement as a dangerous mix of spiritualism, free love, free divorce, family limitation, and agitation for the ballot.[3] By 1874 her concern for the rising tide of feminism seemed no less urgent. By dedicating *Educational Reminiscences and Suggestions* to those "who as Housekeepers, Mothers, and Schoolteachers, are to decide the Safety and Prosperity of our country," Beecher exhorted her constituency of middle-class white women to continue advocating the philosophy that had guided her half-century career as an educational reformer and advocate of domestic female autonomy.[4]

Catharine Beecher's reform impulse, like that of so many women and men of her generation, originated in the economic, social, and cultural transformations that characterized the first half of the nineteenth century. The decline of self-sufficient family farms in portions of the Northeast, coupled with the opening of the West, drained a significant portion of land-hungry, marriageable-age men from the older, settled region. At the same time, many of these older agrarian communities were undergoing an urban metamorphosis as a result of nascent industrial development. These economic and demographic changes influenced cultural developments, especially in the areas of religion, family, and gender relations. Concomitant with the flowering of evangelical Protestantism, which attributed human agency to personal salvation and linked an individual's salvation to that of society, was the emergence of a gender ideology that ascribed mutually exclusive interests and responsibilities to men and women. If men claimed the public world of business and politics for themselves, which they did, then the private world of the family became the purview of women.

Through thought and deed, Beecher, who never married or managed her own household, contributed to the formation of this new ideology of domesticity. Her version of the ideology, however, contained a subversive twist. Central to the public–private dichotomy was a corresponding set of assumptions about men's and women's characters: men were inherently aggressive, competitive, and individualistic; women were naturally passive, nurturing, and pious. Although Beecher, like so many nineteenth-century reformers, believed in the redemptive power of American women, she disagreed vehemently with those who argued that female moral agency was innate. Even as she extolled the virtues of female benevolence and self-sacrifice, she stressed that these were not inborn personality traits but acquired characteristics that needed to be taught to young women at an early age. For Beecher, the key to society's salvation lay in educating and training women for their responsibilities.

When Beecher began her work in education in the 1820s, first as a teacher in New London, Connecticut, and then as the founder of the Hartford Female Seminary, public support for educating women beyond the acquisition of ornamental skills was tepid at best, and teaching was still a man's occupation. In the decade and a half following the Civil War, as Beecher's career was drawing to a close, private female seminaries and colleges flourished, several originally all-male private and public colleges became coeducational, state-supported teacher training colleges were in vogue, and teaching was fast becoming a woman's profession. Beecher does not deserve sole credit for these changes, but her literary and institutional contributions definitely shaped the direction American education took in the nineteenth century.

Prior to Beecher's entrance into the area of educational reform, educating women was deemed controversial because it gave them "an identity outside the family."[5] Beecher's genius in promoting an education for women equal to that which their male counterparts received lay in her recognition that the American public feared a classical education might render women unfit for their domestic duties. Beecher effectively defused this argument by linking advances in women's education to their primary social responsibilities as wives and mothers, which she identified as women's true profession. Her views first appeared in 1827 in the *American Journal of Education*:

When we consider the amazing responsibilities resting upon the mother of a family, and the fact, that her own characteristics, feelings and sentiments will inevitably be impressed upon the plastic mind of her offspring, it would seem as if this alone would render the subject of female education an object of the highest interest.[6]

Beecher's convictions appear evolutionary rather than revolutionary. She and her contemporaries in educational reform—Emma Willard, Mary Lyon, and Zilpah Grant—built their arguments favoring a classical education for women on the foundation laid by Revolutionary era educational reformers like Benjamin Rush and Judith Sargent Murray. Rush explicitly advocated advances in women's education by attaching significant political weight to the social responsibilities of mothering. According to the tenets of "Republican Motherhood," the new nation's success depended on knowledgeable women because they bore the primary responsibility for supervising their children's early education. This maternal duty was especially weighty in the case of sons, who needed careful training before claiming their rightful place as citizens.

Beecher's generation of educational reformers, with her in the lead, made more explicit the connection between a woman's influence on her family and her influence on society:

But it is not in domestic relations alone that the female character operates. There is no refined, well educated woman, but can exert an immediate influence upon a father, husband, or brother, and thus upon the general interests of society.[7]

However indirect a woman's influence might appear, Beecher presented a convincing argument that society gained when women received an education comparable with that of men.

Beecher believed that women coming of age in antebellum America needed an education superior to that which their mothers had received because this generation confronted a world far different from that of their predecessors. She emphasized this point by linking her philosophy of education and womanhood to the demands of a modernizing society. Mastering the environment depended on acquiring knowledge, especially of science and technology, and learning "time management" skills rather than relying on instinct and traditional modes of thought and action. Beecher underscored this point in her advice manual, *A Treatise on Domestic Economy*, which was a best-seller from its publication in

1841 until the mid-1850s and was adopted as a textbook by the Massachusetts state board of education in 1842:

There is no one thing more necessary to a housekeeper in performing her varied duties than a *habit of system and order.* . . . A wise economy is nowhere more conspicuous, than in a systematic *apportionment of time* to different pursuits.[8]

No longer could young women learn the arts of household management from their mothers' personal, informal instruction. Modern times demanded a more rigorous and systematic formal education. Women needed instruction, Beecher wrote, "in the formation of habits of investigation, of correct reasoning, of persevering attention, of regular system, of accurate analysis and of vigorous mental action."[9]

Beecher not only advocated an education for women that went well beyond the limitations of ornamental instruction, but she also provided a powerful rationale for training women for the profession of teaching. Since the stated purpose of female education was the production of better wives and mothers, it seemed obvious that the task of preparing young women for their domestic duties properly belonged to women. Here, too, Beecher's philosophy built on educational concepts embedded in the ideology of "Republican Motherhood." She adroitly assisted in the shift from public acceptance of educating mothers so that they could instruct their children at home to educating women "to teach the children of others."[10] She did so by reconceptualizing and expanding the mothering role to include a teaching function. That this teaching duty eventually led women out of their households and into schools and academies confirmed Beecher's belief that the boundaries separating the private, domestic sphere from the public, social sphere were flexible rather than fixed. A nagging question remained, however: How could women instruct the next generation unless they themselves were knowledgeable? Beecher's answer was succinct and to the point: women needed to be schooled in how to teach.

Beecher was hardly the product of the systematic and rigorous training she advocated for women; nor in her youth had she anticipated that she would carve out a professional career for herself and for the generations of women educators who followed in her footsteps. In fact, until her twenty-second year, Beecher expected that her life would follow a different, much more traditional course.

Born in East Hampton, New York, on 6 September 1800, to Lyman Beecher and Roxanna Foote Beecher, Catharine was the oldest of eight surviving children from her father's first marriage. Schooled at home by her mother and her Aunt Mary (Roxanna's sister became part of the Beecher household when Catharine was born) until the age of ten, she was a reluctant student of the domestic arts. According to Beecher's preeminent biographer, Kathryn Kish Sklar, the young pupil chafed under her mother's strict instruction.[11] Aunt Mary's coaxing achieved better results from Catharine, who remembered that "She [Aunt Mary] secured my enthusiastic devotion by the high appreciation she seemed to have of my childish services.''[12]

When the Beechers moved from the village of East Hampton to the bustling town of Litchfield, Connecticut, in 1809, Catharine left her mother's ''parlor'' school for Sarah Pierce's academy. Begun in 1791, Pierce's school drew its pupils from leading families in the region. Although Pierce offered her female students a ''full academic curriculum,'' it was not a demanding one; the emphasis was on instruction in the ''social graces.''[13] Beecher flourished in this environment. Mastering the academic component of the curriculum was easy for her, and she earned top honors in the school's first competition in 1814. She enjoyed her years at Pierce's academy because the school provided her with an outlet for her sociability; ''concocting plans for amusement'' was far more important to her than studying.[14]

Beecher's carefree childhood came to an abrupt end in 1816 when tuberculosis claimed her mother's life; Aunt Mary had succumbed to the same disease three years earlier. At her mother's death, Beecher left school to take charge of her father's household. Even after Lyman Beecher remarried the following year, she remained at home, assisting her new stepmother, Harriet Porter. To Catharine fell the task of caring for her siblings, especially after the arrival in 1818 of Frederick, the first of four children born to Harriet and Lyman Beecher.

In 1819 Beecher escaped the confines of the Litchfield household by embarking on an extended visit to relatives living in Massachusetts and Rhode Island. Six months later, when she returned home, she focused her energies on polishing her ornamental skills—painting, poetry writing, and piano playing—and her domestic arts—needlework—in preparation for a temporary teaching position at a girls' school in New London. She also met Alexander Metcalf Fisher, a brilliant professor of mathematics and natural philosophy at Yale. After a bumpy courtship (to which her father contributed), the couple became engaged in January 1822. They planned to marry the following year, after Fisher returned from a year of study abroad.

Beecher's carefully orchestrated life, revolving around her impending marriage and the eventual assumption of maternal duties, came to an abrupt and tragic end in April 1822, when Alexander Fisher died in a shipwreck off the coast of Ireland. Grief-stricken, she received no solace from her father. The close, loving, supportive relationship of her early childhood had become strained even before her father's meddling in the courtship.

Simultaneous to but independent of Beecher's acquaintance with Fisher, her father had begun pressuring her to start the process of religious introspection that would culminate in her conversion and mark her entry into adulthood. However, she found it difficult to adhere to her father's Calvinist teachings, which stressed the sovereignty of an angry God, the doctrine of human depravity, the need for repentance, and total submission to God. Beecher was beginning the process of parting company with her father over the concept of human depravity and original sin in favor of a theology that stressed free will, the uncorrupted nature of the individual, and ''the conviction that God was just and merciful.''[15] Adding to the growing tension between father and daughter was the fact that Fisher, although a religious man, had not had a conversion experience before death claimed him. Beecher found it difficult to reconcile her father's teachings with the thought that Fisher's unconverted soul was doomed.

It was only a matter of months before Beecher left her father's house, seeking refuge first with her Boston relatives and then with Fisher's parents. Her conflict with her father continued, albeit through correspondence. In January 1823 she wrote:

When I think of Mr. Fisher and remember his blameless . . . life, his . . . efforts to do his duty both to God and man, I believe that a merciful Savior has not left him to perish at last . . . and that in the Day of Judgement we shall find that . . . God is influenced in bestowing his grace by the efforts of men . . . and that there was more reason to hope for one whose whole life had been an example of excellence, than for one who had spent all his days in guilt and sin.[16]

The strain between father and daughter eventually abated. Although Catharine returned to the Beecher fold, she continued to assert her independence from her father by remaining unconverted. In 1823, still unconverted, she joined his church; three years later she led a revival at her school. Nonetheless, as her voluminous writings on theology, ethics, and moral instruction indicate, Beecher had rejected the religious orthodoxy of her father. Shortly before his death in 1863, she made a complete break with Lyman Beecher's faith by joining the church to which her mother had belonged in her youth, the Episcopal Church.

Her stay at the Fishers' home provided Beecher with the opportunity to reflect on her future. Poring over Alexander Fisher's books, she discovered the pleasures of intellectual stimulation; self-discovery also revealed the deficiencies in her formal education at Pierce's academy. A chance remark by a family friend concerning the lack of a good school for girls in Hartford, the necessity of earning a living if she wanted to remain independent of her father, and the bittersweet windfall of $2,000 from Fisher's will constituted all the impetus she needed. Moving to Hartford, she rented a room above a harness shop and founded Hartford Female Seminary.

Beecher took a gamble when she opened her school in 1823. Although she wrote to her father that ''there seems to be no very extensive sphere of usefulness for a single woman but that which can be found in the limits of a school room,'' she was mistaken.[17] In the 1820s, when she opened the doors of Hartford Female Seminary, the majority of young women who worked outside the home were domestic servants, milliners, seamstresses, and factory operatives. If women found employment in schools during the 1820s, they were more than likely hired for summer terms, when boys were absent. Until late in the century, male-dominated school boards in communities across the country clung to the notion that women could neither supervise boys nor serve as appropriate role models for them, even while they were hiring women as cheap replacements for men. The feminization of the teaching profession, which began in Massachusetts during the mid-to-late 1830s, was complete by the 1880s. Beecher was indeed ahead of her times.

Of the five institutions Beecher was instrumental in founding, Hartford Female Seminary was the most successful. By the time she left Hartford in 1832 to follow her father to Cincinnati, where he became president of Lane Theological Seminary and where she founded, a year later, the short-lived Western Female Institute, Hartford Female Seminary had acquired a widespread reputation for academic excellence. The school's eventual decline was due, in part, to the rise of the public high school movement. Beecher's resumption of the principalship near the end of her life did little to revive the faltering institution. Of the three remaining institutions that were founded under the aegis of Beecher's organization, the American Woman's Educational Association, only Milwaukee Female Seminary (later Milwaukee Female College) endured.

Hartford Female Seminary stands out because the school was truly a family affair. Beecher's first venture at running a school, like many of her future endeavors, depended on the support of her siblings and, in later instances, in-laws. She and several of her siblings created a second home in Hartford, living together, studying together, and sometimes working together. Her brother Edward was her mentor (and Latin tutor) until he left the city in 1824 to pursue theological studies. Her sister Mary shared teaching responsibilities at the school until her marriage to Thomas Perkins in 1827. Harriet, who later became a teacher at the school, began there as a pupil, as did a younger brother. Catharine relied heavily on Harriet after Mary's retirement into domesticity. In fact, Harriet assumed responsibility for running the school in 1829 when Catharine, suffering from "nervous prostration," retreated to Boston, where her father resided.

Beecher's depression in the fall of 1829 had its root cause in a recent setback she had suffered while striving to implement facets of her educational philosophy. Although Hartford Female Seminary began as a modest one-room school above a harness shop, it became something much larger and more significant than its name implied. The school served as Beecher's educational laboratory, where over the course of nine years she experimented with and refined many of her ideas about the future direction of women's education. Twice during her tenure she attempted to alter its function and structure. Her professed goals were threefold: to transform the instruction offered at Hartford Female Seminary in order to make it equivalent to that available at any endowed institution of higher education available to men; to professionalize teaching for middle-class white women like herself, who, for a variety of reasons, remained single; and, in keeping with her evolving theological stance, to create an environment conducive to molding the moral character of her students and faculty. Her first attempt to implement her educational goals met with modest success; her second venture did not.

Three years of teaching had allowed Beecher ample time to observe and experience the "defects and difficulties in the mode of teaching and conducting [female] schools," points she addressed in the 1827 article she published in the *American Journal of Education*.[18] Simply put, women's schools were not equal to men's schools. The breadth of the curriculum offered to women and men was similar, but the depth of knowledge was not. Beecher blamed the difference on the structural and organizational limitations imposed on women's education. The limited physical space of women's schools—often one or two rooms stuffed with teachers, tutors, and pupils all reciting at once—was detrimental to learning. Moreover, the division of labor of the faculties at men's and women's schools differed significantly. Beecher preferred the "college plan," an organizational innovation recently adopted at some of the leading men's schools. Under this plan, administrators, faculty, and boards of trustees had separate but complementary duties. At women's schools the principals were responsible for the administrative, financial, and maintenance functions of their institutions, and they taught. Unlike their male counterparts, principals and teachers at women's schools were expected to offer instruction in a variety of subjects rather than specialize in a specific discipline. Although this instructional mode might have sufficed a decade earlier, Beecher wrote, "the amount of knowledge required to complete the education" of young women in the 1820s rendered this system obsolete.[19]

Beecher was determined to transform her "private school into an endowed seminary."[20] With an endowment, the school's immediate future was secured and she could turn her attention to expanding the school's physical facilities and introducing (in however modified a form) the "college plan." Much to Beecher's surprise, her plans received a cool reception from Hartford's leading male citizens, who were "surprised and almost dismayed" by her request for an endowment.[21] Undeterred by their rebuff, she turned to their wives and found success. Fund-raising among women provided Beecher with the capital she needed to expand the school and taught her a valuable lesson about the importance of cultivating a female network. When Hartford Female Seminary opened its doors in the fall of 1827, Beecher, in her capacity as principal, supervised eight teachers in a beautiful new building that "contained ten recitation rooms, a lecture room, and a study hall that could accommodate 150 pupils."[22]

The reluctance of the city's most influential and powerful men to support Beecher's educational endeavors left a lasting impression. In her memoir she recalled, perhaps with a trace of bitterness, that while the city fathers refused to endow her school for girls, there were several endowed colleges for men within a thirty-mile radius of Hartford. Men, she could only assume, were not committed to putting women's and men's education on an equal footing. From her creation, in the mid-1840s, of the Central Committee for Promoting National Education to her founding of the American Woman's Education Association in 1852, Beecher cultivated the support of middle- and upper-class white women for her goal of establishing endowed institutions of higher education for women.

The aim of these institutions was to train women for their "true professions": teaching, health care, and domestic economy.[23]

Between 1829, when Beecher wrote *Suggestions Respecting Improvements in Education*, and 1831, when she published *The Elements of Mental and Moral Philosophy*, the theological underpinnings of her educational philosophy became more pronounced. Her intellectual journey, which began in 1828, when she took charge of a course in moral philosophy previously taught by a member of her staff, also had a practical bent. Within a year she had determined to take her school in a new direction by proposing the addition of a department of moral instruction and the transformation of Hartford Female Seminary into a boarding school. Both objectives were revolutionary. The former implied that the school and the female teacher, not the church and a male minister, would be responsible for instilling morality in young women; the latter removed daughters from the confines of private homes to a dormitory where they lived with other young women and were supervised by a spinster teacher.

Integral to Beecher's philosophy was her positive view of human agency and reason, and her belief that habit, or training, was essential to the formation of an individual's character. Moreover, because of the influence of personal habits (good or bad) on the human will, she stressed the need for early intervention in a child's moral training, lest the mind become "disordered." "A well managed child could not turn out badly," wrote an observer of Beecher's school.[24]

Cultivating good habits, which Beecher defined as obedience, self-denial, self-sacrifice, and self-government, depended not only on moral instruction in the classroom but also on management of the environment beyond the classroom. "The hours spent outside the classroom," she wrote, "are the hours of access to the heart, hours in which character is developed, and in which opportunities for exerting beneficial influence are continually occurring."[25] The construction of a residence hall at the school met both Beecher's requirements for a managed environment for her teaching staff and students and her personal need for independence from her family by providing her with an inexpensive, secure, and comfortable home.

For Beecher, the proper formation of a child's mind was essential not only to the salvation of an individual's soul but also to that of the nation's spirit. Such high stakes required that those who engaged in this business be trained, rewarded, and honored. In *Suggestions Respecting Improvements in Education*, she broadened the scope of motherhood to include teaching and ministerial duties and called for its professionalization: "What is *the profession of a Woman*? Is it not to form immortal minds, and to watch, to nurse, and to rear the bodily system?"[26] Beecher's philosophy also struck a careful balance between empowering women like herself, for whom marriage was not an option, and upholding the gender conventions of her society:

The writer cannot but believe that all female institutions . . . ought to be conducted exclusively by females, *so soon as suitable teachers of their own sex can be prepared. . . .*

Until this day no other profession could with propriety admit the female aspirant, nor till this day has the profession of a teacher been the road to honour, influence, and emolument. But the feelings of an enlightened society are fast changing. . . . The time is not far distant when it will become an honourable profession . . . [to which] woman is gladly welcomed. . . . *She*, also, can discern before her the road to honourable indepen- dance [*sic*] . . . where she need not outstep the proscribed boundaries of feminine mod- esty, nor diminish one of those retiring graces that must ever constitute her most attractive charms.[27]

Beecher's educational philosophy may have been visionary, but she wisely tem- pered it with a bow to gender conventions. After all, how could Americans quibble with a profession that gave women economic independence and the esteem of a grateful society while ensuring the protection of their feminine charms?

Beecher's success with her second reform effort hinged on three objectives: hiring a leading woman educator to head the proposed department of moral instruction, raising a tidy sum for construction of a residence hall, and overcom- ing any prejudices parents might harbor about boarding their daughters in res- idence halls located on school grounds rather than placing them with individual families living near the school. Unfortunately, her plans went awry. Beecher was unsuccessful in her attempt to lure Zilpah Grant, a woman with impeccable religious and educational credentials, from her post at Mary Lyon's school; she was stymied in her effort to raise the school's endowment (her goal was $20,000); and she was unprepared for the community's lack of support for the dormitory concept. Upon receipt of Grant's rejection of what she considered a generous offer, Beecher went into a depression that lasted through December 1829.

Although Beecher returned to her school in 1830, she longed for something else. When the trustees of Lane Theological Seminary in Cincinnati offered her father the presidency, and he suggested that she join the family pilgrimage to the Queen City of the West, she seized the opportunity. Economic promise had enticed both New Englanders and immigrants to move west. Fearful that "Cath- olics and infidels" would dominate (and debase) the region, father and daughter viewed the West as the battleground for the nation's soul. Although their means differed (Lyman training young men for the ministry and Catharine training young women for the teaching profession), their ends were the same.

Unfortunately for the Beechers, Cincinnati was unlike either Hartford or Bos- ton. Their initial reception by Cincinnati society was warm, but relations be- tween the "better sort" and the Beechers soon cooled. The Beechers' air of superiority did not sit well with Cincinnatians. In particular, Catharine's impe- rious manner alienated influential members of society whose financial support she so desperately needed for her educational cause. Cincinnatians also were extremely skittish about the escalating controversy over slavery. Many of the leading merchant families, who made their money in the Southern trade, were not inclined to support abolition. Moreover, during the previous few years, whites from all levels of society had grown increasingly uncomfortable with the city's free black community because of its reputation for harboring fugitive slaves; working-class whites resented competing for jobs with free blacks. The Beechers unwittingly found themselves embroiled in a community conflict over slavery in 1834 when Lane Theological Seminary students, led by Theodore Dwight Weld, began a series of debates on immediate abolition versus gradualism and colonization, and put their abolitionist views into practice in the black community. Although the Beechers had not raised the issue, and in fact were supporters of the more moderate stance, they were tarred with the brush of radicalism.

A year before the controversy at Lane, Beecher opened the doors of her second school, Western Female Institute. Less interested in either teaching or the day-to-day management of the school, which she turned over to her sister Harriet and Mary Dutton (a friend from the Hartford school), she preferred to promote her cause of training teachers to "save the West from darkness and damnation."[28] She also joined forces with leading education reformers of the day—William Russell, William C. Woodbridge, George B. Emerson, and Horace Mann—in their drive to eradicate the pernicious use of competition (emulation) and ranking in American schools. Yet even as Beecher gained national prominence in the field of educational reform, Beecher's popularity sank. Her school suffered the loss of patronage by Cincinnati's social and economic elite. With students and funding in short supply, she sought assistance for her cause outside the local community. Just as she had done in her Hartford Seminary days, Beecher looked to middle- and upper-class white women for that support.

In 1836 Beecher planned a promotional tour through the East that kept her out of Cincinnati for six months. This action suited her because it allowed her to ignore the intertwining of professional and personal problems associated with the imminent collapse of her school and new arrangements within the Beecher household. Catharine's stepmother, Harriet Porter Beecher, had died the previous year, and her father had wasted little time in finding a third wife, Lydia Beals Jackson. Although the grown Beecher children and the new Mrs. Beecher never developed a comfortable relationship, Lyman's third marriage was especially stressful for Catharine, who increasingly felt unwelcome in her father and stepmother's household.

Beecher's Eastern tour netted a collection of potential benefactors and teachers. But a combination of circumstances limited her success: the loss of her institutional base when Western Female Institute finally closed in 1837, the lingering ill effects of the antiabolition and antiblack mob violence that had wracked Cincinnati the previous summer, and a perceived challenge to Beecher's prominence as an advocate for American women's unique social identity and responsibilities. While traveling in the East, Beecher discovered that a woman who had once considered enrolling in the Hartford school was poised to tap Beecher's sources for a cause that she and her family found troublesome. The person was Angelina Grimké, and the cause was the creation of "Abolition Societies among ladies of the non-slave-holding states."[29]

It was within this context that Beecher decided to counter Grimké's ideas by firing the first salvo of what became a public debate over the social responsibilities of American women. In 1837 Beecher published *An Essay on Slavery and Abolition, with Reference to the Duty of American Females*, which began by distinguishing between the "moral and conscientious character" of abolitionists and their misguided support for measures that were neither "peaceful [n]or Christian . . . but calculated to generate . . . recrimination and angry passions."[30] In particular, Beecher found fault with the movement's emphasis on immediate emancipation, which she viewed as "unduly provocative," and the decided lack of concern by abolitionists for the consequences of their actions. She abhorred social strife and remained steadfast in her belief that American society was best served by a gradual approach to ending slavery. She believed that this solution, which was less disruptive to social harmony, would achieve the greater goal of establishing a "peaceable Kingdom" in America. Grimké apparently thought otherwise. In *Letters to Catherine E. Beecher, in Reply to an Essay on Slavery and Abolitionism* (1838), she accused Beecher of "bartering principle for an unholy peace."[31]

Central to Beecher's and Grimké's debate over means versus ends within the abolition movement was a second, and very much related, issue: "the just bounds of female influence, and the times, places, and manner in which it can be appropriately exerted."[32] Beecher favored an orderly, hierarchical society ordained by God: child to parent, pupil to teacher, servant to master, wife to husband, citizen to magistrate, and man to God. Although female subordination did not imply female inferiority, she believed that men and women differed in temperament, and that these differences called forth separate spheres of duty and social responsibility. Women legitimated their social power by appealing to Christian principles of kindness, generosity, peace, and benevolence, and they exerted their influence within the domestic and social circle.

Beecher's vision of American womanhood was not hidebound, nor did it advocate female submissiveness. The source of female power was not innate and God-given; instead, female authority was based on principles (albeit Christian ones) that were learned through moral instruction. By treating the "domestic and social circle" as a single sphere, Beecher provided a convincing rationale for women to expand their influence beyond their households and into society. Moreover, by infusing mothering with a teaching function that extended beyond the family circle, she created a useful and honorable position for single women as "mothers" of society's children. As the historian Kathryn Sklar has noted, the subtlety of Beecher's philosophy of womanhood derived from its ability to glorify domesticity even as it reconceptualized and politicized it.[33] There were, however, limits to female power. Women exerted their influence on society indirectly through their social roles as wives, mothers, and teachers. Thus, the home and the classroom were their stage. Beecher abhorred a more direct representation of female influence, especially in the realm of politics. Political power was something men exercised. Beecher believed that it was foolhardy for women to engage in this pursuit because it undermined the gender hierarchy that was central to the maintenance of the social order.

Drawn into a controversy she had not necessarily intended, Grimké replied to Beecher in a series of letters published in the abolitionist press during the latter months of 1837. The bulk of her response addressed various points of disagreement between the two reformers pertaining to the abolition movement and the character of its participants: the strategy of immediacy, colonization, the Christian impulse of abolitionists (or lack thereof), the consequences of abolition on society, and prejudice. In three concluding letters Grimké sketched out her theory of womanhood, which stood in stark contrast to Beecher's. Rejecting Beecher's belief in an ordained social hierarchy in favor of the principle of equality, Grimké labeled the former "an assertion without proof" and used Christian doctrine—"in Christ Jesus there is neither male nor female"—in support of the latter.[34] Even as she clothed herself in her religious faith, however, Grimké rejected the notion that "rights" were a gift from God; without respect to differences based on color, sex, or status, she insisted that humans had rights "because they are moral beings" endowed with the "same moral nature."[35]

Grimké's repudiation of differences between men and women "based on the mere circumstance of sex" paved the way for her rejection of the doctrine of separatism, which she held as injurious to both sexes:

By this doctrine, man has been converted into the warrior, and clothed with sternness . . . ; whilst woman has been taught to lean . . . to sit as a doll . . . to be admired for her personal charms . . . caressed and humored as a spoiled child, or converted into a mere drudge [for] the convenience of her lord and master.

No artificial boundary separated men's and women's social responsibilities or their exercise of power: "whatever is morally right for a man to do, it is morally right for a woman to do."[36] Logic dictated that the opposite dictum also held. Questioning Beecher's view that it was the peculiar duty of women to educate society's children, Grimké concluded that it was the duty of men to cooperate with women in this "high and holy venture."[37] No matter the consequences, Grimké did not shy away from expressing her convictions, even if they challenged Beecher's lifework.

The implications of Grimké's views were not lost upon Beecher. Grimké had raised important questions about the limitations of women's social power and had offered an alternative vision of womanhood in which power was exercised directly, through the political process. While Beecher shrank from the idea that women should engage in politics, Grimké called for women to claim political participation as their birthright:

Now, I believe it is woman's right to have a voice in all the laws and regulations by which she is to be *governed*, whether in Church or State; and that the present arrangements of society on these points, are *a violation of human rights, a rank usurpation of power*. . . . I contend that woman has just as much right to sit in solemn counsel in Conventions, Conferences . . . and General Assemblies, as man—just as much right to it . . . in the Presidential chair of the United States.[38]

As Beecher's and Grimké's ideological clash suggests, the influence and exercise of female power in American society, so integral to feminism, was contested terrain in the antebellum era. In 1837 it was not a foregone conclusion that Beecher's vision of womanhood would falter while Grimké's conceptualization would prevail. Over the next two decades, American women pressed forward with their competing claims for the source and direction of their influence and responsibilities.

After her clash with Grimké, a depressed Beecher retreated to her father's household. Over the next few years she turned inward. Writing and occasional visits to her favorite water cure establishment became her therapy. By the mid-1840s, buoyed by the financial success of her domestic advice manual, which brought independence from her family, Beecher returned to an active public agenda. She envisioned women's education as the great social leveler, uniting the interests and resources of the upper classes with the faith and industry of the working and middle classes. Pressing forward with her plans for uniting American women of all ranks beneath the democratic banner of a female-led education movement, she turned to former pupils for help, cultivated support from women's church groups, and managed to secure the endorsement of America's leading male educational reformers, Horace Mann and Henry Barnard.

In 1844 Beecher founded the Central Committee for Promoting National Education after persuading her brother-in-law Calvin Stowe to serve as its titular head. Putting a reluctant Stowe at the helm was in keeping with Beecher's belief that men lent prestige to her cause, although she expected to run the Committee. Stowe eventually found his replacement, William Slade, the former governor of Vermont. As the organization's general agent, Slade's responsibilities were limited to making local arrangements and supporting Beecher's endeavors—promotional fund-raising tours in the East and teacher training. Unfortunately for Catharine, Slade was not as malleable as Stowe. In 1848 they parted company, with Slade renaming Beecher's organization the National Board of Popular Education. Working her connections in the East, in 1852 Beecher founded her last organization devoted to the cause of women's education, the American Woman's Education Association. In addition to the support of her now famous younger sister, Harriet Beecher Stowe, Catharine persuaded a number of influential female literary figures, among them Sarah Josepha Hale, Lydia Sigourney, and Catharine Sedgwick, to serve on the organization's board of managers. Over the next four years the American Woman's Education Association sponsored three institutions organized according to the ''college plan'' Beecher had advocated some thirty years earlier.

While Beecher's movement flourished, the ideas that Grimké advocated sputtered along, impeded by the lack of an autonomous institutional base. The "woman's question" tore apart the abolition movement even as Grimké retired from public life after her marriage to the Beechers' old nemesis, Theodore Weld. Nonetheless, a handful of women and men, most of whom were associated with William Lloyd Garrison's radical wing of the abolition movement, nurtured the concept of woman's rights. In 1848 Elizabeth Cady Stanton's meeting at Seneca Falls, New York, produced the famous feminist document "A Declaration of Sentiments," but women registered few concrete gains in promoting their political equality before the Civil War. Not until 1869, when woman's rights advocates founded two suffrage associations, did an autonomous movement exist; success, however, was fifty years in the future.

Early in 1856 Beecher made two decisions that, however unintentional, signaled an end to her career as an educator. She severed her relationship with Milwaukee Female College, and a few months later ended her association with the American Woman's Education Association. Having devoted several years to the Milwaukee venture, she had looked to the school for a permanent home. When the trustees refused to subsidize the building of a private residence for Beecher, she disengaged herself.

Milwaukee Female College endured and became the most successful of the institutions founded by Beecher's organization, although its future was hardly assured when Beecher left. Meanwhile, the other two institutions eventually foundered for lack of resources. After 1856 Beecher never formalized her relationship with the American Woman's Education Association, which limped along until it disbanded in 1862, but she continued to promote its cause long after its demise. The association never realized her goal of securing a sizable endowment for each institution it founded, and scholars have attributed a number of causes to its and Beecher's lack of success.

Beecher's intractability probably led her to reject the advice of those who cautioned her to consolidate the association's resources and urged her to consider denominational support for the colleges. Then, too, as Beecher often lamented, support for private women's colleges was neither as deep nor as widespread as support for private men's colleges. The Civil War also disrupted and redirected the path of American reform. In education the movement to include a teacher training curriculum in the public high schools expanded during the postwar years, and states responded to the Morrill Act of 1862 by promoting vocational education for women through the establishment of state-supported normal schools.

Although Beecher's influence on reform waned after the Civil War, her contributions were noteworthy. Her most important ideas about professionalizing teaching and claiming it as a respectable option for women became part of mainstream thought by midcentury. Her articles criticizing emulation appeared in the leading education journals of her day, and her writings on domestic economy laid the foundations for the field of home economics that emerged after her death. Of equal importance were Beecher's contributions to the emerging debate over the origins and scope of woman's influence on society. Although her ideas about womanhood became more contested in the post–Civil War era, especially when cast in the light of the debates over the Fourteenth and Fifteenth Amendments to the Constitution, Beecher did not relinquish her position without a fight. Retirement from public life was not something she relished. She wrote endlessly, traveled, and lectured whenever possible. As support for woman's suffrage gained ground, she redoubled her critique of the movement. In December 1870 Beecher debated woman's rights activist Mary Livermore at Boston's Music Hall, and expanded and published her address, *Woman's Suffrage and Woman's Profession*, in 1871.[39]

Never having a home to call her own, Beecher moved about in her last years, from relative to relative. In 1877 she made her last move, retiring to the Elmira, New York, home of her brother Thomas. The generosity of her brother and sister-in-law, the availability of a nearby water cure establishment, and the presence of Elmira College, where she could lecture to young women, made her last year tolerable. Two days after suffering a debilitating stroke, Catharine Esther Beecher died in her sleep on 12 May 1878.

NOTES

1. Jeanne Boydston, Mary Kelly, and Anne Margolis, *The Limits of Sisterhood: The Beecher Sisters on Women's Rights and Woman's Sphere* (Chapel Hill, N.C., 1988), 13.

2. Kathryn Kish Sklar, *Catharine Beecher, a Study in American Domesticity* (New York, 1976), 270.

3. Catharine Beecher, *Woman's Suffrage and Woman's Profession* (Hartford, Conn.: 1871), dedication page.

4. Catharine Beecher, *Educational Reminiscences and Suggestions* (New York, 1874), dedication page.

5. Barbara Miller Solomon, *In the Company of Educated Women: A History of Women in Higher Education in America* (New Haven, 1985), xviii.

6. Catharine Beecher, "Female Education," *American Journal of Education* 2 (1827): 219–222, 264–269. The quote is on 221.

7. Ibid., 221.

8. Catharine Beecher, *A Treatise on Domestic Economy* (New York, 1841), 222.

9. Kathryn Kish Sklar, "Catharine Beecher," in G. J. Barker-Benfield and Catharine Clinton, eds., *Portraits of American Women: From Settlement to the Present* (New York, 1991), 178.

10. Joan M. Jensen, "Not Only Ours but Others: The Quaker Teaching Daughters of the Mid-Atlantic, 1790–1850," *History of Education Quarterly* 24 (1984): 3.

11. Sklar, *Catharine Beecher*, 7.

12. Ibid., 7–8.

13. Milton Rugoff, *The Beechers: An American Family in the Nineteenth Century* (New York, 1981), 43.

14. Sklar, *Catharine Beecher*, 18.

15. Boydston, Kelly, and Margolis, *The Limits of Sisterhood*, 34.

16. Ibid., 34–35.

17. Ibid., 35.

18. Beecher, "Female Education," 219.

19. Ibid.; Joan N. Burstyn, "Catharine Beecher and the Education of American Women," *New England Quarterly* 47 (1974): 398–399.

20. Sklar, *Catherine Beecher*, 72.

21. Ibid., 74.

22. Rugoff, *The Beechers*, 56.

23. *Third Annual Report of the American Woman's Education Association and of the General Agent, May 1855* (New York, 1855), 8.

24. The statement is attributed to Angelina Grimké when she toured Hartford Female Seminary in 1831.

25. Beecher, *Educational Reminiscences*, 68.

26. Boydston, Kelly, and Margolis, *The Limits of Sisterhood*, 43.

27. Ibid., 45.

28. Rugoff, *The Beechers*, 174.

29. Catharine Beecher, *An Essay on Slavery and Abolition with Reference to the Duty of American Females* (Philadelphia, 1837), 5.

30. Ibid., 14–17.

31. Esther L. Bruland, "Great Debates: Ethical Reasoning and Social Change in Antebellum America: The Exchange Between Angelina Grimké and Catharine Beecher" (Ph.D. diss., Drew University, 1990), 175. Whether by accident or design, in her reply to Beecher, Grimké misspelled Catharine's name. Beecher also made a mistake, addressing Grimké as Miss A. D. Grimké (her middle initial was E.).

32. Beecher, *An Essay on Slavery*, 98.

33. Sklar, *Catharine Beecher*, 134–136.

34. Angelina E. Grimké, *Letters to Catherine E. Beecher, in Reply to An Essay on Slavery and Abolition, Addressed to A. E. Grimke* (Boston, 1838), 103, 108.

35. Ibid., 114–115.

36. Ibid., 115–116.

37. Ibid., 122.

38. Ibid., 119.

39. Catharine Beecher, *Woman's Suffrage and Woman's Profession* (Hartford, Conn., 1871). Perhaps too close for comfort for Catharine was the conversion to the suffrage cause of her youngest sister, Isabella Beecher Hooker. Twenty-two years younger than Catharine, Isabella represented a new generation of women. Although she grew up under the shadow of her famous sister, and attended the Hartford and Cincinnati schools, Isabella eventually rejected her sister's theory of social power for women in favor of female political power. Hooker's thoughts crystallized during the period in which Catharine Beecher's public career was drawing to a close. See Isabella Beecher Hooker, *Shall Women Vote? A Matrimonial Dialogue* (n.p., 1860) and *A Mother's Letter to a Daughter on Woman Suffrage* (Hartford, Conn., 1870).

BIBLIOGRAPHY

Boydston, Jeanne, Mary Kelly, and Anne Margolis. *The Limits of Sisterhood: The Beecher Sisters on Women's Rights and Woman's Sphere*. Chapel Hill, N.C., 1988.

Bruland, Esther Louise. "Great Debates: Ethical Reasoning and Social Change in Antebellum America: The Exchange Between Angelina Grimké and Catharine Beecher." Ph.D. diss., Drew University, 1990.

Burstyn, Joan N. "Catharine Beecher and the Education of American Women." *New
England Quarterly* 47 (1974): 386–403.

Chambers, Carol L. "Heavenly Influences: Catharine Beecher and the Moral Sphere of
Nineteenth Century Women." M.A. thesis, Indiana University, 1984.

Green, Nancy. "Female Education and School Competition, 1820–1850." *History of
Education Quarterly* 18 (1978): 129–142.

Lindley, Susan H. "Woman's Profession in the Life and Thought of Catharine Beecher:
A Study of Religion and Reform." Ph.D. diss., Duke University, 1974.

Rugoff, Milton. *The Beechers: An American Family in the Nineteenth Century*. New
York, 1981.

Sklar, Kathryn Kish. *Catharine Beecher, a Study in American Domesticity*. New Haven,
1973; New York, 1976.

Solomon, Barbara M. *In the Company of Educated Women: A History of Women in
Higher Education in America*. New Haven, 1985.

Mary Ann Shadd Cary
and Black Abolitionism

PAUL A. CIMBALA

In January 1849, Mary Ann Shadd, a twenty-five-year-old free-born African-American schoolteacher from Wilmington, Delaware, boldly criticized the Northern black leadership in a letter soon published in Frederick Douglass's *North Star*—a forum the leadership was bound to notice. Unleashing one verbal volley after another, she ridiculed black conventioneers who made thumping speeches at their annual meetings, "whining over our difficulties and afflictions, passing resolutions on resolutions to any extent," but who were not very effective in seeing "practical efforts to an end." She chastised a money-hungry, "corrupt clergy" full of "gross ignorance and insolent bearing" for "sapping our every means, and, as a compensation, inculcating ignorance as a duty, superstition as true religion." And she advised free blacks to ignore these "high priests" who urged them to put aside worldly concerns lest they be distracted from devoting themselves to contemplating the next life.

Shadd's letter may have lacked tact, but it embodied a style that would become the hallmark of her career in reform. More important, however, were the ideas outlined along with the personality revealed, ideas that formed the lifelong core of Shadd's reform philosophy. "We should do more, and talk less," she advised. Northern blacks must be world-wise, must think in practical terms, and must take charge of their destiny. They must emphasize "individual enterprise and self-reliance," because by becoming producers, they would earn the respect of the larger white community in which they would continue to live. They must grapple with ignorance, taking "the knowledge of the white man" while avoiding "imitating his follies." And, Shadd warned, they should not allow their preachers to disabuse them of the importance of the political franchise. She saw "no need" for "our distinctive meetings," a conclusion drawn as much from her opposition to segregation, which kept blacks and whites from learning from each other, as from her unfavorable judgment of the antebellum black convention movement's practical accomplishments.[1]

Throughout her public career, Shadd did not veer much from these views. Teacher, editor, publisher, army recruiter, suffrage activist, and lawyer, she remained a tireless advocate of liberation, equality, and self-reliance not only for her race, but for her sex as well. Along the way, her life touched upon the central concerns of the men and women who shaped black abolitionism, a movement much more complex than its white counterpart.

Shadd publicly joined the ranks of an already mature black abolitionist movement when she wrote her letter to Douglass. Indeed, she was a second-generation activist who was brought up in the movement. Shadd, the eldest of thirteen children, was born on 9 October 1823 in Wilmington to Harriet Parnell and Abraham Doros Shadd. Her father was a free-born Pennsylvanian who earned his competency as a shoemaker and had moved to Wilmington to practice his trade. Because of his skill, Abraham Shadd was able to create an economically comfortable existence for his family. Nevertheless, as Abraham Shadd and other free blacks understood, money alone could not purchase an equal place for themselves or their families in American society. It did, however, provide him and other middle-class blacks with the time and the resources necessary for creating a distinct black abolitionist movement that called for an end to racism, as well as the immediate abolition of Southern slavery, a generation before white abolitionist William Lloyd Garrison issued his own January 1831 call for immediate abolition in the inaugural number of *The Liberator*. In fact, black abolitionists in Philadelphia and Boston influenced Garrison's move to radical abolitionism, and black agents helped get his paper off the ground with their subscription efforts in the black community.

During the late eighteenth and early nineteenth centuries, the Northern states witnessed the beginning of the end of slavery and an increase in their free black population, indicating that freedom was to be the legal norm for African Americans there, not the exception. Caught up in the revolutionary rhetoric of the era as well as the knowledge that their economies were not so dependent upon slave labor, Northern states began to wean themselves of the institution. By 1800, most of the 36,505 slaves left in the North resided in only two states—New York and New Jersey. Those states were the last states north of Maryland to adopt gradual emancipation laws, with New York doing so in 1799 and New Jersey in 1804. But ending the institution of slavery was one thing; integrating free blacks into Northern society was something else. The North failed to provide a climate in which free blacks could stand unburdened by prejudice. For black Northerners, freedom was never the absolute status that it was for their white neighbors, an important understanding that would influence the African-American approach to organized abolitionism.

By the time Mary Ann Shadd wrote to Frederick Douglass, the patterns of antebellum Northern race relations were well-defined. In 1830 there were 137,529 free blacks in the North, and by 1860 their numbers had increased to

226,152. Laws, customs, and comments regularly reminded these men and women that, despite their free status, white racist assumptions proved to be stronger than any lingering revolutionary ideology. White Northerners accepted segregation, the restriction of black civil liberties, and limitations on black economic opportunities. Some states prohibited black immigration; others allowed immigration but required black newcomers to post bonds for good behavior. Blacks could not testify against whites in some states and they had their access to the jury box limited in others. Only a handful of states—Massachusetts, New Hampshire, Vermont, and Maine—treated free blacks the same as whites when it came to exercising the franchise; other states that had once allowed black voting—New Jersey, Pennsylvania, and Connecticut—actually disfranchised their Negro population during the antebellum era. Furthermore, black Northerners found their freedom restricted not only by law but also by custom and personal prejudice. The personal affronts they encountered were troubling reminders of their inferior status.

Abraham Shadd's skill earned him a place among the economic elite of the Northern free black community along with men like free-born Philadelphian James Forten, a successful sailmaker who bought his employer's business. Shadd's middle-class circumstances probably shielded his children from some of the worst consequences of racism, as James Forten's daughter Sarah believed the wealth of her family had shielded her. Shadd and Forten, however, were fortunate to be able to ply trades and run their own businesses, for most Northern blacks found their economic opportunities restricted by racism. In 1841, when the runaway slave Frederick Douglass attempted to find work as a skilled ship's caulker in New Bedford, Massachusetts, he learned that "every white man would leave the ship in her unfinished condition if I struck a blow at my trade upon her."[2]

Racism forced Frederick Douglass to earn his bread as a common laborer, a situation that cut his potential income by half. Most Northern blacks shared his experience, finding their access to skilled jobs limited by white reluctance to accept them as apprentices and comrades in the trades. This common prejudice limited most Northern blacks to earning their livelihoods in menial positions or as subsistence farmers. Ironically, white Northerners, ignoring the role played by skilled slaves in the Southern economy, used the small number of skilled blacks in the Northern states as evidence of black inferiority.

Life for most black Northerners was not only economically difficult, but also potentially dangerous. Race riots and mob violence shattered the security of communities in a number of cities, and runaway slaves who established themselves in Northern communities were never completely secure in their new freedom. Even free-born blacks risked kidnapping and enslavement because of their skin color, as Saratoga Springs, New York, musician Solomon Northup discovered. In 1841 he traveled to Washington, D. C., to perform with a circus and wound up spending twelve years as a slave in the deep South.

Violence lurked just below the surface of everyday life, ready to rear up if

someone witnessed a perceived threat to the racial hierarchy. In 1841 David
Ruggles tried to purchase a first-class ticket on a Massachusetts steamer and
instead received a beating from the captain for his alleged insolence. Earlier, in
1835, the future black abolitionist Henry Highland Garnet watched a mob of
white men haul off of its foundation the Noyes Academy in Canaan, New Hampshire, for daring to admit fourteen blacks along with the twenty-eight white
scholars. Indeed, Northerners generally opposed black education because of its
association with abolitionism: the men who removed the Noyes Academy building praised the Constitution and condemned abolitionism once their work was
done. When Northern communities provided for the educational needs of their
black residents, they established segregated facilities.

If the evils of slavery in the South made emancipation the goal of white
abolitionists, Northern racism taught blacks that freedom was just the beginning
of their liberation. For white abolitionists, slavery and freedom were absolutes;
most of them devoted their attention to abolishing the institution of slavery
without seeing beyond that end. Black abolitionists understood otherwise. In
June 1838, Samuel E. Cornish, editor of the *Colored American*, made this point
clear to white abolitionists who "must gird up the loins of their minds for a
conflict with prejudice against color." He demanded that his allies meet the
problem head on, because "Prejudice against color ... is the test question—at
least among us. The mere and direct question of slavery is not."[3] This was a
message that required repeating on a regular basis, one that most white abolitionists found difficult to absorb.

Having experienced first hand the limitations placed on their liberties by
Northern society, black abolitionists understood that they must repair the dev-
astation caused not only by slavery but also by racism. Black abolitionism,
therefore, was a movement designed to free slaves, end racism, and eradicate
the consequences of both. Black abolitionism also embraced moral reform, the
belief associated with Garrisonian abolitionists that right behavior could contribute to human progress and the perfection of society and, in the case of black
people, that improving their condition would help to improve their status in the
eyes of their white neighbors. Consequently, black abolitionism was both pragmatic and idealistic. It was a temperance movement, a self-help movement, an
education movement, an equal rights movement, and, for some, a women's
liberation movement. It was a movement that expected to liberate individuals
from their own weaknesses, thereby allowing them to stand free of drunkenness,
ignorance, sloth, and poverty while proving that blacks were every bit as worthy
of their place in American society as whites. It was a movement that preached
the middle-class values of thrift, sobriety, and education, because the fruits of
such virtues brought dignity and prosperity while contradicting racist stereotypes. And it was a movement that was designed to help black Americans claim
the very things their white neighbors wished to keep from them, including their
humanity, while convincing their white neighbors of their rights to such a claim.

Black abolitionists relied on a variety of tactics to push forward their agenda within their own community and within the white community in the United States and abroad. Northern free people established literary societies to discuss issues and improve their minds, and self-help organizations to attack the specific problems and emergencies of their communities. They founded their own anti-slavery societies and joined white abolitionists in integrated local and national groups. Abraham Shadd, for example, was one of five African Americans who were on the American Anti-Slavery Society's board of managers when abolitionists founded it in 1833.

Black men and women participated in fund-raising activities for these various organizations. They challenged churches that failed to combat proslavery influences within their own ranks. They sent antislavery petitions to state legislatures and Congress, an important avenue of political expression for the disfranchised. They established newspapers, like John B. Russwurm's and Samuel E. Cornish's *Freedom's Journal*; founded in 1827 in New York City, it was the first black newspaper in the United States. They published the autobiographies of runaway slaves to bring to Northern readers first-hand accounts of how slavery destroyed, among other things, black families, female virtue, and white morals. And they planned boycotts of produce grown by slave labor, an idea rooted in American Quaker and British antislavery.

While the antislavery movement in general relied heavily on the printed word, black orators brought the message about the horrors of slavery and the evils of racism to white audiences at home and abroad. Indeed, black men and women traveled to the British Isles during the three decades before the Civil War to spread their message, raise funds, and promote boycotts. These sojourners alerted audiences to the connection between churches and the endurance of slavery and tried to convince their audiences of the power that the slavocracy wielded over American government, all the while expecting to provoke some kind of international ostracism of the United States.

Black Northerners had always assisted and protected runaway slaves; during the 1830s they organized those efforts by establishing vigilance committees to take legal and extra-legal action on behalf of those runaways, sometimes engaging in dramatic rescue attempts to free blacks from white kidnappers. The activities of these committees also suggested that black Americans would not be completely comfortable with the kind of nonresistance philosophy that would become closely identified with the Garrisonian branch of abolitionism. In response to the kidnapping of "a respectable free colored man," black abolitionist David Ruggles acknowledged that all blacks were liable to similar treatment, regardless of their legal antecedents, and demanded independent and unambiguous action from the black community. "We must no longer depend on the interposition of the Manumission or Anti-Slavery Societies, in the hope of peaceable and just protection; where such outrages are committed, peace and justice cannot dwell," he argued. "While we are subject to be thus inhumanly practiced upon, no man is safe; we must look to our own safety and protection from kidnappers! remembering that 'self-defence is the first law of nature'."[4]

Black abolitionists were always eclectic in their concerns, but the critical issue that sparked a distinct, organized black reform movement was colonization. The American Colonization Society, established in 1816, proposed to encourage the removal of freed slaves to Africa. Free blacks, however, considered the American Colonization Society to be dangerous because it encouraged racism and the abandonment of the South's slaves. Colonization, more than anything else, meant that neither Southern slaves nor Northern free men would ever be accepted as fully fledged members of American society.

As early as January 1817, Philadelphia blacks condemned the American Colonization Society. It also was one of the white institutions attacked by David Walker in his 1829 *Appeal*, a tract that called for a black uprising. A more moderate yet still forceful attack against the Society came from a meeting held in Wilmington, Delaware, in July 1831. A committee issued a strong statement against the efforts of the Society, whose work it charged with being ''unchristian and anti-republican in principle, and at variance with our best interests as a people.'' Its goal, the committee believed, was to ''deprive us of our rights that the Declaration of Independence declares are the 'unalienable rights' of all men.'' All things considered, the Society was ''a barrier to our improvement.''[5] Abraham Shadd, along with two other committee members, composed and signed the statement.

There is some irony in the father attending those very conventions later criticized by the daughter, but Abraham Shadd also showed his children that they must do more than talk about their concerns. Abraham Shadd's feelings about the importance of education's role in developing black independence and Delaware's lack of educational opportunities for African Americans no doubt influenced his return to Pennsylvania in 1833. At the old Shadd family home in Wilmington and then at the family's new residence near Philadelphia in West Chester, Pennsylvania, Abraham assisted runaways along the Underground Railroad; thus he joined the ranks of other black abolitionists who risked their own freedom to help the slave. He helped spread the antislavery word by acting as a subscription agent for reform newspapers, including William Lloyd Garrison's *Liberator*. He was in the forefront of the unsuccessful protest against Pennsylvania's 1838 disfranchisement of black voters, and when he moved to Canada in 1852, he became involved in local electoral politics. Education, temperance, runaway slaves, abolitionist literature, and the franchise—all of these things became prominent in his daughter Mary Ann's reform agenda as well as those of several of his other children.

It was fitting that when Mary Ann Shadd entered the public arena after six years at a Quaker school in West Chester, she did so as a teacher. It probably said much about her father's influence and her desire to right past wrongs that before leaving the United States for Canada in 1851 she returned to Wilmington, Delaware, to organize a school for black children. She also taught in New York City, West Chester, and Norristown, Pennsylvania. Her early teaching career was not a string of successes, however. In 1844 she failed to establish a school in Trenton, New Jersey, a failure that hinted at the personal and systemic problems she would encounter in her subsequent attempts to finance schools.

Shadd complained to her father that Trenton blacks were not giving her school adequate support. Her abrasive personality might have alienated the local parents, but it was likely that class differences played at least some role in her failure. Education was a key to real freedom for the Shadd family and other middle-class blacks, but for working-class blacks—and most urban blacks were laboring people—food and shelter took precedence. Even solvent Northern black families often depended on the income of working women to make ends meet; few of those women had the opportunity to engage in genteel or lucrative employment. Freeborn black New Englander, writer, and orator Maria W. Stewart understood this situation. "Look at our middle-aged men, clad in their rusty plaids and coats," she declaimed to an audience in Boston in September 1832; "in winter, every cent they earn goes to buy their wood and pay their rents; the poor wives also toil beyond their strength, to help support their families."[6] Perhaps most black Trentonians simply did not have the wherewithal to support a school and by necessity rejected Shadd's efforts. Regardless of the reasons for the Trenton community's less-than-enthusiastic response to Shadd's educational plans for them, Shadd apparently showed little sympathy for individuals who did not support her agenda.

The Shadd family's concern for education was true to the black abolitionist belief that the eradication of ignorance was a necessary part of black liberation. Southern laws denied slaves an education; Northern prejudices made it difficult for free blacks to obtain one. Complete emancipation had to address the consequences of these white actions. Education directly attacked the damaging stereotype of the ignorant Negro. Also, the expectation was that education would make blacks more likely candidates for new economic opportunities, the franchise, and other rights and opportunities denied them by white society. But the fact that Mary Ann Shadd and many other black women entered the public sphere through a schoolhouse door was indicative of what was considered an acceptable role for black middle-class women reformers and a reflection of the era's expectations concerning gender roles.

Black women reformers, like their white counterparts, grappled with the implications of the ideal of true womanhood, an expectation that women would work within their separate sphere to provide the emotional support for their families while exemplifying moral purity and nurturing domesticity. Such gender expectations complicated the role of all women in the abolitionist movement, but this ideal of true womanhood had special ramifications for black women reformers. "True womanhood" imposed limits and caused conflicts for them, but at the same time living up to the ideal provided them with an important weapon in their fight against racism and slavery.

Northern black women reformers, who generally were from the middle class, understood the ideal's potential because it provided them with an image that directly contradicted the stereotypes of slavery, especially that of the wanton jezebel. There was also an acceptance of and pride in the duties of motherhood, duties that the institution of slavery treated with contempt. "O, ye mothers, what a responsibility rests on you!" Maria Stewart wrote in the 8 October 1831 edition of Garrison's *Liberator*. "It is you that must create in the minds of your little girls and boys a thirst for knowledge, the love of virtue, the abhorrence of vice, and the cultivation of a pure heart."[7] Even as black women pushed back the boundaries of acceptable public roles, the old image of the true woman gave power to black femininity and remained a useful tool for combating racism.

On one occasion, Mary Ann Shadd's own public presence provided an example of how the careful reporting of the apparently unfeminine activity of public speaking could combat charges not only of moving beyond woman's proper sphere but also of racial inferiority. After witnessing Shadd speak in March 1856, a newspaper editor praised her presentation. "It was replete with original ideas and soundest logic, and unmistakeably showed that she is a woman of superior intellect, of high literary cultivation, and of most persevering energy of character," he reported. He also noted that "Her manner is modest, and in strict keeping with the popular notions of the 'sphere of women'." Shadd was "truly a superior woman," the editor stressed, a quality that made her too good to be considered inferior to her white counterparts.[8]

The editor's assessment struck at black stereotypes, but also illustrated the cautious words required to praise an active woman, lest any praise have the opposite effect and damage her reputation. Other women before Mary Ann Shadd's public time as well as Shadd herself felt the sting from black and white male critics when they intruded into the unwomanly sphere. In September 1832 Maria Stewart began speaking in public, years before white abolitionists Angelina and Sarah Grimké caused a stir in 1837 by standing in front of mixed crowds of men and women—"promiscuous" audiences as they were called—or the more famous Sojourner Truth began her public ministry in 1843. Influenced by fellow Bostonian David Walker, Stewart challenged slavery, racism, and sexism in presentations laced with biblical references and evangelical zeal. She also rang out the common black abolitionist theme of self-reliance. In September 1833, however, she retired because of the criticism provoked by her activities.

Later, in 1840, when the question about the active participation of women in the American Anti-Slavery Society contributed to a schism in the abolitionist movement, some black men opposed admitting women into the more public activities of their abolitionist movement. However, black men by necessity accepted female activism to varying degrees. Some understood the value of female participation in the abolitionist movement, if women followed accepted roles or if they did not challenge black men. Others, like Frederick Douglass and Charles Remond, put aside notions of limited participation and supported women as speakers and even as voting delegates at their conventions. In October 1855, for example, Mary Ann Shadd ran into opposition from delegates to the National Convention of Colored Men held in Philadelphia in her effort to be admitted as an elected member. Some men protested that the meeting "was not a Women's

Rights Convention."[9] Frederick Douglass came to her support and she won the day.

Black women stepped beyond their purely domestic roles and participated in all aspects of the tactical side of the antislavery campaign, contributing literary pieces to antislavery newspapers and fundraising. Furthermore, they actively engaged in the organization of antislavery activities. In 1829 women from Philadelphia's Bethel African Methodist Episcopal Church organized the short-lived Colored Female Free Produce Society of Pennsylvania, part of the movement designed to encourage the purchase of crops grown without slave labor. In 1831, Philadelphia black women organized the Female Literary Society, a consequence of their desire for self-improvement and their exclusion from black male literary societies (it took another decade before the city's blacks established a society open to men and women). In 1832, black women in Salem, Massachusetts, established the first women's antislavery society, and in 1834, their Middletown, Connecticut, counterparts established the Colored Female AntiSlavery Society.

Black women also participated in the politically charged antislavery petition campaign. In November 1839, for example, an anonymous black woman urged the free women of Connecticut to rouse themselves to participate in petitioning Congress and to canvass their neighbors on the issue. "Do you say you have so many family cares you cannot go?" she chided. "Thousands of your sisters may never hear the word *family* but to mock their desolation."[10]

At the same time, the gender-specific organizations of the free women activists reflected all the larger goals of black abolitionism, engaging in activities that transcended neatly defined reform boundaries. The Salem antislavery society's constitution, for example, noted that the female founders "have associated ourselves for our mutual improvement, and to promote the welfare of our color."[11]

Black women, like their male counterparts, also participated in racially mixed organizations. Some even exercised leadership roles, but their experiences were similar to those of their fathers, husbands, and brothers because the white racial attitudes they encountered were ambiguous. "Even our professed friends have not yet rid themselves of [prejudice]," Philadelphian Sarah Forten explained to Angelina Grimké. "To some of them it clings like a dark mantle obscuring their many virtues and choking up the avenues to higher and nobler achievements."[12]

During the 1840s, the relationship between black and white women reformers was further strained when white women entered a new feminist movement. The Seneca Falls convention of 1848, for example, produced a Declaration of Sentiments that did not address the concerns of most black women, slave or free, perhaps because there were no black women in attendance. The oppressive nature of marriage and family and the institutional and societal discrimination against women who desired higher education were not relevant concerns for most black women. Most Northern free black women had to work outside of the home to keep their families in food, clothing, and shelter, circumstances that Sojourner Truth later pointed out made it unlikely that they would have the opportunity to challenge gender boundaries in higher education. Also, free black women may have found it difficult to condemn the oppressive nature of marriage when they understood that one of the means by which Southern slaveholders dehumanized blacks was by denying the legitimacy of slave unions and the permanency of slave families. Nevertheless, if black women failed to find the feminist organizations of white women very appealing, they spoke out for women's rights on their own and at black conventions. They continued to pursue feminism and abolitionism even as white women began to lose their commitment to the latter as they came to focus on the former.

By the 1840s, black abolitionists were frustrated with their inability to bring slavery to an end. It was during this decade that black abolitionists strove for their independence from their white sponsors as they pushed their multifaceted agenda. Black abolitionists, always eclectic and pragmatic in their approaches, began to feel that the Garrisonian tactic of moral suasion required the more vigorous assistance for which Ruggles had called in 1835. In a direct challenge to the philosophy of Garrisonian non-resistance, black abolitionist leaders accepted the need to attack slavery with political action and discussed the role that violence might play in their movement. Henry Highland Garnet, Frederick Douglass, and other black abolitionists rejected Garrisonian pacifism by openly calling for slave revolts. Later Mary Ann Shadd would hint at her own views on violence when she referred to slave insurrectionist Nat Turner as having lived an "eventful but heroic life."[13] In 1858 she met John Brown and came to admire him because he did more than just talk about ending slavery. Also, as late as December 1872, she honored the memory of a former *Provincial Freeman*'s printer's devil who had followed John Brown to Harper's Ferry when she addressed a meeting that had assembled in Washington, D. C. to raise money to reinter the body of Osborne Anderson.

While black abolitionists explored different tactical approaches to ending slavery, they did not jettison all of the old ideas that gave their movement such breadth. Frances Ellen Watkins Harper's September 1860 argument for continued efforts at moral reform, for example, suggested the powerful connection that many black Northerners continued to see between improving their own conditions and attacking Southern slavery. "Upon our alleged inferiority is based our social ostracism and proscription," she wrote to Ohio Quaker abolitionist Jane E. Hitchcock Jones. "To teach our people how to build up a character for themselves—a character that will challenge respect in spite of opposition and prejudice; to develop their own souls, intellect and genius, and thus verify their credentials, is some of the best anti-slavery work that can be done in this country."[14]

Mary Ann Shadd's 1849 demand for vigorous action, a reflection of the growing militancy of a movement becoming impatient with talk, also touched on themes that remained important to black abolitionists, especially that of self-improvement. It was a theme she revisited in her pamphlet *Hints to the Colored People of the North*, also published in 1849. In that work, however, she made it clear that she was in tune with the new sentiments of black abolitionism:

blacks should act independently of their white allies if their friends lagged behind black expectations in the fight against slavery. The developments of the 1850s gave even greater urgency to such a view.

Antebellum free black Northerners had been discussing the possibility of leaving the United States for more congenial environs since 1829, when anywhere from 1,000 to 2,000 Cincinnati blacks left their oppressive city for Canada. Their hatred of the American Colonization Society, however, limited the appeal of and prompted opposition to emigration. The Fugitive Slave Law of 1850 changed matters. Designed to remove the return of fugitive slaves from ordinary judicial procedures and reassure Southerners that the federal government was intent on protecting their right to slave property, it denied the accused the right of habeas corpus and the right to testify in his or her own behalf. Now many African Americans assumed that the Northern states no longer provided even a flawed haven, no matter whether they were runaways or free born; as many as 3,000 blacks sought refuge in Canada during the fall of 1850. The other critical events of the 1850s were equally discouraging to Northern blacks. Indeed, the Dred Scott decision of 1857 clearly stated that the federal government rejected the notion of black citizenship, dashing the hopes of free blacks who had worked under the premise that they would eventually claim all of the benefits commensurate with their birthright as Americans.

During the 1850s, blacks developed several colonization schemes, but Canada remained the favorite and most practicable destination. In the decade before the Civil War, upwards of 20,000 blacks from the United States emigrated to Canada, raising its total black population to approximately 60,000. For some of those African Americans, Canadian residency was a temporary measure until conditions changed in the United States; for others, it was a permanent solution to the problem of second-class citizenship. Mary Ann Shadd was among those immigrants who believed the latter.

In 1851 Shadd and her brother Isaac, after attending a convention in Toronto, settled at Windsor, across from Detroit, a common destination for black emigrés. Her father followed her to Canada the next year to explore the land's potential and decided to relocate his family there. No doubt he was content with his decision. In 1859 he won a place on the Raleigh Town Council, thus becoming the first black to win elected office in Canada, and he remained in Canada after the American Civil War. The elder Shadd's commitment to Canadian settlement evidenced the increasing black frustration with life in the United States.

The Shadd family's enthusiasm for emigration was apparent in Mary Ann Shadd's 1852 pamphlet *A Plea for Emigration: or Notes of Canada West*. Shadd intended to provide useful information for immigrants and to show that blacks would be better off emigrating to points outside of the United States, excluding the African destination of the American Colonization Society, than staying in the United States. Among her arguments and data was a point that would appeal to blacks who had experienced economic discrimination in the cities of the Northern states. "It will suffice," she wrote, "that colored men progress to all the different trades; are store keepers, farmers, clerks, and laborers; and are not only unmolested, but sustained and encouraged in any business for which their qualifications and means fit them.'' She conveyed an optimistic outlook to her readers. ''As the resources of the country develop, new fields of enterprise will be opened to them, and consequently new motives to honorable effort.''

Shadd also explained the benefits of an integrated Canadian society to her American readers who had suffered humiliation not only in the workplace and on the streets, but in churches as well. While in Toronto, she ''was forcibly struck'' by the congregations of the churches ''originally built by the white Canadians'' there. ''The presence of colored persons, promiscuously seated,'' she noted, ''elicited no comment whatever.''

She was severely critical of blacks who continued to segregate themselves from the mainstream of Canadian society. Such separation, she argued, would only encourage assumptions of black inferiority and suspicion among whites and paranoia and prejudice concerning whites among blacks. In contrast to integrated churches, Shadd viewed an exclusive black Canadian church as damaging of good race relations. She was convinced that ''In her bosom is nurtured the long-standing and rankling prejudices, and hatred against whites, without exception, that had their origin in American oppression, and that should have been left in the country in which they originated.''[15] Indeed, Shadd, a one-time African Methodist in the states, refused to renew her membership in Canada because of the denomination's ''distinctive character.''

Shadd's attack against separate black institutions was rooted in her own sensibilities brought with her from the United States, where segregation was the consequence of the white assumption of black inferiority. It also came from her desire to settle roots into the Canadian landscape, where she believed the law was on the side of racial equality, even if the authorities were at times lax in its enforcement. However, after she moved to Canada, a feud with the fugitive slave, abolitionist, and leader of the black Windsor settlement Henry Bibb and his wife Mary gave her an occasion to expound further her personal philosophy, one that directly clashed with that of the Bibbs. The incident acts as a reminder that while black abolitionists shared major concerns, they, too, fought over the most efficacious route to uplift and freedom. Those ideological fights could become heated and could degenerate into personal vendettas.

After arriving in Windsor, Shadd opened a school for ''children of all complexions,'' because she believed there was no excuse for separate institutions in Canada. Despite Shadd's desire to run an integrated school, it was unlikely that white Canadians would send their children to her when they already had adequate public institutions of their own. Despite her earlier flattering account of white Toronto churches, Shadd recognized that there was racism in the Windsor area; her argument for establishing a school was that the trustees of the local government schools refused admission to black children on some technicality and that it would take legal action to open their doors to them. Shadd also observed that the Canadian government provided inadequate support for its black public schools. She later compared the fine buildings of the white government schools to the delapidated black structure and pointed out that the black children who attended it had little hope of advancing beyond the lower grades. Consequently, because she would by necessity direct the efforts of her private school primarily to black scholars, Shadd encountered a problem among the impoverished Windsor blacks that she had faced before in Trenton, New Jersey. Poor black parents could not pay her tuition, or at least that was the "excuse" they used for "not sending [their children] or attending now." Shadd solved that problem by turning to the American Missionary Association, which assisted her school until it withdrew its support in 1853. Shadd did not publicly admit to holding reservations about potentially compromising her independence by accepting "foreign aid," but the problem and its solution did indicate the precarious financial circumstances that black teachers encountered when trying to do good.[16]

It was opposition to this integrated school from Mary Bibb, who conducted the exclusively black government school at nearby Sandwich, and others in the black community who accepted the Bibbs's vision of black separatism as being the best route for black advancement that provoked the feud that would last until Henry Bibb's death in 1854. Mary Ann Shadd's opposition to Bibb's separatist ways found further provocation in his involvement with the Refugee Home Society. Founded in Detroit in 1851 and controlled by white abolitionists, the Society was an organization that had as its purpose the acquisition of Canadian land and the resettlement of blacks on that land. To help carry out these goals, it raised funds by sending representatives on tours to solicit contributions.

The Society, Shadd argued, was not needed because the Canadian government offered land "cheaper and on better conditions." Its segregated nature "arrays the whites against the blacks, because of the superior political privileges sought to be given to ignorant men, by which in petty elections, black men may control, when the provisions made by Government affect all alike." The Society "fosters exclusive institutions, making a line between black men [and white] men." Furthermore, because the character of its settlers was not good, "The Home is looked upon as a lounging place for worthless, shiftless men." In other words, Bibb's Society contradicted Shadd's particular views about black independence and integration. Furthermore, Shadd believed that Bibb was "a dishonest man and as such must be made known to the world."

Shadd opposed the Refugee Home Society's fundraising methods because its "begging" system diverted money "from efficient missionary organizations."[17] Furthermore, she believed that it was an embarrassment to Canadian blacks. Indeed, she objected to the whole begging scheme because it gave a false impression of the plight of the fugitives. New arrivals, Shadd optimistically told William Lloyd Garrison in early 1853, could find gainful employment almost immediately after setting foot on Canadian soil.

The feud between Shadd and the Bibbs, propelled by personal animosity, degenerated into a conflict that went beyond ideology. Also, Henry Bibb's attacks against Shadd were attacks against a woman who stepped beyond accept-able gender boundaries by challenging a black male leader. Shadd in turn attacked the character of both Bibbs and went on to challenge the honesty of the Refugee Home Society, fanning a factionalism within the Canadian black community that contributed to the Society's failure to leave much of a legacy to Canadian blacks. Before the end of the decade, Shadd leveled similar acidic criticism at John Scoble, the secretary of the British and Foreign Anti-Slavery Society, for his involvement with Dawn, another exclusive black settlement. She also severed ties with the Canadian Anti-Slavery Society in part because of the racism of its members and in part because she perceived a personal slight when she wrongly assumed that the Society raised money for Frederick Douglass's journalistic endeavors but ignored her own. Still, Shadd's battles had origins in her views about racism and prejudice and the best ways to deal with them. Her fight with Bibb, for example, began in a legitimate difference of opinion over whether it was best to integrate into white society or remain a separate black community, as well as whether black Canadians were either sojourners awaiting changing circumstances in the United States or settlers intent on making new lives for themselves in their new home. For Shadd the answer was the latter; she became a British subject in 1862.

Her feud with Bibb made Mary Ann Shadd realize that she was at a disad-vantage when competing with someone who controlled a newspaper, in this case Bibb's *Voice of the Fugitive*. "What a vast amount of mischief a man like *H. Bibb* can do with an organ of his own to nod, insinuate and 'fling' away at the reputation of others," she complained.[18] Her efforts to find a larger voice beyond letters to acquaintances and newspaper editors led her to establish her own news-paper, the *Provincial Freeman*, in March 1854. Shadd was technically the pub-lishing agent with Samuel Ringgold Ward publicly acknowledged as the editor, as much a nod to the sexism of the day as to Ward's reputation. Ward, who had taken refuge in Canada after assisting in the rescue of a fugitive slave in Syracuse, New York, in October 1851, contributed little more than his name to the endeavor. Over the years Shadd would hold various titles and there would be other editors listed on the paper's masthead, including H. Ford Douglas and her brother Isaac, but she remained the paper's driving force. It was her vision that dominated the *Provincial Freeman*, and she was well aware of the gender boundary that she had broken as the first black woman editor in North America. She urged other black women to follow her lead into newspaper editing.

It took Shadd almost another year to find sufficient backing to begin publish-ing the *Provincial Freeman* on a regular basis, this time from Toronto with Shadd's philosophy giving the paper its motto: "Self Reliance Is the True Road to Independence." The move to Toronto was a futile attempt to locate the paper where it might find sufficient support in the larger, more prosperous black com-munity. A move the next year to Chatham was also most likely a search for a base of support within a larger black community. The paper's financial stability, however, remained precarious. It went through different periods of fruitful activity, laying fallow during others. By the end of the decade, it was no longer publishing.

While it was in print, the *Provincial Freeman* provided Shadd with an independent public forum for addressing in her own inimitable way the issues—especially black self-reliance, racial discrimination, and the integration of blacks into Canadian society—that were important to her. In a February 1857 circular designed to help raise funds for the paper, Shadd, along with her co-editors H. Ford Douglas and Isaac Shadd, clearly stated her editorial expectations, which encompassed some of the common themes of black abolitionism: "Ignorance and inexperience of individual responsibility, are bitter fruits of the Institution of Slavery; as an anti-slavery instrumentality, then, the *Freeman* aims in an humble way to uproot the tree, by inculcating a healthy anti-slavery sentiment, in a country which though under British rule, is particularly exposed, by intercommunication, to proslavery religious and secular influences to encourage the colored people to improve their minds, and to hold fast by their religious faith, and thus to dissipate the dark cloud hovering over their intellect, the direct result of their former condition."[19] For Shadd, improving the lives and futures of black refugees now residing in Canada was truly antislavery work, a necessity to counter the "injury done to [them] intellectually, physically, [and] morally" by the institution that they had escaped.[20]

During her years involved with the *Provincial Freeman*, she pressed forward with her agenda, continuing to condemn black churches that fostered racism, white Canadian churches that refused to sever ties with their congregations in the United States that refused to condemn slavery, begging agents who embarrassed her vision of self-help, and individuals and their institutions that disagreed with her vision. Even when traveling to raise funds for the paper, she still appeared in its pages as a correspondent describing her experiences and criticizing communities that did not live up to her expectations.

In her fight against oppression, she made it clear that society had to deal with the problem of sexism as well as racism. Women as well as men were created in the image of God, Shadd once wrote, and "We cannot successfully evade duty because the suffering fellow woman is only a *woman*! . . . The spirit of true philanthropy knows no sex."[21]

It seems that Shadd's feminism also included the belief that women had something distinct to offer their communities. After attending a meeting of the voters of Chatham, she remarked on the number of women present and suggested that their presence at political gatherings would change the tone of those meetings by introducing a feminine quality to them. "I like that new feature in political gatherings," she commented, "and you will agree with me, that much of the asperity of such assemblies will be softened by their presence."[22] She seemed to ignore the fact that she was often the source of such "asperity."

Shadd also expounded on her favorite themes when she visited the various meetings of African Americans during her travels. At the National Convention of Colored Men's October 1855 meeting in Philadelphia, Shadd defended emigration to Canada, where there were opportunities for the energetic and where former slaves now owned acres of land; she challenged those delegates who wished to "stifle" the right of black Americans to go anywhere they wished on the continent. And once again, she prodded delegates to action, telling them "that they were not simply sent here to make speeches, but to act upon matters by which the elevation of coloured persons would be accomplished." [23]

Even some of those who were present who disagreed with her views on emigration were impressed by her confident demeanor. One observer reported his favorable opinion of Shadd's presentation, despite their differences of opinion. He noted that Shadd's eyes "fairly flash when she is speaking. Her ideas seem to flow so fast that she, at times, hesitates for words; yet she overcomes any apparent imperfections in her speaking by the earnestness of her manner and the quality of her thoughts." Shadd captured the crowd with her "masterly exposition." [24] But unfortunately for Shadd, her performance did little to raise any significant sums of money to help her paper.

Along with her efforts to establish a newspaper and her travels to raise funds and spread her ideas, Shadd began her own family. On 3 January 1856 Shadd married Thomas F. Cary, a Toronto barber who had three children from an earlier marriage. At times she pursued the role of the domestic nurturer by caring for her stepchildren and having two children of her own, Sarah Elizabeth (born in 1857) and Linton (born in 1860). She conventionally took her husband's last name, signing her correspondence and newspaper pieces with it, but the Shadd-Cary marriage was far from conventional. Only five days after her wedding, Mary Ann left her new husband to travel through the midwestern United States for six months. Thomas Cary remained in Toronto while his wife traveled or edited her paper in Chatham. Mary Ann also felt an obligation to travel even when her daughter was a baby; she was able to do so thanks to the assistance of a younger sister. Sometime by 1858, her ailing husband joined her in Chatham; he died there in November 1860.

As the sectional crisis came to a crescendo, Mary Ann Shadd Cary kept her readers apprised of her views of the situation in the United States. After the election of 1856, she presciently warned that the quiet south of the Canadian border was just the calm before the storm. The Democrats may expect deference to their views now that they had won the electoral contest, Cary observed, "but the genius and spirit of liberty is against them." Violence in Kansas and in the halls of Congress as well as the "demon-like attitude of the South" have made many white Northerners abolitionists by necessity; they feared the further transgressions of slaveholders "because of their tyrannical and dictatorial policy towards them." For the new breed of antislavery activist, Cary noted that "Compassion for the slave in his chains is but secondary to the great necessity of a decided struggle for his own liberties, by the white man of the country." Her views were the pragmatic views of many black abolitionists who would take their allies where they could find them, but she also looked forward to slavery being consumed by a terrible conflagration. "Depend upon it," she

warned, "there will be hard and bloody work before the struggle termi-
nate[s]. . . . [N]ow we contemplate a great but gory struggle."[25]

With the demise of her paper, Mary Ann Shadd Cary returned to education,
teaching for a short time in Michigan during 1862 and then at Chatham, again
with the assistance of the American Missionary Association. Her need for financial aid even prompted her to swallow her pride and unsuccessfully approach
the Refugee Home Society for funds. Her activism, however, ran unabated and
continued to transcend the classroom. In 1860 she assisted Osborne Anderson
in preparing for publication his account of John Brown's raid, *A Voice from
Harper's Ferry*, which appeared in early 1861. Also, the lack of her own personally controlled journalistic forum did not stop her from continuing to make
known her views to American editors. Her work was recognized and in demand.
In 1859 Thomas Hamilton recruited her to contribute to his shortlived *Anglo-
African Magazine*, and in November 1861, Garrison published one of her letters
in *The Liberator*, which reminded Americans that, as they embarked on their
Civil War, the Canadian fugitives "have keen sympathies for friends and kindred left behind; their better selves remember for ever [sic] the friends who
helped them on, and aid others with help when needed here."[26]

Cary also continued attending meetings and making her presence felt at them.
In March 1861, Cary offered a resolution at a meeting that entertained black
physician, editor, and emigrationist Martin R. Delany's plans to establish a col-
ony in the Niger Valley of Africa. Cary, still committed to Canada, did not
endorse Delany's plan. She acknowledged Delany's work for African emigration, resolving that black Canadians would be able to accept it or reject it "as
their best judgement shall dictate."[27] Later in October 1861 Cary confirmed her
affection for Canadian emigration when she referred to Haitian emigration,
which she opposed, as a "new fangled movement."[28] In the end, while some
African Americans exhibited a new willingness to listen to Delany and the other
emigrationists, the reasons that prompted their fathers to oppose the American
Colonization Society still resonated with them.

With the secession and the coming of the Civil War, black Americans focused
their attention on the United States, understanding that this fight would determine their fate. A successful Southern rebellion could only strengthen the institution of slavery, they understood, but a Union victory just might alter the
nature of race relations in America. Consequently, even as black abolitionists
debated exactly what role they should play in the crisis, they devoted much
effort to keeping emancipation at the center of wartime antislavery.

One thing that black Americans understood that they could do to further their
cause was to volunteer to carry arms in the fight. Initially rejected as soldiers
by the Lincoln administration, black Northerners rushed to the colors after Lincoln issued his Emancipation Proclamation on 1, January 1863. There was no
question that the Civil War was now their fight. Sattira Douglas, H. Ford Douglas's wife, understood the significance of her own husband's enlistment and
expected others to follow his example to learn the lessons of sacrifice and cour-

age. "It is true that now is offered the only opportunity that will be extended, during the present generation, for colored men to strike the blow that will at once relieve them of northern prejudice and southern slavery," she wrote in June 1863. "If they do not enroll themselves among those other noble men who have gone forth to do battle for the true and right, it will only prove the correctness of the aspersions indulged in by our enemies, that we are unworthy of those rights which they have so long withheld from us, and that freedom would not be appreciated by us, if possessed." In the end, black men had much to gain, for the war had placed "liberty, honor, social and political position . . . within their grasp."[29]

In 1863, Cary returned to the United States and became involved in assisting the ex-slaves caste adrift in the wake of advancing Union armies. She worked as a fundraiser for the Colored Ladies Freedmen's Aid Society of Chicago to help support its efforts to provide relief for ex-slaves residing in contraband camps. Later that year, however, Martin Delany, one of the most successful black army recruiters, invited Cary to recruit black troops, which she did. In March 1864, the Connecticut state recruiting service requested her assistance, and in August 1864 the adjutant general of the state of Indiana officially commissioned her as a recruiter. It could be a rewarding assignment for someone who needed to repair her finances; a recruiter received a fee for each able-bodied slave, freedman, or free black that he or she brought into the service. Still, self-interest did not diminish the nobility of the work and now Cary had a message that appealed to working-class African Americans. Even the dullest recruit understood the abolitionist relationship between killing white Southerners and ending slavery. By Appomattox, over 34,000 of the nearly 180,000 blacks who served in the Union Army were black Northerners, including Mary Ann Shadd Cary's brother Abraham W. Shadd, a sergeant major in the 55th Massachusetts.

During the war and after the victory, black abolitionists participated in the shaping of postbellum America in other ways. Not only did black women abolitionists use their organizational experience to raise money for the ex-slaves, they participated in the freedom experience close to the front lines. The courageous Maryland ex-slave Harriet Tubman, who had returned South on numerous occasions to rescue other slaves, served the Union cause as a nurse, a scout, and a spy. Other black women may not have engaged in such dramatic ventures, but they also took serious risks when they eagerly volunteered to go South to teach and to do missionary work among the freedpeople. Their work was truly heroic. In the South, they entered a harsh, dangerous environment created by hostile white Southerners as well as the lingering prejudice and paternalism of their white associates.

Once in the South, black women taught ex-slaves the middle-class virtues they believed were essential for their future independence. Sojourner Truth, for example, taught ex-slaves "the habits of industry and economy" while instructing them in "order, cleanliness and virtue."[30] They were lessons repeated by black middle-class women steeped in the traditions of the work ethic of the antebellum North. They believed these lessons had been useful for their own families and that now they would have equal value for the newly freed slaves.

Reconstruction provided new opportunities for a new generation of black women abolitionists, too young to have participated in the battles of the 1850s but old enough to have learned of their importance from their elders, to test themselves and their commitment to improving their race. Charlotte Forten, the granddaughter of James Forten and the niece of Sarah Forten, for example, completed her education in 1855, taught school, and nursed her health until 1862 when she traveled to Port Royal, South Carolina, teaching freedpeople there until May 1864.

Black and white abolitionists also participated in the debates over the proper course for reconstructing the South, perhaps suggesting that it became easier for white abolitionists to accept the need to root out the vestiges of slavery and the power of the slavocracy in the South than it had been to fight racism in the antebellum North. For black abolitionists, their position remained a familiar one. John Mercer Langston, president of the National Equal Rights League, made it clear in his speeches that black Americans still required more than the abolition of slavery before they could claim their movement to be a success; legal equality and "the free and untrammelled use of the ballot" were also the freedmen's due.[31]

The debates over the nature of citizenship that were central to Reconstruction policy led to problems for black women abolitionists who, like Mary Ann Shadd Cary, believed they should not be pushed aside by the racism of white feminists or the sexism of black men. The Fourteenth Amendment adopted in 1868 defined citizenship for black men, but excluded women from its attempt to encourage states to grant blacks the vote by inserting the word "male" for the first time into the Constitution. Both white and black women reformers were disappointed by the Fifteenth Amendment adopted in 1870 because it did not specifically grant them suffrage. The struggle for woman's suffrage would continue into the next century until the Nineteenth Amendment granted women the ballot in 1920. But woman's suffrage came when Jim Crow and disfranchisement reduced most African Americans to second-class citizens in the South. For most black women, real enfranchisement did not come until the civil rights movement began to enjoy some success during the 1960s. Along the way, the fight for women's rights brought with it racial tension that reenforced black women's understanding that both racism and sexism needed to be eradicated. Black women remained committed to multifaceted reform that was the hallmark of black abolitionism.

During the war, Mary Ann Shadd Cary watched as many of her black Canadian neighbors returned to the United States after the fight became one for freedom. After the war, she observed the serious needs of the freed population. Consequently, she decided to reside in her native land. After her stint as a Union Army recruiter, Cary settled in Detroit and taught school there. In 1869 she moved to Washington, D. C., where from 1872 to 1884 she served as principal of a black school.

Cary continued to express her views in the press and on the lecture circuit. While she no longer advocated emigration, she held to her views about black advancement, black equality, and woman's suffrage while also addressing the need for black women to become more involved in the public life of their communities. She continued to maintain a full lecture schedule until her health prevented such activity, but while doing so, Cary remembered the youthful criticism she had leveled at black conventioneers in 1849 to "do more, and talk less." She testified before the House Judiciary Committee in favor of expanding the scope of the Reconstruction amendments to include women. In March 1874 she joined a group of women that unsuccessfully attempted to register to vote. In 1880 she founded the Colored Women's Progressive Franchise Program, an organization that was true to the black abolitionist legacy; while the organization diverged from her earlier integrationist views (as did her position at a black school, which perhaps suggests her recognition of the unhappy facts of American life and the need for black organizations to make headway in a racist society), it did present a multi-faceted program for black advancement. And in 1883 she received a law degree from Howard University. Rheumatism and cancer finally stopped Mary Ann Shadd Cary from "doing." She died in Washington, D. C., on 5 June 1893, having lived long enough to see the hopes and expectations of black abolitionism stymied for the time being by white America's abandonment of its black citizens. After a lifetime of activism, there was still much left to do.

Mary Ann Shadd Cary placed great demands on black Americans. Her expectations were high and her criticism of those who failed to accept her challenge was unforgiving. While recognizing the inequities of the society in which they lived, she prodded blacks on to take control of their destiny and to claim what was rightfully theirs. She had, however, never asked anyone to do what she was not willing to do herself.

NOTES

1. *North Star*, 23 March, 1849, reel 5, George E. Carter and C. Peter Ripley, eds., *Black Abolitionist Papers, 1830–1865* (17 reels, New York, 1981; Ann Arbor, Mich., 1984) (hereinafter referred to as *Black Abolitionist Papers*). The Black Abolitionist Papers Project collected almost 14,000 documents produced by approximately 300 African-American men and women. A selection of these documents has been annotated and published in C. Peter Ripley et al., eds., *The Black Abolitionist Papers* (5 vols., Chapel Hill, N.C., 1985–1992). An even more select group of documents from the letterpress edition appears in C. Peter Ripley et al., eds., *Witness for Freedom: African American Voices on Race, Slavery, and Emancipation* (Chapel Hill, 1993). *The Black Abolitionist Papers* in its various forms are critical for understanding the movement. Peter Ripley's introductions to the various published volumes were essential in shaping my views of black abolitionism, as was the time I spent working with him on the Canadian volume,

the second volume of the letterpress edition. Other essential works on black abolitionism, black life in the North, and black women used for this essay are listed in the following bibliography. Two books were published too late to be used in writing this essay, but are of interest to those students who wish to pursue this topic: James O. Horton and Lois E. Horton, *In Hope of Liberty: Culture, Community, and Protest Among Northern Free Blacks, 1700–1860* (New York, 1996) and Nell Irvin Painter, *Sojourner Truth: A Life, A Symbol* (New York, 1996).

2. Frederick Douglass, *Life and Times of Frederick Douglass* (1892; New York, 1962), 211.

3. C. Peter Ripley et al., eds., *The Black Abolitionist Papers*, Vol. 3: *The United States, 1830–1846* (Chapel Hill, 1991), 265.

4. Ibid., 169.

5. C. Peter Ripley et al., eds., *The Black Abolitionist Papers*, Vol. 5: *The United States, 1859–1865* (Chapel Hill, 1991), 102–106.

6. Marilyn Richardson, ed., *Maria W. Stewart: America's First Black Woman Political Writer, Essays and Speeches* (Bloomington, 1987), 49.

7. Ibid., 35.

8. *Provincial Freeman*, 29 March, 1856, reel 10, *Black Abolitionist Papers*.

9. *British Banner*, 20 November, 1855, reel 9, ibid.

10. C. Peter Ripley et al., eds., *The Black Abolitionist Papers*, Vol 2: *Canada, 1830–1865* (Chapel Hill, 1986), 326–327.

11. Dorothy Sterling, ed., *We Are Your Sisters: Black Women in the Nineteenth Century* (New York, 1984), 113.

12. Ripley et al., eds., *Black Abolitionist Papers*, 3: 222.

13. *Provincial Freeman*, 3 June, 1854, reel 8, *Black Abolitionist Papers*.

14. Ripley et al., eds., *Black Abolitionist Papers*, 5: 82.

15. Mary A. Shadd, *A Plea for Emigration: or, Notes of Canada West, in its Moral, Social, and Political Aspect: With Suggestions Respecting Mexico, W. Indies and Vancouver's Island, for the Information of Colored Emigrants* (Detroit, 1852), 7, 8, reel 7, *Black Abolitionist Papers*.

16. Mary Ann Shadd to Rev. George Whipple, 27 November, 1851, ibid.

17. Mary Ann Shadd to Rev. George Whipple, 28 December, 1852, ibid.

18. Mary Ann Shadd to Rev. George Whipple, 21 July, 1852, ibid.

19. Mary Ann Shadd Cary, Henry Ford Douglas, and Isaac D. Shadd, Feb. 1857, reel 10, ibid.

20. *Liberator*, 29 November, 1861, reel 13, ibid.

21. Mary Ann Shadd Cary, 6 April, [1858?], reel 11, ibid.

22. *Provincial Freeman*, 6 October, 1855, reel 9, ibid.

23. *British Banner*, 20 November, 1855, ibid.

24. Sterling, ed., *We Are Your Sisters*, 171.

25. *Provincial Freeman*, 6 December, 1856, reel 10, *Black Abolitionist Papers*.

26. *Liberator*, 29 November, 1861, reel 13, ibid.

27. *Chatham Planet*, 29 March, 1861, ibid.

28. *Weekly Anglo-African*, 19 October, 1861, ibid.

29. Ripley et al., eds., *Black Abolitionist Papers*, 5: 212.

30. Sterling, ed., *We Are Your Sisters*, 253.

31. Ripley et al., eds., *Black Abolitionist Papers*, 5: 376.

BIBLIOGRAPHY

Blackett, R.J.M. *Beating Against the Barriers: Biographical Essays in Nineteenth-Century Afro-American History.* Baton Rouge, 1986.

———. *Building an Antislavery Wall: Black Americans in the Atlantic Abolitionist Movement, 1830–1860.* Baton Rouge, 1983.

Blight, David W. *Frederick Douglass' Civil War: Keeping Faith in Jubilee.* Baton Rouge, 1989.

———. "They Knew What Time It Was: African-Americans and the Coming of the Civil War," in Gabor S. Boritt, ed., *Why the Civil War Came.* New York, 1996.

Curry, Leonard P. *The Free Negro in Urban America, 1800–1850.* Chicago, 1981.

Dillon, Merton L. *Slavery Attacked: Southern Slaves and their Allies, 1619–1865.* Baton Rouge, 1990.

Hancock, Harold. "Mary Ann Shadd Cary: Negro Editor, Educator, and Lawyer," *Delaware History* 15 (1973): 187–194.

Hine, Darlene Clark, ed. *Black Women in America: An Historical Encyclopedia*, 2 vols. Brooklyn, N.Y., 1993.

Horton, James Oliver. *Free People of Color: Inside the African American Community.* Washington, D. C., 1993.

Litwack, Leon F. *North of Slavery: The Negro in the Free States, 1790–1860.* Chicago, 1961.

McPherson, James M. *The Struggle for Equality: Abolitionists and the Negro in the Civil War and Reconstruction.* Princeton, N. J., 1964.

Pease, Jane H., and William H. Pease. *They Who Would Be Free: Blacks' Search for Freedom, 1830–1861.* New York, 1974.

Quarles, Benjamin. *Allies for Freedom: Blacks and John Brown.* New York, 1974.

Silverman, Jason H. "Mary Ann Shadd and the Search for Equality," in Leon Litwack and August Meier, eds., *Black Leaders of the Nineteenth Century.* Urbana, 1988: 87–102.

Venet, Wendy Hamand. *Neither Ballots nor Bullets: Women Abolitionists and the Civil War.* Charlottesville, Va., 1991.

White, Deborah Gray. *Ar'n't I a Woman? Female Slaves in the Plantation South.* New York, 1985.

Yee, Shirley J. *Black Women Abolitionists: A Study in Activism, 1828–1860.* Knoxville, 1992.

Yellin, Jean Fagan. *Women & Sisters: The Antislavery Feminists in American Culture.* New Haven, 1989.

———, and John C. Van Horne, eds. *The Abolitionist Sisterhood: Women's Political Culture in Antebellum America.* Ithaca, 1994.

Elizabeth Cady Stanton
and the Woman's Rights Movement

ANN D. GORDON

Advocates of woman's rights in nineteenth-century America declared no new or special rights, but claimed rights that were acknowledged for men within the family and outside it in civic life. Exact legal parallels between men and women could not be drawn. The women's realization that their relationship to men was prescribed in both spheres—in the family circle and the political arena—drove woman's rights activists to explore new and multiple meanings of equality. They attacked men's arbitrary power in familiar language derived from the colonial protest against a king and in new language aimed at the patriarchal authority preserved in common law, customs, and cultural institutions.

Elizabeth Cady Stanton was the chief writer and intellectual of the woman's rights movement during the decade before the Civil War, when the new reform found its voice and revealed its objectives. After the war, her renown spread beyond reformers. On the national lecture circuit she commanded high fees and drew good audiences year after year. Editors sought her opinion not only about women but also about street cleaning, child rearing, and fashion. Her name became synonymous internationally with the cause of women's equality. Stanton also served as an officer of national associations representing the movement's interests, beginning with the Women's Loyal National League (1863–1864), rallying support to outlaw slavery; the American Equal Rights Association (1866–1869), advocating universal suffrage; and both the National Woman Suffrage Association (1869–1890) and its successor, the National American Woman Suffrage Association (1890–1892), pressing for federal protection of woman's right to vote. She presided over the founding meeting of the International Council of Women in 1888.

Historians usually reserve the term "woman's rights" for the antebellum phase of the nineteenth-century movement, replacing it after the war with the term "woman suffrage movement." This shift in terminology echoes the language of the times; the National Woman's Rights Committee dissolved itself into the American Equal Rights Association, and that in turn produced woman suffrage associations. The new term underscores, without defining, an effect of the Civil War on this reform. But attention to "rights" survived the war and characterized the postwar movement through the years of Reconstruction and its demise. A case can be made that greater differences separated the early from the late stages of the woman suffrage movement than marked the transformation wrought by war.

Along with her good friend and invaluable coadjutor Susan B. Anthony, Elizabeth Cady Stanton promoted the idea that the basic tenets of American political ideology dictated women's political participation. It was an imperfect republic and an incomplete revolution that left women taxed without representation and subject to laws to which they gave no consent. She took women's fundamental equality with men for granted. Her reforms would remake law and institutions to reflect the fact. The woman suffrage movement ceased to agree on those principles sometime in the early 1880s. Suffrage attracted women who were concerned with increasing their power rather than establishing their equality and who brought late nineteenth-century political values to the cause. Many late suffragists shared the conservative mood that accompanied the end of Reconstruction, and they welcomed the drive for national unity that would replace a war over human rights. By the end of her career, Elizabeth Cady Stanton and equal rights were controversial among woman suffragists.

Born in Johnstown, New York, 12 November 1815 to Daniel and Margaret Livingston Cady, Elizabeth Cady came from an atypical background for a pioneer of woman's rights. She grew up in a well-to-do household with parents who gave her as good an education as a girl of her generation was likely to get. When she exhausted the resources of the Johnstown Academy, she attended the famous Troy Female Seminary, where Emma Willard pioneered a secular, academic education for girls. In the year of her birth, her father served in Congress; throughout her childhood, he practiced law and trained lawyers at Johnstown; after she left home, he was a member of the New York Supreme Court. From the heights of local society, Elizabeth knew no limits she was bound to respect—save her sex.

Looking for the precipitating causes of her career in her youth, the mature Stanton credited herself with early perspicacity about the injustice of being female in antebellum America. She described rebellion against the dour and fearsome theology of her family's Scotch Presbyterianism. She recounted the injustice she suffered when boys who were her intellectual inferiors at the Academy went on to college while no such opportunity was offered her; the pain of realizing, when her one surviving brother died, that sons meant more to a father than his daughters; and the woes of wives and widows consulting her father, their rights to property not protected by law.

During his courtship of the twenty-four-old Elizabeth Cady, the antislavery orator and agent Henry B. Stanton, then at the peak of his career, saw in her a woman undecided about two paths that beckoned: "the giddy whirl of fashionable follies" and the religious duty of "a person of so superior a mind & enlarged heart" to do something for "a wicked world's salvation."[1] Opting for "duty," Elizabeth Cady married Henry Stanton on 1 May 1840.

By 1848, when Elizabeth Cady Stanton called the first woman's rights convention at Seneca Falls, New York, she had blended diverse experiences into a new perspective on reform and women's part in it. Because Henry Stanton agreed to study law with his father-in-law in order to support a wife and family, marriage for Elizabeth reinforced the legal training she had begun with her father and his students who gathered around him. Yet she was attracted to reformers who spurned law for moral suasion, and to Quakers who regarded the practice of law as amoral. Marriage introduced her to the most radical women in the land: to Angelina and Sarah Grimké, who had linked antislavery activism to the liberation of women; to the Quaker preacher and abolitionist Lucretia Mott, who had joined the causes of religious individualism and equal rights; and to the Garrisonian radicals who led female antislavery societies in Rochester, Philadelphia, and Boston. But marriage also had put her at the very center of the antislavery division over the efficacy and rectitude of political action. While she learned to admire William Lloyd Garrison, Henry Stanton defied him by building the Liberty party in Massachusetts and later in New York. She had a front-row seat on the future, when political abolitionism would dominate the reform and marginalize its women.

At the Seneca Falls convention, women demanded "immediate admission to all the rights and privileges which belong to them as citizens of the United States." Most notable among these were political rights. Women wanted representation and a voice in the making of law; they wanted "their sacred right to the elective franchise." Of a generation that was familiar with ceremonial readings of the Declaration of Independence each Fourth of July, and whose grandfathers fought in the American Revolution, the women at Seneca Falls turned to the Declaration to indict men's tyranny and to declare, in language hallowed in American politics, their inalienable rights. All laws that made woman the inferior of man or conflicted with her pursuit of happiness were, they declared, "contrary to the great precept of nature, and therefore of no force or authority." Laws of marriage and property were singled out for special condemnation, as were limits placed on her pursuit of education and employment. Overarching all the specifics in their "Declaration of Sentiments" and their resolutions was their claim to individuality, to being philosophically like men, similarly "endowed by their Creator," and entitled to follow their own consciences. Man had "usurped the prerogative of Jehovah himself, claiming it as his right to assign for her a sphere of action, when that belongs to her conscience and to her God."[2]

Not all of these ideas were new in 1848. Stanton's coauthors and many in attendance at the convention were veterans of women's fight to join the antislavery cause. At the Anti-Slavery Convention of American Women at New York in 1837, the language was more religious but the points were similar. Bearing equal moral responsibility with men, women needed the freedom to pursue moral causes—to lecture and preach, to educate, to petition, to join men in abolishing slavery. They resolved, in the words of Angelina Grimké, "That the time has come for women to . . . no longer remain satisfied in the circumscribed limits with which corrupt custom and a perverted application of Scripture have encircled her."[3] Although women's claims divided the antislavery forces, defense of women's right to a public role in the movement became part of the credo of the American Anti-Slavery Society.

Legal reform that would rid state codes of their most egregious examples of women's subordination to men's control of property had begun before the 1848 meeting. In Stanton's home state of New York, new law in 1848 protected the property that married women inherited from their fathers, though few women had yet seen the cause of legal reform as their own. Stanton knew that statutes were replete with exclusions aimed at women, children, idiots, and prisoners. "Think you," Stanton asked in 1848, "if woman had a vote in this government, that all those laws affecting her interests would so entirely violate every principle of right and justice?"[4]

While taking ideas from familiar reforms, the Seneca Falls convention broke with the past most decisively in its claim that woman's moral responsibility extended to herself. "The question now is," Stanton said, "how shall we get possession of what rightfully belongs to us."[5] This movement would seek women's rights because they were entitled to them, not because rights were tools in the struggle to free slaves, improve the lives of children, or purify the community.

From Seneca Falls the ideas spread, sprouting up in woman's rights conventions in New York, Ohio, Indiana, Massachusetts, and Pennsylvania within a few years. Broad principles were reiterated, the Declaration of Independence was cited, and precise objectives were spelled out. A letter from Stanton was standard fare at these meetings; her brood of young children (seven were born by 1859) kept her tied to home. Her wit as much as her wisdom won an audience. The antislavery press, the women's press, the temperance press, the health reform press—all gave space to Stanton for appeals and articles. The National Woman's Rights Convention resolved that she should write for Horace Greeley's *New York Tribune*, and she did, firing her opening shot at the midterm elections of 1854.

[R]eally, if all the women on the footstool, of every color, nation and tongue, had combined together to see what confusion they could make, they could never have equaled the men of the Empire State in this last campaign. Who ever saw such a botch, such a game at cross-questions, and silly answers. . . . Now, Greeley do you suppose the women could do worse than the lords of creation have done for the last four years?[6]

The clearest achievement of the movement in this early phase was to stimulate debate by introducing the ideas of women's subordination and resistance into political and social culture. Less obvious was the rapid schooling in political practice that activists acquired. In state after state, women petitioned their legislatures and constitutional conventions, learned to write memorials, and mastered the mysteries of legislative procedure. At the state capitals they assigned someone to oversee legislation and mobilized crowds of lobbyists as needed. Year by year their skills improved. In 1859 Clarina Nichols, an early ally, a newspaper editor from New York and Vermont, and an emigrant to Kansas, led a sophisticated and remarkably successful campaign at the Kansas constitutional convention to gain rights for women. Committee members consulted her, and the delegates asked her to address an evening session.

With Susan B. Anthony as her partner, Stanton put her ideas to the political test in New York State. Single and willing to travel ceaselessly, Anthony became the agent of the woman's rights movement who scheduled lectures, accompanied speakers into every county, distributed petitions and shepherded them back to the legislature, published pamphlets, and raised money. In 1854, assisted by their many friends in the legal community, Stanton and Anthony prepared for the legislature an itemized list of "the legal disabilities under which we labor." It included the absence of classic rights—government by consent, representation, and trial by a jury of their peers—and the imposition of disabilities by laws of marriage, widowhood, and motherhood. It defined an agenda for reform. "We ask no better laws than those you have made for yourselves," Stanton assured the legislators. "We need no other protection than that which your present laws secure to you."[7] Persistence won them rare allies and small victories before the war, especially in revised laws on women's economic rights.

Equality in the private relations of families proved early to be the most controversial part of the woman's rights agenda, though no more difficult to achieve legislatively than suffrage. When Stanton first broached her demand, in 1852, that more grounds be allowed women for obtaining a divorce, the clergy attacked her swiftly; clerical opposition would plague her for years. If marriage was a sacred institution, she asked them, then why did state law govern it so minutely? Marriage was a civil contract, and, she argued in 1860, a flawed one: the "marriage contract [is] based in the idea of the supremacy of man, as the keeper of woman's virtue, her sole protection and support," and most of the disabilities that women sought to overcome could be traced to marriage. "Out of marriage," Stanton wrote, "woman asks nothing at this hour but the elective franchise. It is only in marriage that she must demand her rights to person, children, property, wages, life, liberty, and the pursuit of happiness."[8]

Stanton continued to explore private equality through and after the Civil War. In 1869 she announced to an audience in New York City a new mission: "that as I had devoted my life heretofore to the enfranchisement of woman, my future work should be to teach woman her duties to herself in the home. . . . Thus far we have had the man idea of marriage. Now the time has come for woman to give the world the other side of this question.''[9] She overstated how she would allocate her time thereafter, but she affirmed how the personal dimension of women's lives remained central to her political agenda for woman's rights. Equality in marriage and at home supplied her with themes for many of the lectures she took to the public in the 1870s.

Before considering the contentious history of woman's rights during and immediately after the Civil War, it is useful to review the relationship between woman's rights and abolitionism. It had its troubles even before war began, but everyone seemed surprised when these problems produced serious disagreement during and after the war. Abolitionists were the best friends the woman's rights movement had. The spots in the North where agitation took root were antislavery communities, and most woman's rights leaders moved easily back and forth to meet the immediate needs of one movement or the other. The *Liberator* and the *National Anti-Slavery Standard* were the media of woman's rights as they were of abolition. However, opinions about what tied the one movement to the other varied.

Stanton, like most of her colaborers, relied on an analogy between women and slaves. Writing to the Ohio woman's rights convention at Salem in 1850, for example, she noted that a married woman ''has no more absolute rights than a slave on a Southern plantation. . . . Civilly, socially, and religiously, she is what man chooses her to be—nothing more or less—and such is the slave.''[10] A decade later she ventured to compare not only their conditions but their subjective experience as well. Men, she told the American Anti-Slavery Society, might describe ''the general features'' of the slave system, ''but a privileged class can never conceive the feelings of those who are born to contempt, to inferiority, to degradation. Herein is woman more fully identified with the slave than man can possibly be, for she can take the subjective view.''[11] She was the slave.

Antislavery feminists constructed this equation early. Celebrating her own liberation through antislavery activism, Angelina Grimké said in 1838: ''For many years I felt as if I was compelled to drag the chain and wear the collar on my struggling *spirit* as truly as the poor slave was on his body.'' A metaphor about oppression and liberation had obvious utility when explaining their oppression. It also posited a sisterhood that bound even privileged white women in the North to the antislavery cause. But did they believe it as social reality? Historian Jean Fagan Yellin observes that in time the metaphor permitted women ''to collapse the racist, sexist, and class oppression of black women into a common expression of gender.''[12] The analogy ceased to particularize the horrors of American slavery. When emancipation became a possibility and then a reality, history required that the equation be questioned. People who had implicitly accepted that women and slaves shared a common oppression did not agree about the social and political priorities for emancipation when the fate of ex-slaves hung in the balance.

Unanimity in the two antebellum movements about the need to redefine American rights as individual human rights obscured another problem—that woman's rights depended on abolitionists for power—and dependency undercut claims of equality. The women were, after all, lacking in the currency of politics. In theory, women's citizenship within the reform community was a prototype of long-range goals; in practice, women were dependents. In 1856, when violence broke out in Kansas over slavery and John Charles Frémont ran for president on the new Republican party's ticket, Stanton's male allies expected her to hold woman's rights demands in abeyance so as not to divert attention and resources from the national crisis or to complicate the election by raising extraneous controversies. Abolitionists needed the male electorate at this moment more than they needed their female allies, if their ideas were to gain popular support. Implicit in that judgment was a decision that slavery's abolition could occur without addressing the related question of woman's rights. During the war, the decision became explicit.

Most deeply buried of the tensions within the antebellum alliance were the implications of an independent political movement among women. Sharing the abhorrence of slavery, women had stepped easily into the opening that male antislavery leaders allowed them. Side by side they worked in an established cause with recognized leaders. Stanton venerated William Lloyd Garrison, Wendell Phillips, and their colleagues as the premier reformers of the age. Only gradually did advocates of woman's rights articulate positions that went beyond the antislavery consensus. And when they did, most often in discussions of marriage and divorce, antislavery leaders acted as if they had never heard or heeded Stanton's early proclamations that men could not represent women, that women would define issues for themselves. Instead, the men presumed not only to represent but also to lead her movement because they were leaders in their own.

In the cauldron of civil war, the demand for woman's rights was transformed, most dramatically by its becoming national in scope and federal in focus. That the cause became national during the war had less to do with the activists themselves than with national crisis. Like men, women experienced the war as an unprecedented mobilization for national ends, whether their role was to relinquish the lives of husbands and sons to battle or to serve the war machine as nurses or managers of relief efforts. They were drawn into national organizations far more centralized than anything in their previous experience, such as the U.S. Sanitary Commission. As the chief architect of the new federal focus for woman's rights, Stanton redirected women's national identities. She transformed the movement and in the process helped to fragment it.

In 1863 Stanton revived one of women's earliest political activities—petitioning Congress for an end to slavery—and created a new organization to coordinate it rather than work through the antislavery societies. Under the motto ''In Emancipation Is National Unity,'' her Women's Loyal National League set itself the goal of gathering 1 million signatures on petitions demanding slavery's end. The names of 265,000 men and women, gathered by the League, were delivered to Congress during the winter and spring of 1864 by Massachusetts Senator Charles Sumner, as evidence that public opinion favored emancipation.

Some women were confused by the League. Drawn by its call, they expected more soldiers' relief and found its antislavery focus puzzling. Others accepted the centrality of abolition but balked when woman's rights topics surfaced. Stanton envisaged a League that would imitate, under new circumstances, the advent of women into the antislavery cause. The League would once again tie women's liberation to the emancipation of slaves. Just as Angelina Grimké had, while emancipating herself, become one of the best antislavery orators, proven women's value to the cause, and opened the way for women's equality as abolitionists, so the League, in the midst of war, would position women at the forefront of republican ideology, where their value to the nation would be appreciated. The League demanded "for ALL the people the exercise of those rights that belong to every citizen of a republic."[13] Congress passed the Thirteenth Amendment, ending slavery, and the League's members awaited the next step.

Reconstruction absorbed women's attention because Congress, for the first time, debated the issues that their movement had articulated since 1848. It asked what made a citizen; it examined how to create representation of an unrepresented group; it wondered how to protect new rights; it debated whether voting rights were necessary for citizenship; and it looked at how voting rights might be extended despite states' rights to regulate the franchise. Stanton seized the moment. With Anthony, Lucy Stone, and a handful of other prewar leaders, she appealed to Congress in January 1866 for universal suffrage that would enfranchise former slaves and all women. That Congress never intended to push the cause of universal liberty and rights slowly dawned on the petitioners. Woman suffrage was the demand crafted from the failure to win universal suffrage, and it was a demand now more difficult to achieve because the amended Constitution linked manhood to voting rights. Very few male abolitionists had stood with women in the fight, and none shared their bitterness at defeat. Woman's rights activists found themselves alone for the first time.

Between 1869 and the mid-1870s, the woman's rights movement struggled for a strategy that would make woman suffrage a significant national demand, take advantage of a new precedent for federal action on voting rights, and capitalize on the new use of constitutional amendments for reform. A few supporters introduced a sixteenth amendment in Congress that would match the Fifteenth and complete in tandem what could not be accomplished in a sweeping reform. Women converged for the first time on Washington, as they had on state capitals before the war, but the measure died. The constitutional amendments of Reconstruction were completed without removing what Stanton had called "the inconsistencies of our theory and practice" in this republic.

Suffragists divided over their response to this failure. Stanton turned against the Fifteenth Amendment for establishing the principle of man government and enshrining women's exclusion from the franchise in the Constitution. Many of her oldest friends from the woman's rights movement were appalled that she would thus attack the delicate balance that protected voting rights for the men who had been slaves. She offended them further by defining an independent political agenda for woman suffragists. Her National Woman Suffrage Association (NWSA), established in 1869, did not allow men to hold positions of leadership, refused to be guided by the Republican party, and dismissed out of hand the new Republican faith that women should go back to winning their voting rights state by state. Many of her critics found their home in the rival American Woman Suffrage Association headed by Lucy Stone.

Although Stanton and the NWSA sought a national, federal solution for obtaining woman's right to vote, they lacked a more precise strategy for several years. In fact, the initiative lay elsewhere, as women new to the cause tried to establish that their voting rights were in fact protected by the combination of the Fourteenth and Fifteenth amendments. Stanton adopted and popularized their reasoning: that by virtue of their national citizenship, women were now protected in their right to vote. By taking direct action at the polls and pursuing court cases, dozens of suffragists looked to the Supreme Court to settle the question. At the same time, others appealed to Congress for legislation that would enable their interpretation of the amendments. Congress rejected their argument, and the Supreme Court ruled that citizenship implied nothing about voting rights. In decisions that imperiled the voting rights of Southern black men as well, the Court in fact reaffirmed the right of states to regulate the franchise. By 1875 Stanton's wing of the suffrage movement faltered.

Stanton, however, revived the movement and led it through its most important campaign until the twentieth century by taking it back to the lessons of Reconstruction and reprising the demand for a sixteenth amendment. In an appeal issued in the fall of 1876, she wrote: "Having celebrated our Centennial birthday with a National jubilee, let us now dedicate the dawn of the Second Century to securing justice for Women." She acknowledged the decisions of the Supreme Court but condemned them. "If this Magna Charta of Human Rights [the Constitution] can be thus narrowed by judicial interpretations in favor of class legislation, then must we demand an amendment that in clear, unmistakable language, shall declare the equality of all citizens before the law."[14] For the next five years Stanton and the NWSA worked ceaselessly to mobilize women around this demand.

Their success with women owed a great deal to Stanton's parallel career as a popular lecturer. In the decade since the war, women of quite different experiences and values had learned to recognize her as a leader who embodied their aspirations. A call for proof that women wanted the vote elicited several thousand signatures from more than half the states, all of them gathered informally in neighborhoods and at meetings of women who came together for purposes other than gaining suffrage. Some of the writers echoed Stanton's belief in woman's rights. "I want the ballot," wrote a woman from Oshkosh, Wisconsin. "1st Because it is mine by a right, withheld by the 'powers that be'[.]" Others spoke a new language that wedded a belief in woman's moral superiority with her political ambition. "[P]eople are beginning to see," wrote a woman from Breckinridge, Missouri, "that if this hydra headed demon of Intemperance is ever subdued, *woman must have a voice in Legislation*." Women recalled occasions when they had heard Stanton speak, and thanked her. One sent her preserves along with the list of signatures.[15]

Among men, the battle by the late 1870s was more difficult. Even to propose federal action for woman suffrage required a confrontation over states' rights, and states' rights were gaining political power. "National Protection for National Citizens" was the suffragists' theme and the title of one of Stanton's greatest speeches, delivered to senators in 1878. She combined the ideals of Radical Reconstruction with answers to the Supreme Court's denial of a federal interest in voting rights. A republic, she insisted, could not survive the separation of citizenship from voting rights that the United States attempted. Voting rights were too important to the republican idea to be left to states.

"Inasmuch as we are, first, citizens of the United States, and, second, of the State wherein we reside, the primal rights of all citizens should be regulated by national government, and complete equality in civil and political rights everywhere secured." The paralysis that kept the government from protecting the political rights of Southern freedmen she condemned as evidence of "the imperfect development of our own nationality," of the nation's historic failure to define "the limit of State rights and Federal power." On behalf of woman's rights Stanton reaffirmed the vision of universal rights. "The kind of government the people of this country expect, and intend to have, State rights or no State rights . . . is a government to protect the humblest citizen in the exercise of all his rights."[16] For nine years the Senate kept the amendment alive but locked in committee. When it finally came to a vote in January 1887, the measure failed.

Stanton retired from the lecture circuit in 1881 and spent a considerable part of the next decade abroad, where her grandchildren were growing up in England and France. Thereafter, she spoke publicly only a few times a year at special events. Although nominally the president of the NWSA until 1892, she missed many meetings and spent little time with the members. Personal pulls and political pushes alike contributed to this change in her life. Aged sixty-six, she was weary of travel. When her youngest child reached legal maturity, Stanton gave up housekeeping, and for the next twenty years relied on her children to provide her with homes, as if collecting on the debt of their childhoods, when she had paced "like a caged lioness," longing to be free of "nursing and housekeeping cares."[17]

Privacy also allowed Stanton to distance herself from the woman suffrage movement and its new demands. Success was changing the movement's membership and the leadership it required. More and more of its adherents wanted the vote to express female superiority and to empower their religious or regional views; only a faction expressed itself in the language of equal rights. Compromise with these new voices did not appeal to Stanton. With the principles in place and support growing for the idea that women deserved a political voice, agitation for woman suffrage required organizing and lobbying skills of a sort that Stanton neither enjoyed nor excelled in. It needed builders of institutions and planners of political strategy. It called for dull meetings and simplification of ideas. By removing herself from the daily demands of leadership, she could write and criticize. In the two decades that remained of her life, Stanton produced five books and hundreds of articles, published in everything from Hearst's daily newspapers to free-thought journals. She became a reformer in her own reform movement, suffragism's independent voice. She died in New York City, 26 October 1902.

Late in life Stanton had summed up the role of the reformer as she understood it. "Let us remember," she wrote in the introduction to her *Woman's Bible*, "that all reforms are interdependent. . . . Reformers who are always compromising, have not yet grasped the idea that truth is the only safe ground to stand upon. The object of an individual life is not to carry one fragmentary measure in human progress, but to utter the highest truth clearly seen in all directions, and thus to round out and perfect a well balanced character."[18] A lofty and difficult mission, this was also a strikingly individual mission measured by personal integrity, not social effect or acceptance. In its immediate context, the passage rationalized Stanton's controversy with suffragists over her critique of clerical and biblical authority. But it clearly addressed a sense of her vocation. It recalled her admiration for William Lloyd Garrison, and it suggested tension in her own career between realizing the objectives of a reformer and those of a leader. Written when suffragists had stalled in their pursuit of winning the vote state by state and when black men were losing the right in one Southern state after another, Stanton may also have affirmed a belief that those who freed the slaves without regard for universal liberty were in error—that it was they, not she, who had compromised and overlooked the interdependence of reform.

NOTES

1. Henry B. Stanton to Gerrit Smith, 27 February 1840, Gerrit Smith Papers (Syracuse University).

2. "Declaration of Sentiments and Resolutions, Adopted by the Woman's Rights Convention at Seneca Falls, New York, 19–20 July 1848," in Mari Jo Buhle and Paul Buhle, eds., *Concise History of Woman Suffrage: Selections from the Classic Work of Stanton, Anthony, Gage, and Harper* (Urbana, Ill., 1978), 94–97.

3. Dorothy Sterling, ed., *Turning the World Upside Down: The Anti-Slavery Convention of American Women, Held in New York City, May 9–12, 1837* (New York, 1987), 13.

4. Untitled address, 1848, excerpted in Ellen C. DuBois, ed., *Elizabeth Cady Stanton, Susan B. Anthony: Correspondence, Writings, Speeches*, rev. ed. (Boston, 1993), 32.

5. Ibid.

6. Letter to the Editor, *New York Semi-Weekly Tribune*, 28 November 1854.

7. "Address to the Legislature of New York on Women's Rights," 20 February 1854, excerpted in DuBois, ed., *Stanton, Anthony*, 44–52.

8. Letter to the Editor, *New York Daily Tribune*, 30 May 1860.

9. "Speech to the McFarland-Richardson Protest Meeting," May 1869, excerpted in DuBois, ed., *Stanton, Anthony*, 125–130.

10. Letter to the Ohio Women's Convention, 7 April 1850, in *Liberator*, 17 May 1850.

11. "Speech to the American Anti-Slavery Society," May 1860, excerpted in DuBois, ed., *Stanton, Anthony*, 79–85.

12. Jean Fagan Yellin, *Women & Sisters: The Antislavery Feminists in American Culture* (New Haven, 1989), 171; quotation from Grimké's speech, p. 42.

13. "To the Women of the Republic," *New York Daily Tribune*, 24 April 1863.

14. Appeal for a Sixteenth Amendment, 10 November 1876, *Ballot Box* (Toledo, Ohio), December 1876.

15. Mrs. L. M. Stephenson to Stanton, undated, and Mrs. Josephine B. Humphrey to Stanton et al., 31 May 1880, in National Woman Suffrage Association Collection (Chicago Historical Society).

16. Stanton's testimony, *Arguments Before the Committee on Privileges and Elections of the United States Senate, in Behalf of a Sixteenth Amendment to the Constitution of the United States . . . January 11 and 12, 1878 . . .* (Washington, D.C., 1878), 4–17.

17. To Susan B. Anthony, 10 June 1856, in DuBois, ed., *Stanton, Anthony*, 63.

18. Introduction, *The Woman's Bible* (1898; repr. Boston, 1993), 11.

BIBLIOGRAPHY

Aptheker, Bettina. *Woman's Legacy: Essays on Race, Sex, and Class in American History*. Amherst, Mass., 1982.

Buhle, Mari Jo, and Paul Buhle, eds. *Concise History of Woman Suffrage: Selections From the Classic Work of Stanton, Anthony, Gage, and Harper*. Urbana, Ill., 1978.

DuBois, Ellen C. *Feminism and Suffrage: The Emergence of an Independent Women's Movement in America, 1848–1869*. Ithaca, N.Y., 1978.

———. "Outgrowing the Compact of the Fathers: Equal Rights, Woman Suffrage, and the United States Constitution, 1820–1878." *Journal of American History* 74 (December 1987): 836–862.

———, ed. *Elizabeth Cady Stanton, Susan B. Anthony: Correspondence, Writings, Speeches*. Rev. ed. Boston, 1993.

Flexner, Eleanor. *Century of Struggle: The Woman's Rights Movement in the United States*. Rev. ed. Cambridge, Mass., 1975.

Griffith, Elisabeth. *In Her Own Right: The Life of Elizabeth Cady Stanton*. New York, 1984.

Hewitt, Nancy A. *Women's Activism and Social Change: Rochester, New York, 1822–1872*. Ithaca, 1984.

Holland, Patricia G., and Ann D. Gordon, eds. *Papers of Elizabeth Cady Stanton and Susan B. Anthony*. Microfilm ed. Wilmington, Del., 1991.

Stanton, Elizabeth Cady. *Eighty Years and More: Reminiscences, 1815–1897*. 1898; repr. Boston, 1993.

Stanton, Elizabeth Cady, Susan B. Anthony, and Matilda Joslyn Gage, eds. *History of Woman Suffrage*. 3 vols. 1881–1886; repr. New York, 1969.

Venet, Wendy Hamand. *Neither Ballots nor Bullets: Women Abolitionists and the Civil War*. Charlottesville, Va., 1991.

Yellin, Jean Fagan. *Women & Sisters: The Antislavery Feminists in American Culture*. New Haven, 1989.

Dorothea Dix
and Mental Health Reform

ELISABETH LASCH-QUINN

"I am the Revelation," Dorothea Dix once wrote, "of hundreds of wailing, suffering creatures hidden in your private dwellings, and in pens, and cabins,—shut out, cut off from all healing influences, from all mind restoring cares."[1] Nineteenth-century reformer, author, teacher, and Civil War superintendent of nurses, Dix helped usher in a revolution in the way Americans thought of and treated those considered mentally ill. Incensed by her firsthand observations of the living conditions of the insane confined in her local jail, she began a lifelong project of examining such conditions and bringing them to public attention primarily through her memorials, which were presented for government action by members of the legislatures of the various states. These elaborate testimonials raised general awareness of the most shocking and tangible details of cruel treatment and confinement, and through the nineteenth-century reformer's method of moral suasion, Dix managed to compel legislatures to appropriate funds for the construction of new hospitals for the treatment of the insane and for improvements to extant ones, thus abetting the transition to institutionalization already under way. Dix's reform work struck her as the humanitarian imperative of her life: "I am the Hope of the poor crazed beings who pine in cells, and stalls, and cages, and waserooms," she wrote.[2]

When Dix promoted institutions for the insane, she pictured benevolent hospitals in which treatment would be the province of enlightened doctors who saw madness as a disease, albeit one with a moral component. Far from the authoritarian and inhumane psychiatric hospital of the modern American cultural landscape—as depicted, for instance, in Ken Kesey's *One Flew over the Cuckoo's Nest*—or the overcrowded place of confinement, not cure, described by discouraged asylum superintendents, Dix's ideal asylum was a place of kindness, order, and decency. Part of a larger movement that sought to revise older ways of viewing insanity, Dix advocated the application of science and medicine to madness, which by the early nineteenth century was presumed to possess a discrete and unique character. Like many doctors, asylum superintendents, and reformers, she was outraged at what many mistakenly considered the colonial custom of mass confinement of all dependents, often in deplorable conditions. Confinement of the insane together with criminals, or the poor, came under constant attack in her memorials, as did forcible restraint of the insane more generally. She considered institutions for the insane an alternative to dehumanizing methods of confinement. Dix's writings on behalf of the insane offer remarkable testimony, as does her entire life of reform, to the rise of a new sensibility concerning insanity in the late eighteenth and early nineteenth centuries.

The notion that insanity was a unique condition that set its victims apart from the rest of the population replaced the colonial tendency to view it as part of life and to integrate the afflicted into the other structures of community life. During the interim between colonial methods of provision for the insane and nineteenth-century institutionalization, the heightened sensitivity toward insanity as a separate condition buttressed the emerging notion that the insane should be separated from society. Coupled with such forces of drastic social dislocation as population growth, industrialism, and urbanization, this sensitivity led to changes that included the passage of a law in Massachusetts in 1796 that required the confinement of those considered "furiously mad" in jail.[3] Once policies concerning the insane were initiated, and confinement began to appear appropriate, "the right to confine extended to all classes." According to Mary Ann Jimenez, "Insanity had now taken on an independent status, and the insane, whether paupers or not, were the object of policies designed especially for them."[4]

Driving the movement to institutionalize the insane was the belief that it was not only the violent insane that required confinement—a central irony of the work of reformers like Dix. While decrying the confinement of the insane in *"cages, closets, cellars, stalls, pens!"*[5] Dix promoted confinement in institutions, which entailed other forms of maltreatment. Reformers generally thought they were freeing the insane from abuses inherent in colonial custom, but actually, Jimenez writes, "those insane who suffered the difficulties of confinement in the beginning of the nineteenth century had been subject to a more insistent rationality that characterized the early Republic," when "the anxiety about madness apparently led to a new pattern of confining the non-violent insane."[6]

Unfortunately, the abuses prevalent in the period that witnessed the decline of colonial traditions became wedded in many people's minds with colonial traditions themselves. Those who considered themselves compassionate rejected earlier customs as a whole, without salvaging what was useful and beneficial to the community, such as the integration of nonviolent troubled individuals into family and community life. Practices that publicly singled out the insane for special attention only when they became dependent on the community protected the privacy and encouraged the self-reliance of anyone who managed to cope with the demands of daily life. This guideline, at its best, could keep the focus on the objective need for care and support instead of on subjective conceptions of normal behavior. Once judgments about normality began to be the criteria for insanity, the population considered insane mushroomed and therapeutic procedures eventually insinuated their way into the innermost realms of private life. Although it would be naive to idealize colonial custom as a whole, given that it veered off at times into witch-hunting or ostracizing misfits, many have erred in dismissing it as inhumane in all aspects. In the nineteenth century, partly because of reformers like Dix, the colonial failure to distinguish between insanity and other forms of dependency became associated with the most cruel forms of confinement, which were actually more prevalent in the early national period and all melded into one bogey—tradition. As a result of their faith in newness and progress, nineteenth-century asylum superintendents, prompted by conscientious reformers, perpetuated a shorter-lived practice whose particular flaws they tried to remedy but whose larger misdirection they overlooked—confinement.

Dorothea Lynde Dix was born on 4 April 1802, in Hampden, Maine (then part of Massachusetts), to Joseph and Mary Bigelow Dix. Her parents apparently did not provide a very stable, comforting, or inspiring environment for the young girl. Her father, Joseph Dix, began his studies at Harvard but dropped out to marry the impoverished Mary Bigelow, twenty years his senior, who was considered an unsuitable addition to the respected Dix family. Joseph's inability to provide for the family, which came to include two sons, combined with Mary's physical infirmities to put unusual burdens on young Dorothea. When Joseph turned to the itinerant Methodist ministry, she spent her days sewing his tracts. Her life contrasted markedly with the order and plenty of the elegant Boston estate of her grandparents. On visits there, until he died when she was seven, Dorothea was inseparable from her grandfather, whom she loved to accompany on walks around his gardens, on drives to historical Boston sites, and on outings to his place of work.

At age twelve Dorothea ran away from her parents to live with her grandmother, Dorothy Dix, the widow of Elijah Dix, a prosperous physician, chemical manufacturer, and land promoter. When her grandmother, a strict disciplinarian, tried to educate Dorothea in proper decorum and other social skills, she encountered a headstrong girl with ideas of her own, formed by the demands of frontier life. Dorothea was sent to live with her great aunt in Worcester, where she found a more congenial environment in a home filled with children. At age fourteen, she set up a little school in a vacant building and became a "school marm," dressing severely to appear older than she was. In the course of teaching "reading, writing, manners, and sewing," she proved herself a harsh disciplinarian, whipping her pupils for misbehaving and making one walk to and from school with a sign on her back reading "A Very Bad Girl Indeed."[7]

Dorothea returned to her grandmother's house in Boston and pursued her own education with the help of her grandfather's substantial library and private tutors. Driven by the need to support her mother and two younger brothers and to become financially independent, she soon opened a school with a special section for needy children that was inspired by the work of Hannah More in England. Dorothea became engaged to a cousin, Edward Bangs, but as her work expanded to fill her waking hours, the engagement was broken off. A key figure in her emotional life stepped in; Ann Heath, who then lived with her family in Brookline, became a lifelong friend and confidante. Dorothea did not participate in social events—ignoring her grandmother's encouragement to enter society as an eligible young lady—not even those arranged around intellectual and reformist endeavors. One biographer wrote:

In her nature there lodged an intensity, a search for perfection, an awful seriousness, dwelling there side by side with an unyielding reserve, that made for a deportment considered old-fashioned, ultra-ladylike, even in those days of gentle manners. It is not hard to see that this young woman of unbending dignity and serious purpose might have been a damper on any assemblage not committed to improvement of the human lot.[8]

From an early age, Dorothea avoided frivolity in attire, preferring dark, simple dresses and wearing her hair parted down the middle of her head and stretched across her ears to a tight knot in back, and expressed a conscious dislike for "fashionable dissipation."[9] Perhaps it was the unreliability of her parents and the contrasting model of order and respectability provided by her grandparents that steered her toward a heightened sense of purpose, order, seriousness, and self-control. She mentioned to friends that she had always to counteract an innate tendency to avoid work; such self-criticism seemed to ensure that little of her life would be spent in relaxation.

In her twenties Dix wrote a science text titled *Conversations on Common Things* (1824), a book of poems titled *Hymns for Children* (1825), and numerous other works for young people. From early on, however, she thought teachers had the responsibility to inculcate in children a self-critical moral awareness, as illustrated by her book, *American Moral Tales for Young Persons* (1832), and by previous students' comments about the strict decorum she required and a curious technique she had of soliciting quasiconfessions from her students. In her grandmother's house, where she ran a boarding school for young women, Dix kept a large shell, "a sort of ear of God,"[10] in which she asked her students to place daily letters spelling out the results of constant self-examination. Dix wrote extensive replies, encouraging students to forsake greed and vanity, and on Saturday evenings discussed their shortcomings with them in individual consultations.

Dix's teaching, writing, and studying occupied nearly all her waking hours. Lack of rest, combined with physical ailments, resulted in periodic infirmity, including a full-scale collapse in 1836 and numerous other battles with illness throughout her life. To recuperate, she traveled to Liverpool, England, and, through William Ellery Channing's introduction, stayed with a Unitarian merchant and philanthropist, William Rathbone. While living with Rathbone and his family, she may have met—and certainly became acquainted with the ideas of—one of the leading reformers of conditions for the insane in England, Dr. Samuel Tuke, son of William Tuke, a Quaker who founded the York Retreat in 1792. Upon her return to America, Dix traveled, avoiding teaching because of the potential strain. In 1841, at the age of thirty-nine, she taught a Sunday school for women at a prison in East Cambridge, Massachusetts. There she encountered mentally ill women confined in an unheated section of the jail. Horrified at both the inhumane living conditions and the confinement of prisoners and the insane together, she launched a career in the reform of conditions for the mentally ill in America.

Dix began her life's work by conducting an intensive survey of all Massachusetts jails, almshouses, and houses of correction. Finding atrocious conditions, she spelled them out in detail and used them as a basis for a moral appeal to the Massachusetts legislature in the form of an 1843 memorial written by her and presented by Samuel Gridley Howe. Along with Charles Sumner and Horace Mann, Howe supported Dix's efforts and championed her cause, taking public stands against those who accused her of sensationalism and inappropriateness. The result was a triumph for Dix—the appropriation of more funds for Worcester State Hospital. Drawing on this experience, she went on to conduct surveys of Rhode Island and New York, and then many other states, presenting numerous memorials. Her inspections entailed thousands of miles of traveling in often grueling conditions. At times, she participated in other reforms, as when she conducted research on prison conditions and published the results in *Remarks on Prisons and Prison Discipline in the United States* (1845).

In 1848 Dix had Senator John A. Dix of New York present a different kind of memorial—one asking Congress to set aside millions of acres of public land as a perpetual trust, the income from which would fund the treatment of the insane. For six years she lobbied Congress to pass the bill, but when both the House and the Senate finally did vote in favor of it, President Franklin Pierce vetoed the measure on the grounds that the responsibility for public welfare rightly belonged to the states. Nevertheless, Dix's agitation for better treatment of the insane resulted in the allotment of state funds for new or improved facilities. In the 1850s, she continued her work abroad in Scotland, Italy, France, Turkey, and Russia.

During the Civil War, Dix served as superintendent of nurses for the Union. Before undertaking this role, she tried to continue her efforts on behalf of the insane without speaking out about slavery, for fear it would close all doors to her reform work in the South. But when the war broke out, she immediately boarded a train for Washington, in order to volunteer for nursing duty. She was assigned the responsibility of hiring nurses and placing them in military hospitals, along with other duties. The idea that one woman could perform such

work, which derived from misconceptions about the war's duration and seriousness, was mistaken. In addition, Dix's experience in reform work had taught
her to be independent and to answer only to her own high standards of morality
and organization. Faced with the exigencies of war and administration, which
called for practical solutions, compromises, and cooperation with other workers,
she sought much more single-handed control than was possible. Even her friends
spoke of the difficulties she encountered working with others, the impossibly
high level of "pure consecration to duty" she demanded of her nurses, and her
inability to tackle effectively the problems at hand with her usual tone of moral
righteousness. She sought out abuses, fought with surgeons, and "tried to stand
over the sick and wounded soldiers as the avenging angel of their wrongs," as
a biographer put it.[11]

Observers like Elizabeth Blackwell and Louisa May Alcott thought Dix a
difficult or arbitrary administrator, and she was formally reprimanded by removal of the ultimate authority over nurses from her hands. In spite of her
unsuitability for the work and her unpopularity in this position, she never took
a day's vacation during the war. She spent the duration organizing nurses, ar-
ranging for medical supplies, inspecting hospitals, and exposing poor conditions
in them. Undoubtedly Dix's efforts led to the saving of many lives. Nevertheless,
looking at her Civil War work, she said, "This is not the work I would have
my life judged by!"[12]

After the Civil War, Dix again visited hospitals and prisons, particularly those
in the South, lamenting the decline in conditions. She came to symbolize the
movement to institutionalize the insane, and worked in concert with the Association of Medical Superintendents of American Institutions for the Insane,
founded in 1844. At least partly because of her efforts, by 1850, 123 hospitals
for the insane existed in the United States (in 1843 there were only thirteen);
Dix had helped found thirty-two of them and had inspired many more. She was
particularly proud of the New Jersey State Hospital for the Insane in Trenton,
New Jersey, which she called "my first-born child."[13]

Lobbying for the establishment of this hospital, Dix had her memorial concerning conditions in New Jersey presented to the state legislature by Joseph S.
Dodd. It stressed that the asylum was the only viable alternative to physical
restraint of the insane at home, indicating that it was not only the indigent who
were treated in that manner. One well-known former judge, lawyer, and member
of the state legislature, Dix said, had fallen from a place of "honor and trust"
to one of loneliness and despair because he had lost his wealth through economic
"fluctuations" and his mind had begun to drift with age.[14]

Behind the scenes, Dix worked from before dawn to late night, writing letters
and editorials, meeting with legislators individually and in small groups, in attempts to influence those who did not favor increasing taxes in order to finance
the building of a hospital for the insane at Trenton. She wrote to a friend: "You
cannot imagine the labor of conversing and convincing."[15] Viewing her endeavor as a purely humanitarian one, Dix approached her political maneuvering

as a missionary cause, as is evident in her description of her conversation with one doubting Thomas:

The last evening, a rough country member, who had announced in the House that the "wants of the insane in New Jersey were all humbug," and who came to overwhelm me with his arguments, after listening an hour and a half with wonderful patience to my details and to principles of treatment, suddenly moved into the middle of the parlor, and thus delivered himself: "Ma'am, I bid you good-night! I do not want, for my part, to hear anything more; the others can stay if they want to. *I am convinced*; you've conquered me out and out; I shall vote for the hospital. If you'll come to the House, and talk there as you've done here, no man that is n't [*sic*] a brute can stand you; and so, when a man's convinced, that's enough. The Lord bless you!"—and thereupon he departed.[16]

When the vote was finally taken, on 14 March 1845, the bill for the establishment of the New Jersey asylum passed into law, as did many others that Dix was to initiate. Her desires for a homey place of order and pleasantness were seemingly fulfilled; she visited the asylum on numerous occasions and returned there to spend her last years. She died there on 18 July 1887.

Although it might be tempting to view Dix as inaugurating drastic social changes nearly single-handedly, her work can be understood only in the context of nineteenth-century social conditions and cultural transition. Stirred by the reform fervor of the period, particularly strong in Boston in the 1830s, Dix responded to particular circumstances when she decided to devote her life to altering the ways that the insane would be treated. She was one of a small but growing number of women, for instance, who fashioned an expanded female sphere from the imperatives of the emerging "cult of true womanhood," with its emphasis on the superiority of women in the moral and domestic sphere and its view of the inherent differences between men and women. Although she criticized politicians for their petty partisanship and disputes driven by self-interest, she was as politically active as it was possible for a woman to be, given the lack of the right to vote, the capacity to hold public office, and approval for speaking in public. In fact, Dix was not known to speak to a group of more than about a dozen people at a time throughout her life.

Although Dix had sympathy for the cause of women's rights, she criticized the extremism of some reformers, drawing on notions of "respectable womanhood" to advance her cause. She asserted that her femininity compelled her to bring to the attention of the public the horrifying details of conditions in prisons and almshouses. She called on the "Men of Massachusetts": "I beg, I implore, I demand, pity and protection for these of my suffering, outraged sex."[17] At the same time, she apologized for stepping out of the modest reserve of ladylike behavior to convey the abuses she witnessed: "I shall be obliged to speak with great plainness, and to reveal many things revolting to the taste, and from which my woman's nature shrinks with peculiar sensitiveness. But truth is the highest consideration."[18] Like Catharine Beecher, Frances Willard, and others, Dix used her femininity to argue, as moral guardian, for a political goal she thought transcended traditional politics:

Fathers, Husbands, Brothers . . . Here you will put away the cold, calculating spirit of selfishness and self-seeking; lay off the armor of local strife and political opposition; here and now, for once, forgetful of the earthly and perishable, come up to these halls and consecrate them with one heart and one mind to works of righteousness and just judgment. Become the benefactors of your race, the just guardians of the solemn rights you hold in trust. Raise up the fallen; succor the desolate; restore the outcast; defend the helpless; and for your eternal and great reward, receive the benediction. . . . "Well done, good and faithful servants, become rulers over many things!"[19]

Dorothea Dix also belonged to a generation of reformers who interpreted their religious views as a mandate for social reform. Although she criticized revivalists as succumbing to an "age of impulse," Dix partook of that aspect of reform Christianity that rejected determinism and emphasized the possibility for earthly perfection through ideal, man-made institutions. In addition, her agitation for federal land that would provide a fund for care of the insane made her part of the longer-term movement to expand the realm of the federal government into public welfare that came to fruition in the twentieth century. It was, however, the successful movement for the appropriation of federal land for internal improvements that laid the immediate groundwork for Dix's demand.

Most crucial for understanding Dix's life and role in the movement on behalf of the insane is, of course, the major transformation in attitudes toward madness already under way by the time Dix became involved in furthering such change at age thirty-nine. The debate over the ultimate significance of this transformation has centered on basic differences over how reformers, self-appointed humanitarians, philanthropists, and other do-gooders should be understood.

Some scholars have stressed the humanitarian motives of reformers, viewing the results of their efforts as advancements from an inferior set of arrangements to a rational order more conducive to the needs of beneficiaries. Others have criticized this progressive view, citing the class interests and ulterior motives of reformers as evidence that behind the eleemosynary expressions lurked a desire to control the poor and deviant, to rein in the disorder they appeared to cause. Others see reformers as seeking to impose their middle-class morality in order to discipline the work force, and as representing a larger shift in attitudes that included the families of the insane as well as the insane themselves. The asylum, in sum, symbolizes a fundamental change in American culture. It marks the shift from local, familial, and community arrangements for the care and control of those who failed to function as fully in society as their neighbors, to centralized, bureaucratized solutions that subjected to scrutiny the most private preserves— the body and the mind—in order to classify individuals as either insane or sane. In order to explain the nature and significance of Dorothea Dix's reform work, it is important to place it in its larger context—the rise of new institutional forms that accompanied a wholesale shift in sensibility about insanity.

A radical change in social policies and popular attitudes toward the insane occurring in America at the end of the eighteenth and beginning of the nineteenth century resulted in the erection of asylums. In the colonial period, families who could afford to do so cared for their own members, allowing them to participate in family life to the degree of their capacity. In the case of the dependent, colonists aimed primarily to mitigate the individual's economic stress; they did not single out the ''distracted'' as having public needs different from those of paupers. The primary rule governing the care of the poor was that communities should shoulder responsibility for the support of their resident needy. In *The Discovery of the Asylum* (1971), David Rothman writes that ''poor relief was a local system, towns liable for their own, but not for others.''[20] Colonial adherence to local care translated into practices such as bidding-out, contracting, warning-out, and confining the insane in an almshouse. Laws absolved towns of responsibility for nonresident dependents. Warning-out, a practice consisting of warnings or forceful removal, enabled residents to rid their towns of the burden of illegitimate dependents, who had no choice but to move on.

In the case of resident paupers, communities arranged for their care locally. Towns gave donations raised from taxes to support at home those individuals requiring only partial aid. In the case of total dependents, towns auctioned them off to the lowest bidder, that is, to the person who offered to house and support the dependent for the least cost to the town. Contracting, basically a system of labor, hired out a group of paupers to a single household for a fixed price. Bidding-out and contracting usually took place yearly, thus exacerbating the insecure, volatile living conditions of the poor. According to David Rothman, the last alternative was the almshouse, which provided the cheapest answer to the problem of the poor. Workhouses provided yet another deterrent to outsiders by threatening them with hard labor.

These methods allowed towns on the brink of survival to devote their limited resources to caring for their residents. They also grew out of the Elizabethan poor laws, which, in response to the perceived increase of vagrancy and vagabondage, assumed the existence of two kinds of poor—the deserving poor and the shiftless. Bidding-out and contracting represented the belief that the deserving poor should receive aid. Warning-out gave communities the right to make the distinction. Although these customs left much to be desired when applied to the insane, especially for unclaimed dependents, they rested on the notion of family and community responsibility. At their best, they led to the integration of the insane as much as possible into the regular life of the community, rather than placing them in special institutions at a remove from society, as Dix and others later favored.

A variety of demographic, economic, intellectual, and social changes prepared the ground for the growth of asylums and other Jacksonian reforms. An increase in population and in population density occurred in the new republic and magnified the visibility of the insane. Historian Gerald Grob indicates that most large urban areas built almshouses before 1800 because of population growth and its destructive effect on other local solutions. Geographic mobility and population increase rendered obsolete old forms of poor relief; communities could no longer solve the problem on an individual basis because of expense and impracticality. Almshouse incarceration presented a cheaper, though least desirable, alternative.

Another condition setting the scene for the appearance of asylums was the intellectual impact of the Enlightenment. According to Grob, social reform movements developed from a new intellectual stance.

The new outlook stressed the desirability of innovation, condemned stagnation and sought a greater application of human intelligence to social problems. The result was a widespread conviction not only that the conquest of disease was merely a matter of time, but that many of the perennial dilemmas of humanity—including poverty, vice and ignorance—could be minimized if not abolished altogether.[21]

Rationalist activism invaded all aspects of life, including attitudes toward the deviant. Whereas insanity appeared to be folly or "demoniacal possession" to colonists, Americans increasingly considered it not only a disease with definite somatic causes but also one more curable than most diseases. The Second Great Awakening, with its message of individual conversion and regeneration as the means of establishing a good society, added impetus to reform as well as a moralistic mission of eradicating impurities from society. Thus science and religion became intertwined in the crusades of reformers like Dix.

Institutions for the confinement of paupers, the insane, and criminals had provided a solution for the homeless or burdensome dependents since the seventeenth century in Europe. Almshouses and jails increasingly served this purpose in America. The novelty of nineteenth-century institutionalization was that it pointed to the asylum as the preferred solution to the plight of the insane and singled out the insane for separate curative treatment. By the end of the eighteenth century, partly because the early hospices brought about an unhealthful and undesirable amalgam of the diseased, the criminal, and the indigent, reformers perceived a need to separate these groups.

Associationist philosophy, a dominant strand of medical thought at the time, underpinned the belief that insanity was a medical problem. Charles Rosenberg sums up this school of thought as rooted in a metaphor of the body as "a system of dynamic interactions with its environment." Associationism embodied the tenets that each part of the body was related to every other, that the body was "a system of intake and outgo," and that "equilibrium was synonymous with health, disequilibrium with illness." Madness was the culmination of both physical and moral afflictions, all part of one disease, for "just as man's body interacted continuously with his environment, so did his mind with his body, his morals with his health.''[22] This interpretation of insanity paved the way for a system of active therapeutics including the regulation of a system's intake and outgo, usually through drugs, as well as active treatment of the nonsomatic causes and symptoms of insanity.

"Moral treatment," the primary treatment employed for the nonphysical aspects of madness, occupied center stage in the era of the founding of American asylums. This entailed sequestering a patient from the environment producing or aggravating the disorder, and placing him or her in an atmosphere completely dedicated to therapy. This environment was to resemble a well-ordered family and to instill disciplined behavior through the example of the superintendent, the staff, and the well-behaved patients. Classification of patients by sex and by type and extent of illness created a ward system in which patients could proceed to convalescent and privileged wards as a reward for good behavior. As the father of the asylum family, the superintendent was to exert the kind but strict authority he might use in bringing up his own children. Treatment enlisted the active participation of the patient, who was to acknowledge his or her disease and learn self-control in order to overcome it. The success of moral treatment thus required a sort of conversion experience on the part of the patient.

This treatment assumed the existence of a genre of curable insanity that later acquired the title "moral insanity," for a long time a catchall for any form of insanity in which the intellect survived intact but the moral sense was impaired. English physician James Pritchard defined it in 1835 as any affliction that left the intellect untouched but injured "the state of feelings, temper or habit."[23] Patients with moral insanity primarily lost inhibition; they proved "incapable of conducting [themselves] with decency and propriety."[24] In other words, this disease indicated a loss of moral intuition and was the diagnosis for individuals who "had lost their ability to accept society's judgments about what constituted moral behavior."[25]

The notion of moral insanity caused an expansion of the boundaries of insanity, for it encompassed not only the indigent and helpless "feebleminded" but also members of any social class who had difficulty abiding by society's moral code. Moral treatment thus took root in a belief that asylums could restore lost moral sense to individuals. Moral treatment, based on the concept of moral insanity, thus relied on the superintendent and the asylum to restore patients to a semblance of self-control.

Moral treatment had grave implications for what the asylum was to become. It established physicians as guardians of the moral order within the asylum and endowed them with a large share of the responsibility for defining that moral code. They did not possess absolute power, however, for families and neighbors played a large part in deciding who required moral education. Asylum officials ultimately had the authority to determine whose moral sense had been regained enough to merit that person's return to society.

Moral treatment came to the awareness of American reformers like Dix through the ideas of William Tuke and Philippe Pinel, both of whom stressed the need for a combination of kindness and authoritarianism. Pinel deemed the asylum a laboratory for studying mental illness as well as a place for humanitarian treatment, "a mode of care that made an institutional setting a sine qua non." He believed that the treatment of the insane demanded the creation of a separate environment and that insanity "was a curable disease, given understanding, patience, guidance, and proper treatment." Although Pinel is best known for the image of removing female lunatics from chains at the Bicêtre in Paris in 1793, he also believed in a highly authoritarian approach to the care of the insane. Institutionalization was necessary because only within walls could a physician establish himself as the dominant influence in the patient's life and thus instill "an appreciation of normal behavior."[26] The relationship between doctor and patient took on a paternalistic character, and the successful physician would achieve the "happy effects of intimidation, without severity; of oppression without violence; and of triumph, without outrage."[27] To an extent, moral treatment assumed that a departure from social norms consisted of willful misbehaving, lack of discipline, or ignorance of social hierarchies of authority. Moral treatment applied psychological force with the goal of triumphing over behavior and thought considered immoral or abnormal.

Another figure who influenced Americans was William Tuke, who helped found the York Retreat in 1792, a model for American asylums. Founders of this Quaker hospital perceived the need to mitigate the corrupting influence of other patients' unclean or unacceptable behavior on convalescing or well-behaved individuals. Therapy aimed to "develop patients' internal means of self-restraint and self-control" with humane rather than cruel or harsh punishments. Instead of corporal punishment, Tuke applied the "principle of fear" and fostered the "desire for esteem."[28] Tuke likened this treatment to the indoctrination of children. Moral treatment as defined by Pinel and Tuke came to Americans as a fully formed justification for establishing asylums. To Dix, whose moral righteousness seemed to equal her sensitivity to abuse, both humanitarian and authoritarian treatment might have appeared logical and legitimate explanations for institutionalizing the insane.

In assessing the results of these drastic changes in the way the insane were viewed and treated, historians differ over the reasons for the emergence of the asylum in early nineteenth-century America, and their interpretations in turn color their view of its subsequent history. In short, those who deem the mental institution a positive invention believe it emerged from advances in medical opinion inspired by Enlightenment optimism and rationalism. Grob and other scholars who share this view understand the widely proclaimed failure of asylums by the late nineteenth century to deliver on their promises of ideal therapeutic environments and high cure rates as having resulted from parsimonious state legislatures and inexorable demographic forces that caused overcrowding and derailed the best intentions of reformers and physicians.

Critical of the notion that asylums resulted from a humanitarian impulse and a progressive medical profession, other scholars stress reformers' concern for combating the forces of social disorder they feared would burst the seams of early nineteenth-century American society. Historians who emphasize motives of social control, such as David Rothman, contend that reformers anticipated that the patient population would be largely lower class, and consider their reforms a conscious effort to control what the reformers saw as the chaos and dangerous excitement of workers and the poor, as well as an attempt to restore traditional social structures, which they thought were threatened by urbanization and social mobility.

Structuralist historians trace this concern for disorder to reformers' class interests. Some write that reformers, doctors, and other asylum advocates sought to instill the discipline of a well-ordered family in order to develop the regular work habits needed in an industrial labor force. Michel Foucault emphasized the rise of a new bourgeois ideology that legitimized the imperatives of capitalism. The middle class's growing sensitivity to harsh public punishment helped to foster the acceptance of separate institutions and to discourage tolerance of the association of people of a wide range of capabilities, classes, and behaviors. The possibility of exerting psychological rather than physical restraint in a controlled, separate environment best suited this new middle-class sensibility.

The abuses of asylum treatment revealed in the late nineteenth century were, in this view, natural outgrowths of an oppressive regime. Christopher Lasch argued that asylums and other institutions of confinement represented the growing class consciousness of the middle class, which brought with it "a decline in the sense of collective responsibility" and an urge to avoid "the spectacle of suffering and depravity" and "the contamination of the lower orders."[29] Drawing on the theory of "total institutions" articulated by Erving Goffman and Gresham M. Sykes, Lasch asserted that asylums developed according to their own internal, bureaucratic needs; healing was sacrificed to administrative efficiency. Ironically, the "humanizing of the asylum" set this new machine in motion: "Once therapy became the object of confinement, however, and once therapy had been defined as learning to submit to moral discipline, efficient administration came to be so closely identified with treatment that in practice the distinction between them was almost impossible to maintain."[30]

This kind of institution thus resulted less from a vanguard of reformers than from a basic shift in thinking about the place of the insane in the social order. Richard Fox, for instance, has shown that families willingly committed their members to psychiatric hospitals. Patient records show, further, that the mentally ill sometimes volunteered themselves for admission, finding the institution preferable to the world outside. This evidence correlates with the testimony of numerous people who wrote to Dix, thanking her for the work she did on their behalf. Any view of Dix must take into account that many of her contemporaries, well and unwell, praised her efforts. They were not so much participating in their own oppression as agreeing that current methods of confinement required serious change, and that some better form of care was needed. Hindsight suggests that this dire set of circumstances, and the limited notion of what could be done to remedy it, resulted from the decline of older customs and the rise of a new sensitivity to, and even terror of, insanity. Because of the change in sensibility, older customs that benefited communities were abandoned along with the unsatisfactory, even brutal ad hoc measures resulting from the break-down of traditions. Out of this strange blend came a belief in engineered ther-apeutic environments, the need for intense personal scrutiny of others for signs of madness, confinement of the insane away from the rest of society, and the use of insanity as a way of classifying people and segregating communities.

The portrait of reformers like Dix has tended to be oversimplified; the most basic versions of the social control and progressive views have reigned, failing to take into account the much more illuminating interpretations that illustrate the role of both long-term structural changes and more precise short-term shifts in cultural practices. On the one hand are the many biographies full of praise for Dix as a great humanitarian crusader, quoting her contemporaries' view of her as "the chosen daughter of the Republic," "the angel of mercy," or "the apostle of humanity."[31] On the other hand are a number of psychology texts that question the ultimate benefit of her work. Critics focus on her embrace of institutionalization, blaming her for helping to usher in custodialism. Both views simplify the significance of Dix's life by portraying her as either a saint or Nurse Ratched in disguise; neither image can suspend disbelief.

The depiction of Dix as an agent of social control or custodialism fails to appreciate the depth of her commitment to what she considered better treatment, the energy she devoted to exploring actual conditions and exposing desperate neglect to the public eye, and her example of a life dedicated to moral principle. Poet John Greenleaf Whittier, among many others, wrote letters of admiration to Dix, lamenting how far short he fell when he measured himself against her model of generosity and devotion toward those less fortunate. On the other hand, the glorified portrait of Dix as a superhuman champion of the downtrodden, a compassionate samaritan whose moral sense placed her apart from her contem-poraries, takes her completely out of the context of her times. She is better understood as one of many reformers who, for a number of reasons based on her personal circumstances and the tenor of her society, decided to devote her considerable moral energy to a reform already under way by the early nineteenth century.

Dix undoubtedly drew attention to a vital subject—the abusive practices that prevailed in the treatment of the insane in her time. She did so by traveling thousands of miles in the United States and abroad, examining such treatment firsthand and exposing it through her persuasive testimony. She lobbied furiously at a time when women were largely shut out of the political system and achieved many concrete political objectives, securing funds to establish numerous new asylums and to expand ones already in existence. Dix influenced mental health reform by helping ally it with other humanitarian causes, persuading many that increased appropriations for the insane was a moral imperative. But far from the simple matter of moral righteousness that she considered it, the treatment of the insane she favored was only one of the possible alternatives.

Dix's moral appeals on behalf of the insane underpinned her particular view that institutions provided the best treatment, that the state and the national government should assume responsibility for matters of individual welfare, that the treatment of the mentally ill rightly fell to the medical establishment, and that asylums could provide the benefits of a well-ordered family. The persuasiveness of her appeals, the extensiveness of her own fieldwork, and the tirelessness of her lobbying efforts made a huge impact on the direction of mental health reform. The securing of funds from the state would have been met with much fiercer resistance had not Dix disarmed the opposition with her stature, argument, and unassailable moral stance. Above all, perhaps, her life was devoted to defining decent treatment of troubled individuals as a moral issue; indecent treatment that later emerged in many contexts, including in the asylum, did so in spite of her efforts.

In sum, Dorothea Dix helped usher in a major shift in public opinion that designated insanity as the special province of asylum superintendents and doctors, a discrete condition requiring special and humane treatment, and an affliction best treated in institutions apart from society. Her shortcomings and those of the movement for mental health reform lay in the belief that their plans for change needed to entail a wholesale rejection of earlier customs as well as their failure to distinguish colonial custom from early national practice.

Dix and fellow reformers were blind to the possibly devastating effects of the larger movement toward incarceration even of the nonviolent insane, the subsequent expansion of the population considered insane, the invasion of the psychological realm necessitated by the new institutions and treatment, and the replacement of individual, family, and community obligations with governmental and institutional responsibility. Unquestioning faith in the new forms and a certain righteous impatience helped complete a revolution in the way Americans thought about madness. Thus were buried the best along with the worst customs of long past generations—to the detriment of future ones.

NOTES

1. Dorothea Lynde Dix, "Memorial to the General Assembly of North Carolina" (1848), quoted in Helen Marshall, *Dorothea Dix: Forgotten Samaritan* (Chapel Hill, N.C., 1937), 15.

2. Ibid.

3. Mary Ann Jimenez, "Madness in Early American History: Insanity in Massachusetts from 1700 to 1830," *Journal of Social History* 20 (Fall 1986): 35.

4. Ibid., 36.

5. Dix, "Memorial to the Legislature of Massachusetts" (1843), in Dix, *On Behalf of the Insane Poor: Selected Reports* (New York, 1971), 4.

6. Jimenez, "Madness in Early American History," 36.

7. Gladys Brooks, *Three Wise Virgins* (New York, 1957), 14.

8. Ibid., 18.

9. Ibid.

10. Marshall, *Dorothea Dix*, 45.

11. Francis Tiffany, *Life of Dorothea Lynde Dix* (Boston, 1891), 339.

12. Ibid.

13. Dorothy Clarke Wilson, *Stranger and Traveler: The Story of Dorothea Dix, American Reformer* (Boston, 1975), 336.

14. Tiffany, *Life of Dorothea Lynde Dix*, 111, 110.

15. Ibid., 115.

16. Ibid.

17. Dix, "Memorial to Massachusetts," 24–25.

18. Ibid., 3.

19. Ibid., 25.

20. David Rothman, *The Discovery of the Asylum: Social Order and Disorder in the New Republic* (Boston, 1971), 5.

21. Gerald Grob, *Mental Institutions in America: Social Policy to 1875* (New York, 1973), 38–39.

22. Charles Rosenberg, "The Therapeutic Revolution: Medicine, Meaning and Social Change in Nineteenth-Century America," in Morris J. Vogel and Charles Rosenberg, eds. *The Therapeutic Revolution: Essays in the Social History of Medicine* (Philadelphia, 1979), 5–10.

23. Eric T. Carlson and Norman Dain, "Moral Insanity in the United States, 1835–1866," *American Journal of Psychiatry* 118, no. 9 (1962): 795–801.

24. Eric T. Carlson and Norman Dain, "Psychotherapy in the Hospital: 1740–1840," *Current Psychiatric Therapies* 2 (1962): 219–225.

25. Grob, *Mental Institutions in America*, 10.

26. Ibid., 42.

27. Philippe Pinel, quoted in ibid.

28. Samuel Tuke, quoted in ibid., 44.

29. Christopher Lasch, "Origins of the Asylum," in his *The World of Nations: Reflections on American History, Politics, and Culture* (New York, 1973), 13.

30. Ibid., 12.

31. Marshall, *Dorothea Dix*, 122.

BIBLIOGRAPHY

Beach, Seth Curtis. *Daughters of the Puritans: A Group of Brief Biographies*. Repr. Freeport, N.Y., 1967.

Brooks, Gladys. *Three Wise Virgins*. New York, 1957.

Carlson, Eric T., and Norman Dain. "Moral Insanity in the United States, 1835–1866." *American Journal of Psychiatry* 118, no. 9 (1962): 795–801.

———. "Psychotherapy in the Hospital: 1740–1840." *Current Psychiatric Therapies* 2 (1962): 219–225.

Deutsch, Albert. *The Mentally Ill in America: A History of Their Care and Treatment from Colonial Times*. New York, 1949.

Dix, Dorothea Lynde. *On Behalf of the Insane Poor: Selected Reports*. New York, 1971.

Foucault, Michel. *Madness and Civilization: A History of Insanity in the Age of Reason.* New York, 1965.

Fox, Richard. *So Far Disordered in Mind: Insanity in California, 1870–1930.* Berkeley, Calif., 1978.

Gollaher, David L. *Voice for the Mad: A Life of Dorothea Dix.* New York, 1995.

Grob, Gerald. *Mental Institutions in America: Social Policy to 1875.* New York, 1973.

Jimenez, Mary Ann. "Madness in Early American History: Insanity in Massachusetts from 1700 to 1830." *Journal of Social History* 20 (Fall 1986): 25–44.

Lasch, Christopher. "Origins of the Asylum." In his *The World of Nations: Reflections on American History, Politics, and Culture.* New York, 1973.

McGovern, Constance M. "The Myths of Social Control and Custodial Oppression: Patterns of Psychiatric Medicine in Late Nineteenth-Century Institutions." *Journal of Social History* 20 (Fall 1986): 3–24.

Marshall, Helen E. *Dorothea Dix, Forgotten Samaritan.* Chapel Hill, N.C., 1937.

———. "Dorothea Lynde Dix." In Edward T. James, Janet Wilson James, and Paul S. Boyer, eds. *Notable American Women, 1607–1950: A Biographical Dictionary.* Vol. 1. Cambridge, Mass., 1971.

Rosenberg, Charles. "The Therapeutic Revolution: Medicine, Meaning and Social Change in Nineteenth-Century America." In Morris J. Vogel and Charles Rosenberg, eds., *The Therapeutic Revolution: Essays in the Social History of Medicine.* Philadelphia, 1979.

Rothman, David. *The Discovery of the Asylum: Social Order and Disorder in the New Republic.* Boston, 1971.

Schlaifer, Charles, and Lucy Freeman. *Heart's Work: Civil War Heroine and Champion of the Mentally Ill, Dorothea Lynde Dix.* New York, 1991.

Tiffany, Francis. *Life of Dorothea Lynde Dix.* Boston, 1891.

Viney, Wayne, and Karen Bartsch. "Dorothea Lynde Dix: Positive or Negative Influence on the Development of Treatment for the Mentally Ill." *Social Science Journal* 21 (April 1984): 71–82.

Wilson, Dorothy Clarke. *Stranger and Traveler: The Story of Dorothea Dix, American Reformer.* Boston, 1975.

Frances Willard
and Temperance

IAN R. TYRRELL

Frances Willard was one of the towering figures of nineteenth-century American reform. For more than eighteen years after 1879 she led the National Woman's Christian Temperance Union (WCTU) to unprecedented heights of popularity and influence. Journalists hailed her as the "uncrowned Queen of America"; she was treated as a "representative woman" akin to the male business and community leaders whose portraits adorn nineteenth-century biographical compilations. Adored by middle-class American women supporters as "St. Frances," she became a figure on the world stage through the World's WCTU and her visits to England in the 1890s. After her death from pernicious anaemia at the age of fifty-nine, on 17 February 1898, the state of Illinois honored her memory in the Statuary Hall of the U.S. capitol. When Willard's marble statue was placed there in 1905, Senator Albert Beveridge described her as "the first woman of the nineteenth century, the most beloved character of her time."

Born 28 September 1839, in Churchville, New York, and raised on a Wisconsin farm by her devout Christian parents, Frances Willard developed a tomboyish streak that made her feel women could be the equal of men. Her father Josiah's discipline was harsh, and Frances gravitated emotionally toward her mother, Mary Thompson Willard, whom she venerated until the latter's death in 1892. Willard loved her father, or so she said, and nursed him until he died from tuberculosis in 1868. It was "Mother" Willard who encouraged Frances in her desire to obtain an education. Willard first attended college in Milwaukee and then in Evanston, Illinois, where she lived for the last thirty years of her life. She served after graduation from the (Methodist) Northwestern Female College in 1859 as a schoolteacher and then traveled in Europe in 1868–1869 with a wealthy former classmate, Kate Jackson. When she returned, Willard was appointed president of her alma mater; she resigned in 1874 because of a dispute with Charles Fowler, president of Northwestern University, which had taken over control of the Female College. Ironically, Fowler had been Willard's fiancé for a short time in 1861. Fowler later became a bishop of the Methodist Church, to which Willard belonged, and friction between the two persisted for many years thereafter.

The impasse with Fowler was a happy coincidence for Willard. Casting about for a new career, she turned to temperance. Although late nineteenth-century temperance reform became strongly identified with Willard, temperance did not equal women's temperance. The movement to end alcohol in America had deeper roots than the WCTU. Without the preceding decades of agitation, and the evolution of tactics before the Civil War, it is unlikely that Willard could have achieved the considerable impact that she did have.

The temperance movement began on the national stage as part of the evangelical Protestant impulse to reform antebellum society. Temperance lost its original meaning of moderation when the evangelical reformers co-opted the term to mean total abstinence from spirits. From its beginnings in the American Temperance Society in 1826, "temperance" reformers graduated to teetotalism in the 1830s through the American Temperance Union (1836), moved on to prohibition in the 1840s, achieved statewide prohibition in thirteen states and territories from 1851 to 1856, and began to concede a wider role for women in the movement. Still, most temperance organizations kept women in an inferior position; not until the 1870s did women become leaders in the temperance movement with stature equal to that of men. The Good Templars, founded in New York State in 1851, was the first to grant women a theoretical equality with men within the ranks of its organization. After the Civil War, women in the Midwest took the temperance cause into their own hands through an upsurge of social protest known as the Woman's Crusade.

The Crusade was centered in Ohio but spread throughout the Midwest, and it involved more than 56,000 women in direct protests against liquor shops. This was not the first direct action against saloons, nor would it be the last, but it was the most widespread. The impact of women engaged in marches, vigorous picketing, and court attendance in defense of the family stirred public opinion. Legend has it that the WCTU grew out of the Crusade—it was, in Willard's words, "the sober second thought of the crusade"—but recent research has indicated that the focus of the WCTU and the Crusade were different. The women of the Crusade tended to be concerned with immediate threats to the family, in particular to the sons of their own families. The rise in liquor consumption, the spread of immigrant drinking after the Civil War, and the rise of the saloon pressed them into action.

The WCTU, founded in Cincinnati in November 1874 as a response to the new temperance enthusiasm of the Crusade, had a different focus and different leadership. The WCTU sought a broader public role for women and was concerned with changing the law rather than engaging in direct action against liquor sellers. The WCTU had a cosmopolitan focus as well, rather than the local one of the crusaders. Willard fits this pattern. She had not been a participant in the Crusade; she was well educated, well traveled, and middle class. Surprisingly, she had not always practiced total abstinence; she admitted to a medicinal use of alcohol for a time after her visit to Europe. Most important, the WCTU represented a new phase in the history of women and temperance—one of con-solidation and organization on a national scale of diverse women's temperance activities. In a "search for order," American society embraced bureaucratic, specialized organizations in business, politics, and reform. The WCTU, part of this shift, combined bureaucracy in the form of special departments of work with a charismatic leadership and a comprehensive approach that defies easy sociological categorization in terms of specialization.

Willard's rise in the temperance movement was mercurial. Although she had been appointed corresponding secretary at the Cincinnati meeting in 1874, she did not come to full prominence in the organization until her election as Illinois state president in 1878, and national president the following year. After the short reign of the older and more conservative Annie Wittenmyer, Willard seemed a vigorous and attractive new leader. Almost immediately she began to push the WCTU toward advocacy of woman's suffrage as the foundation of what she called "Home Protection." This campaign involved a massive petition signed by over 200,000 people to the Illinois state legislature, calling for women's voting rights on the liquor laws in defense of the family. Willard was the author of many such felicitous phrases as "Home Protection," but this idea of using the Victorian values of "domesticity" to advance the public rights of women was especially important in setting the stage for the further emergence of the WCTU from its formerly narrow base of temperance into the most important organization for women's reform in late nineteenth-century America. Home Pro-tection's organizing success became both a model for future campaigns by tem-perance women and a vehicle that cemented Willard's authority in the WCTU. It was in the Home Protection campaign that she first succeeded in tying the WCTU to support for woman's suffrage, and such arguments of expediency continued to be important in the WCTU suffrage campaigns even after Willard's departure.

Willard's joining the temperance movement was not sheer opportunism. Her father and mother had been abstainers, and the Methodist Church had since the 1840s been firmly in the temperance camp in the Northern states. Willard was on track in arguing that alcohol was a serious problem. Although aggregate consumption had dropped from its reputedly high levels before the 1830s, mid-dle-class youths were increasingly faced with the temptations of drinking through the proliferation of liquor outlets and the increased availability of beer. The WCTU sought to stop this resurgence of drinking after the Civil War by closing saloons. Willard also had personal experience of the dangers of alcohol that reinforced her commitment. After the death of her brother Oliver, she had a considerable involvement in the upbringing of her nephews, Rob and Frank Willard. Frank spent time in a reform school in 1888, and Rob was an alcoholic and a gambler. In 1889 he was sent to the private Christian Home for Intemperate Men. Rob never conquered his drinking habit, and though the scandal was kept private, it intensely affected Frances, bringing home to her the fragility of the middle-class life of purity and abstinence that she valued as the basis of all reform and progress for women.

In the years after her death, historians recalled Willard, if they remembered her at all, as a leader of temperance reform. Yet she was always much more. She remains, after all these years, one of the most difficult to typecast as the representative of a single reform movement. Under her influence as national president, the Woman's Christian Temperance Union embraced an ambitious "Do Everything Policy" that included support for kindergartens, social welfare work, labor reform, woman's suffrage, peace, purity reforms such as antiprostitution and age-of-consent legislation, and campaigns for the Sabbath and against vivisection and drugs other than alcohol. Willard argued, persuasively and self-consciously, that "No one can adequately lead any movement who has not imagination enough to see that movement in its relations to others equally important."[1]

This apparent grab bag reflected the wide impact of the temperance movement, its close connection with other reforms, and the sweeping influence of alcohol as a social problem in nineteenth-century America. Drink damaged families through the propensity of males toward violence and through the loss of family income, which drinking could involve in a society where frugality and industry were pushed ahead of government social welfare or private charities as the basis of social mobility. But drink also served symbolic functions. Alcohol was closely linked to the lessening of control over sexuality. Uninhibited males could frequent prostitutes, and young women could be seduced by predatory companions. In defense of the Victorian middle-class home, temperance reform did battle against the saloon. It was a potent weapon to be able to use an articulate and well-organized lobbying group of women to accomplish this purpose after the Civil War.

While Willard moved to make the WCTU relevant to the Victorian and domesticity-oriented culture of the middle classes, she also strove to make those same classes aware of issues and rights beyond their own narrow and insular outlook. By the late 1880s, she had come to believe that wage reform and trade union development were important components of temperance reform. The Knights of Labor under Terence Powderly banned drink sellers from its membership and allowed men and women to work together as equals in the assemblies of the Knights in promoting labor reforms. Willard found this formula appealing, because she believed that women needed economic independence in order for them to engage in reform and have the economic freedom to choose suitable—that is, Christian, abstaining—husbands.

In the 1890s, Willard's radicalism went further, and she declared herself a socialist. This sprang from her commitment to the Social Gospel, a vital force for reform in urban areas in the 1890s. Willard always justified socialism in terms of "the golden rule" beloved of Social Gospelers, but she gave the cause a radical edge in her critique of great wealth and the use allegedly made of alcohol by wealthy interests. "I charge upon the drink traffic that it keeps people down," she declared in her 1893 presidential address, "and capitalists and politicians know it."[2] This was not anarchism—which she denounced, as did others of her class—nor Marxist socialism but Christian socialism of the variety championed by American reformer Edward Bellamy and some English Fabians. Willard's socialism was, because of its Christian and gradualist disposition, surprisingly influential within the WCTU. A Department of Relations Between Capital and Labor was formed in 1886, and under various names it continued to seek better working conditions for men and women into the 1920s. From its ranks the WCTU contributed a number of members of the American Socialist party, including social justice crusaders like Mary Garbutt, who headed the WCTU in southern California for many years.

Willard's broad-brush approach sometimes threatened to weaken the WCTU. Modern sociological studies confirm that the WCTU developed many ties with other reforms and that these ties reflected the prominence and respectability of the organization. To critics, this web of connections seemed ephemeral, and work done under the WCTU umbrella could be superficial at times. Certainly, much of the value of such reform work was necessarily done in so-called departments sometimes administered as independent fiefdoms by particular temperance women. For this reason, Willard cannot be assessed fairly as an individual leader but as a leader of a complex movement in which many lesser-known women contributed individually: Hannah Clark Bailey dominated peace reform, Mary Hannah Hunt spurred scientific temperance instruction in the American schools, Mary Lovell attacked the killing of animals and birds to produce furs and feathers for women's clothing, and so on. Willard "contextualized" these diverse women's activities, based on her strong friendships with other women. Departmentalization was Willard's master stroke, since it enabled women to do concrete work in their local WCTU. No local was obliged to adopt all of the causes championed at the national level, and the WCTU is best understood as a federation of these local impulses for reform coming together under Willard's galvanizing leadership.

As a symbol of woman's achievements, Willard supported the Woman's Temperance Publishing Association, run by Matilda Carse. All of the WCTU's national publications appeared under this imprint, and WCTU women contributed to the Woman's Temple, an imposing and attractive twelve-story skyscraper in downtown Chicago. Willard, with characteristic hyperbole, called it in 1891 "the noblest architectural pile ever dedicated to business purposes since the world began."[3] Under Willard's leadership, the organization grew in numerical strength from its strongest base of support, the Midwest. She worked tirelessly and made long, arduous train trips to the South, where the organization was weak, and to the West Coast in 1883. She even courted white Southern support by issuing statements that seemed to condone the high incidence of lynching in the South. At the same time, she courted "colored" support in segregated locals. Willard also sought immigrant support, and used women like the German-American Henrietta Skelton of Chicago to minister to the polyglot ethnic communities of the larger American cities. Cordial relations were developed with the Catholic Total Abstinence Union, which favored individual action to achieve temperance reform. Nevertheless, few Catholics joined, and the organization remained overwhelmingly Anglo-Saxon in origin. In this matter, the WCTU reflected the larger tendencies in the prohibition movement; most Catholics opposed the legal prohibition of all alcohol that Willard and her followers sought.

Willard's period as leader was marked by a rapid expansion in the organization both in geography and numbers. From 27,000 in just over 1,000 locals by 1879, the WCTU reached 149,000 paid-up members in over 7,000 locals in 1890. Thereafter, it was hit by the financial crisis of the early 1890s and the failure of the Woman's Temple as an economic venture. By 1897 membership had dropped to 142,000. Willard came under attack after 1895 for her connection to marginal and heretical causes. The advocacy of state-regulated prostitution by her English friend Lady Henry Somerset, and reports that she and Lady Henry had moved away from absolute prohibition toward support of high license laws and municipal management of pubs, damaged Willard's leadership. Willard denied her heterodoxy, and so great was her stature that she retained her presidency unchallenged until her death.

Equally controversial had been Willard's earlier advocacy of the Prohibition party as a third force in the presidential elections of 1884 and 1888. Subsequently, she unsuccessfully sought an alliance with the Populists. These political tactics disturbed some of her supporters in the North, many of whom tended to be Republicans. Judith Ellen Foster, formerly one of Willard's allies, led a breakaway movement in 1889–1890 to found the narrower Non-Partisan Woman's Christian Temperance Union. But the significance of this move should not be exaggerated. Willard's WCTU continued to outnumber the Non-Partisans, who, with a "limited following" in eleven states, never constituted more than a minor annoyance to the main body.

Views of Willard have changed markedly over time. From her late nineteenth-century adoration, Willard's reputation slumped after the repeal of national prohibition in 1933. Only in the 1970s was her reputation as a key woman reformer rehabilitated. The new woman's movement found in her something of a heroine. But whereas early historians had tended to see her simply as a representative of the temperance cause, feminists presented her as moving women forward into the public sphere. In their reading of her life, she emerges as a sagacious and influential woman. However, the reinterpretation can be carried too far. It is too easy to see her as a bearer, in linear progression, of the values of a future woman's movement. Even calling her "feminist" is problematic because of the shifting meanings that feminism has, and still acquires.

Not only was Willard the leader of a complex movement that cannot be reduced to temperance; she herself was a complex character. Especially infuriating is the great gap between public information on her public activities and the ambiguous and fragmentary evidence on her personal life. Like some other prominent women of the temperance cause, Willard was secretive. It is likely that we will never know the full story of the forces that drove her, for she was determined that these remain private. In fact, Willard characterized herself emotionally as "the sphinx that I have always been" on the subject of "life's most intricate equation," love. She was prepared to tantalize, but not to reveal. She wrote: "Of the real romance of my life, unguessed save by a trio of close friends, these pages may not tell." After breaking her engagement to Charles Fowler, she remained single and apparently celibate. Later in life she had a variety of female friends. From 1877 on, she was extremely close to Anna Gordon, who served as her secretary, companion, and lover. Willard also expressed love and affection for various other women. Especially influential in her impact on Willard was Lady Henry Somerset, the president of the British Women's Temperance Association, from whom she was seldom seen apart in the early 1890s.

Willard's affection for other women was not uncommon in temperance ranks. She was part of a group of single, educated, and middle-class women who dominated the reform movement's leadership from the 1870s through World War I. This was also the generation in the larger American community with the greatest number of single, educated women. Being a reform leader required much sacrifice, for the salaries were small. Willard was paid a very modest stipend, which peaked at $2,400 in the 1890s. Much of the help given to temperance, like that given by other women to reform causes, was a form of unpaid work. The women with whom Willard associated became part of what the WCTU called a "sisterhood of service," and close relations with women helped supply the domestic help, secretarial staff, part-time organizers, platform speakers, and fund-raisers the temperance movement needed. Most of the working women in the WCTU held professional and clerical occupations. Teachers and journalists were prominent, and there were also doctors, businesswomen, and lawyers in the ranks.

It would be wrong to see Willard as part of a man-hating generation, the female equivalent of a misogynist. Her study in Rest Cottage was adorned with the portraits of male reformers whom she admired: Neal Dow, Terence Powderly, John Woolley, and others. Willard praised and encouraged the roles of males in the temperance movement, recognizing that their participation was vital if the Victorian family was to be strengthened. She supported, for example, the White Cross campaign, which encouraged male sexual abstinence before marriage. Rather than spinsterhood, she encouraged what she called the "white life for two"—purity in relations between the sexes outside of marriage and an equal and sexually restrained relationship within marriage. Willard advocated women having ultimate control over the sex act; motherhood should be entered into only on terms of women's consent and equality.

Male reform groups were as important to Willard as the love and support of individual males was to the moral well-being of the American home. Since only men could vote in American state or federal elections in the late nineteenth century—with the exception of a few places in the West—it made sense to develop alliances with male-dominated groups such as Francis E. Clark's United Society of Christian Endeavor or the Anti-Saloon League (ASL), the latter group having been founded in 1895. After Willard's death and the coming of the drive for national prohibition after 1907, this alliance with the ASL proved crucial to the success of the Eighteenth Amendment. Prominent supporters of constitutional prohibition, like Representative Richmond Hobson of Alabama, courted the WCTU before and during World War I. Through this strategy of alliance with other temperance organizations, the WCTU increased its membership still further, reaching a peak of over 425,000 members in the late 1920s. But never did the movement regain the innovative leadership that Willard exerted.

Willard's character is difficult to comprehend not only because it was secretive but also because it was often so contradictory. Reared in the traditions of evangelical Protestantism—she was tempted in the 1870s by the idea of working permanently for the famous evangelist Dwight Moody—Willard nevertheless could see, by the end of her life, value in all religions. She was an enthusiastic supporter of the Parliament of Religions at the World's Fair in Chicago in 1893, calling on the Methodists to extend a hand of friendship to all peoples. Willard also differed with many Christians over their treatment of women in the churches. She supported the controversial *Woman's Bible* written by feminist Elizabeth Cady Stanton, and in 1888 she battled with her own Methodist Episcopal Church for the right of women to be delegates—a right won in 1896.

For all that, Willard never abandoned her faith. Rather, she sought to modernize it as part of the Social Gospel. She still strongly believed that Western religion alone, and evangelical Protestantism in particular, gave women hope of advancement. To the end of her life, Jesus Christ was the "Great Emancipator" of women to her, and to most of her followers.

Reform movements require charismatic and effective leaders, and Willard's success in part lies in the uncanny and multilayered appeal that she had for her class of women. This appeal was based on her impressive platform appearances and her physical presence. Willard was by no means the dour person that drab nineteenth-century photographs and the subsequent reputation of temperance might convey. She possessed a strong sense of humor and, well into her forties, a personal attractiveness that reminded followers of a beautiful young girl. She spoke to her followers in strongly rhythmic prose peppered with clever phrases and numerous allusions to the Victorian middle-class culture of polite and uplifting literature. James Clement Ambrose heaped representative praise upon her in *Potter's American Monthly* for May 1882: "As a public speaker, I think Miss Willard is without a peer among women. With much of the Edward Everett in her language, there is more of the Wendell Phillips in her manner of delivery. She is wholly at home, but not forward on the platform, with grace in bearing, ease and moderation in gesture, and in her tones there are tears when she wills."[4]

Despite her enormous appeal as a speaker, Willard preferred the medium of journalism. She especially worked through her contributions to the *Union Signal*, the WCTU's national newspaper. Founded in 1883 by an amalgamation of two earlier papers, it appeared monthly and had a readership estimated at half a million in the early 1890s. Said Willard, ''The true press is a throne of power for good, a pulpit for righteousness, a telephone of heavenly magic, for while the platform speaker is reaching a few thousands, the quiet editor is reaching armies.''[5]

Willard had little time for reflection, and compiled her books, *Woman and Temperance* (1884) and *Glimpses of Fifty Years* (1889) from her diary jottings, newspaper and periodical articles, and platform speeches. She was not an original thinker, but she was quick to grasp the significance of new reforms and changing social conditions for the advancement of both women and the temperance movement. For this reason, she is an excellent person through whom to study the intellectual and social influences of her time.

Willard's involvement in many aspects of health reform for women is a case in point. This included her support for John Harvey Kellogg's sanitarium in Battle Creek, Michigan, her vegetarianism, her advocacy of physical exercise for women, and her embrace of bicycle riding as a form of recreation. Willard even wrote a short book, *A Wheel Within a Wheel: How I Learned to Ride the Bicycle* (1895), to advance the latter cause. She explained there that her own early experience on the frontier had given her a physical freedom absent in the urban, middle-class woman's world, where corsets and drawing room conventions bound women down. Women's sport could become, she felt, a way to repair the physical neglect of women's moral and mental, as well as physical, health.

Willard did not confine her work to the United States. She founded the World's Woman's Christian Temperance Union in 1883 and built an alliance with British temperance women after 1886 that helped to spread American temperance reform, and the institution of the WCTU, to more than forty countries by the 1920s. Willard served as the second president of the World WCTU. She was also influential in the organizing of the International Council of Women (ICW), founded in 1888, and served as the first president of the American National Council affiliated to the ICW. The export of American reform institutions through such groups as the Student Volunteers movement and Young Men's Christian Association and the Young Women's Christian Association after about 1895, and the subsequent expansion internationally of many others, such as Alcoholics Anonymous, testifies to the contribution of American reform movements to the spread of American culture. Willard's WCTU, as one of the earliest and most successful of these organizations, provided a model for other temperance groups, like the ASL, that sought to extend prohibition to other countries after the passage of the Eighteenth Amendment in 1919.

Willard was highly regarded abroad among women's groups. She was a model for Protestant evangelical women in Australia, New Zealand, Canada, South

Africa, Great Britain, and Scandinavia. Kaji Yajima was declared "the Frances Willard of Japan"; portraits of Willard were distributed by missionaries among the mission schools of India. But like the larger temperance movement itself, her reputation never spread to any extent beyond the Anglo-American world and its missionary outposts in such places as China and Japan. Apart from her visits to Great Britain and Europe in the 1890s, to stay with Lady Henry Somerset, and several trips to eastern Canada, Willard did not tour internationally. She suffered severely from seasickness, and her health was failing. So she left the work of international organizing to such missionaries as Mary Clement Leavitt and Jessie Ackermann.

Willard's career shows in particular that American reform had impacts in other countries and at times presented a model for other countries. American reform, in turn, was influenced by events abroad and demands from admirers in those other countries. Willard's views on race, for example, were modified in a more progressive direction in 1895 as a result of British criticism of her failure to condemn lynching in the United States. Her British experience also made her aware of the complexities of alcohol production and consumption, and she was particularly interested, after her British trips in the early 1890s, in the connection of alcoholism to poverty. Her exposure to the international missionary work of the WCTU made her more sympathetic toward religions other than her own evangelical Protestantism. Finally, as part of her international vision for the expansion of the WCTU, she necessarily came to regard the improvement of relations between nations through peace and arbitration as necessary for human survival and prosperity, and pushed the idea of an international arbitration treaty with Britain.

Willard left her mark indelibly upon the WCTU. Her mother's home, Rest Cottage, where Willard lived in Evanston, became WCTU headquarters. It remains so today, and at the same time functions as a de facto mausoleum of women's temperance reform. The furniture and mementos of Willard's time dominate the surroundings and impress the memories of visitors, who are informed that nothing has changed since Willard's death. For all that, Willard's memory lives on in a world vastly changed. Her meaning today is different from that for the nineteenth-century representative woman. Frances Willard still speaks to the role of women with her concerns about the role of the family, moral values, and the tensions between family responsibilities and the search for equality for women.

NOTES

1. *Annual Report of the National Woman's Christian Temperance Union for 1893* (Chicago, 1893), 105. Hereafter these annual reports are cited as NWCTU, AR, and year.
2. Ibid., 104.
3. NWCTU, AR, 1891, 139.
4. Frances Willard, *Woman and Temperance* (Hartford, Conn., 1883), 27–28.
5. NWCTU, AR, 1891, 139.

BIBLIOGRAPHY

Blocker, Jack S., Jr. *"Give to the Winds Thy Fears": The Women's Temperance Crusade, 1873–1874*. Westport, Conn., 1985.

———. *American Temperance Movements: Cycles of Reform*. Boston, 1989.

Bordin, Ruth. *Woman and Temperance: The Quest for Power and Liberty, 1873–1900*. Philadelphia, 1981.

———. *Frances Willard: A Biography*. Chapel Hill, N.C., 1986.

Clark, Norman H. *Deliver Us from Evil: An Interpretation of American Prohibition*. New York, 1976.

Dannenbaum, Jed. *Drink and Disorder: Temperance Reform in Cincinnati from the Washingtonian Revival to the WCTU*. Urbana, Ill., 1984.

Earhart, Mary. *Frances Willard: From Prayers to Politics*. Chicago, 1944.

Epstein, Barbara Leslie. *The Politics of Domesticity: Women, Evangelism, and Temperance in Nineteenth-Century America*. Middletown, Conn., 1981.

Gordon, Anna. *The Beautiful Life of Frances Willard*. Chicago, 1898.

Gusfield, Joseph. "Social Structure and Moral Reform: A Study of the Woman's Christian Temperance Union." *American Journal of Sociology* 61 (November 1955): 221–232.

———. *Symbolic Crusade: Status Politics and the American Temperance Movement*. Urbana, Ill., 1963.

Lee, Susan Dye. "Evangelical Domesticity: The Origins of the WCTU Under Frances Willard." Ph.D. diss., Northwestern University, 1980.

Mezvinzky, Norton. "The White Ribbon Reform, 1874–1920." Ph.D. diss., University of Wisconsin, 1959.

Rorabaugh, William J. *The Alcoholic Republic: An American Tradition*. New York, 1979.

Strachey, Ray. *Frances Willard: Her Life and Work*. London, 1913.

Tyrrell, Ian. *Sobering Up: From Temperance to Prohibition in Antebellum America, 1800–1860*. Westport, Conn., 1979.

———. *Woman's World/Woman's Empire: The Woman's Christian Temperance Union in International Perspective*. Chapel Hill, N.C., 1991.

Willard, Frances. *Woman and Temperance or, The Work and Workers of the Woman's Christian Temperance Union*. 1883; repr. New York, 1972.

———. *Glimpses of Fifty Years: The Autobiography of an American Woman*. 1889; repr. New York, 1970.

Jane Addams
and the Settlement House Movement

LOUISE W. KNIGHT

Jane Addams's contemporaries hailed her as "the leader and prophet of the settlement movement in America" and the movement's "grandmother," and declared Hull House "the Mother House."[1] Such acknowledgments suggest the breadth of her influence but fail to convey its shallow depth. Although her views on settlement purpose and method were respected by those active in the movement, she was more often honored than imitated. This development, often the fate of prophets, was perhaps inevitable in a movement that valued settlement autonomy over conformity to any national definition or standard.

How does one sum up the settlement house movement? Although settlement workers launched or supported hundreds of local, state, and national reforms during the movement's peak years of 1893–1922, no single reform or set of reforms was distinctly identified with the settlement. Indeed, during these years the movement, or elements within it, campaigned for the entire Progressive reform agenda. That agenda included access for all Americans to excellent public education, protective labor laws for women and children, woman's suffrage, municipal reform, recreational facilities, affordable housing for low-income people, and city planning.

Yet the settlement movement was something more than the sum of the Progressive agenda. Although the movement was certainly a source of social reform ideas and social reformers, it was intended by its most visionary leaders as something more—as a reform in itself. The settlement was meant to be a new process by which public policy would be developed and social conditions improved.

An urban minister of the Anglican Church, Samuel A. Barnett, and his wife and fellow worker Henrietta Barnett, founded the world's first settlement, Toynbee Hall, in London in 1884. Believing that university men of the middle and upper classes had a civic obligation to educate themselves about the lives of the working poor in the industrial neighborhoods of London, the couple invited young Oxford graduates to join them in taking up collective residence in the East End. As "residents" of the settlement house, the young men would spend their free time (outside their city jobs) becoming involved in the life of the neighborhood. Clubs, classes, local political organizing, and social reform might follow in response to neighbor interest, but the most important development would be the friendships formed between neighbors and residents, and the mutual education that would result.

The settlement, as Canon Barnett conceived it, was a class-conscious institution—one that acknowledged the existence of class differences. But in conceiving of the settlement, Barnett also challenged the class structure by rejecting the prevailing upper-class prejudices that the working poor did not "deserve" or could not benefit from the "advantages" (education, culture, and the arts) available to the upper classes, and that the working poor were not capable of or interested in being active citizens in a democracy. The residents were meant, of course, to help their neighbors, a fact that made the settlement part of the upper-class tradition of noblesse oblige, but they were also expected to be helped by them, to learn from them. Thus the settlement was potentially conservative and radical, condescending and democratic, all at the same time.

In which of these two directions a settlement went often depended more on the personal style and values of its head resident than on anything else. Barnett, a gentle, spiritual man, treated everyone—neighbors and residents alike—with quiet respect, and his example was an influence on Toynbee Hall residents. But as settlements spread in England and the United States, the conventional expectations and class prejudices of some settlement leaders often served to reinforce the attitudes of class and race superiority that residents brought with them to the neighborhoods. Settlement leaders did not always live up to the high ideals they embraced. This human shortcoming underlines the importance of noting the difference between their words and their deeds, between theory and practice.

One American settlement leader, Jane Addams, stayed closer in practice to the Toynbee Hall model than most of her colleagues. Like Barnett, she believed that the residents had as much to learn from their neighbors as their neighbors had to learn from them. For her, unlike for some head residents, this was not an abstract idea but an insight that grew out of her own experience.

Jane Addams—social reformer, peace activist, author, and lecturer—was born 6 September 1860 in Cedarville, Illinois, a small village fourteen miles south of the Illinois–Wisconsin border. She was the fifth surviving child of John Huy Addams and Sarah Weber Addams. Her mother died when Jane was two and a half, so her early sense of herself was most influenced by her father, a wealthy landowner, miller, banker, investor, and state legislator. His moral rectitude and civic-mindedness made a great impression on his daughter. She also found inspiration in the family and village recollections of her mother as a kind and generous neighbor to the poor of Cedarville.

Determined from childhood to accomplish something in life, Addams became fascinated in high school by social reform. Ralph Waldo Emerson and Charles Dickens were her favorite authors. Her stepmother—her father remarried when Jane was eight—was a woman of culture and social ambition who further broadened Addams's horizons through her love of literature and the arts.

Addams's drive to achieve was strong. Although she was determined to earn a Bachelor of Arts degree at the new Smith College in Massachusetts, her father insisted on sending her to the local Rockford Seminary. The school did not offer the B.A., but she took all the courses she could that would qualify her to receive one. By graduation, her plan was to become a doctor and live and work among the poor.

Still in pursuit of a B.A., Addams planned to attend Smith College before seeking her medical degree. Her parents, feeling she was too ill and weak to go east the following fall, forbade it. Frustrated, Addams lived at home that summer, unsure of her future. Then her father died unexpectedly in August. These two disappointments were followed by a third. That October, while the family was living in Philadelphia, she enrolled with her sister for two semesters of medical studies. Addams did not complete the degree, however, because of back problems that originated in a childhood illness. Major surgery and slow recovery followed.

The years immediately following college were, in some ways, the most difficult of Addams's life. Full of dreams about changing the world, she felt constrained by society's expectations—ones her father had shared and that her stepmother continued to express forcefully—that a single, unmarried daughter of prosperous means (Addams had received a large inheritance upon her father's death) should devote herself to family and travel, and should seek to marry as soon as possible. Addams's letters to her friend Ellen Gates Starr provide a record of her misery during this time.

At first, to compensate, Addams sought meaning for her life in the study of "culture," particularly through books. She read not only her favorite authors from college—Thomas Carlyle, Ralph Waldo Emerson, George Eliot, and Matthew Arnold—but also new ones, such as Leo Tolstoy, Auguste Comte, Herbert Spenser, John Stuart Mill, and Karl Marx. In their various ways, these authors explored the question that came to dominate Addams's life during these years: what was her responsibility as a human being to those who suffered? Slowly, her determination to work with the poor returned, strengthened by her sense that, in their suffering and their joy, they held a key to life's meaning that had escaped her.

By 1886 or 1887 Addams had decided, as she later noted in her autobiography, to rent a house in a poor district of a city where, along with other young women who would join her, she would try to act on the ideas she had absorbed from her extensive education while also trying to "learn of life from life itself."[2] Her ideas about how to reform society, enriched by her wide reading, spurred her to act, but so did her need to feel alive again and her desire to end her isolation from the rest of humanity. Founding Hull House was both an effort to make an objective difference and a personal necessity. She formulated her motives and goals for the settlement house out of her own experience.

Addams does not say when she first learned of Toynbee Hall, but by the spring of 1888 she had decided to visit it. In Madrid at the time, traveling with friends, she confessed her dream to Ellen Gates Starr. They agreed they would start a settlement in Chicago, where Ellen had been teaching school and had many friends. Encouraged by her friend's enthusiasm, Addams departed for London. She was deeply impressed by what she found at Toynbee Hall in the poverty-stricken East End, but most of all by its compassionate head resident, Canon Barnett, who would remain a lifetime friend. By 19 September 1889, Addams and Starr had rented a formerly elegant, now neglected, old house on Chicago's West Side; had lined up several women to join them as residents and volunteers; and had opened the doors to the community of mostly German, Irish, and Italian immigrants who lived in the surrounding tenements. Although Starr was cofounder of Hull House, they agreed Addams would be head resident, probably because her wealth was underwriting the costs of launching the settlement and, having no need to support herself, she had the free time to run it that Ellen, having to earn her living, did not.

Many have assigned the honorific "America's first settlement house" to Neighborhood Guild, which was founded in 1886, three years before Hull House, on the Lower East Side of New York City, and a case can be made for the claim. The Guild rationale, as set forth by its founder, Stanley Coit, sought to give neighbors a voice in governance by organizing entire neighborhoods into self-governing guilds, but it did not emphasize what the residents would learn or the idea of "mutual benefit." Furthermore, the idea of organizing neighborhoods into guilds was adopted in modified form by only a few settlements, and Coit himself, who continued to found guilds in England and America, drew a distinction between his guilds and settlements.

The first two American settlements that adopted the Toynbee Hall model were Hull House in Chicago and the College Settlement in New York City, founded by a group of alumnae (including nongraduates) of Smith, Wellesley, and several other New England women's colleges. The College Settlement opened its doors only two weeks after Hull House, on 1 October. Each settlement had made its initial plans unaware of the other's intent. Thus it was that independent efforts by college alumnae in the Northeast and Midwest launched the American settlement house movement in the fall of 1889.

The settlement idea spread rapidly. In October 1890, an African-American woman and Hampton Institute graduate, Janie Porter Barrett, opened the Locust Street Social Settlement in her home in Hampton, Virginia; the following year three more settlements opened in New York and Chicago. By 1900, fifteen years after Toynbee Hall began, in America alone there were between 50 and 103 settlements, depending on how "settlement" was defined (those with religious affiliations were often excluded). But whichever definition one used, the official figures were always low because the leaders in the field, whose personal networks produced the lists, were all white and from cities in the Northeast and Midwest. Jewish settlements in New York and Chicago were usually known, but Southern, rural, and black settlements were mostly omitted from early counts. By 1922 there were, by one "official" count, 500 settlements in the United States; the number may have marked the movement's peak.

From the beginning, women were drawn in disproportionate numbers to settlements. There were always significantly more women than men residents nationwide, and until the 1950s the majority of head residents were women. Women had always done work for the poor and been active in churches, two traditions that fed into settlements, but the settlement was uniquely appealing to women in that it offered an alternative to marriage—that is, a place to live, a group of people to live with, and a structure that presumed single women would live independent working lives. For the first generation of college-educated women, those graduating in the 1880s and 1890s, these characteristics made the settlement particularly attractive.

With these facts in mind, some historians have argued that the settlement provided a valuable kind of women's community, where they could develop their own strengths as actors in the public realm without interference from men. Many early settlements were sex-segregated and had the potential to be this kind of community (Denison House, the College Settlement in New York City, and Henry Street, for example, accepted only female residents for many years), but some of the settlements whose female residents and head residents were the most active in the "public realm," like Hull House and the University of Chicago Settlement, accepted men residents early. Hull House broke the barrier first, admitting men in late 1891; they soon numbered (and would remain for many years) a third of all Hull House residents. What was significant about Hull House was not the absence of men but their nondominant presence. Masculinity carried no extra authority there. The women of Hull House who emerged as local, state, and national leaders of various Progressive reforms, including Jane Addams, gained valuable experience at Hull House working with and leading men residents.

As the idea's prompt adoption in the United States suggests, the settlement house, although perceived as an innovation, drew on familiar elements in the Anglo-American—and African-American and Jewish—religious charitable traditions. Like a Christian city mission, the settlement came into a poor neighborhood out of concern for the conditions there. But whereas a mission's purpose was conversion, the settlement's was mutual education and cooperation.

Although religious faith often motivated settlement workers, early theorizers about the settlement philosophy, beginning with Canon Barnett, stressed that the settlement did not proselytize. Nevertheless, churches founded religious settlement houses to proselytize to the immigrant and African-American populations in the cities; in fact, among settlements—loosely defined—religious settlements were soon numerous. Between 1897 and 1906, 157 new settlements were established in the United States, 70 of them founded by churches. In 1910, out of 413 settlements that participated in one survey, 167 were religious settlements.

Viewing the movement from this perspective, it was essentially Christian, not only in motive but also in purpose. During the 1890s and after, the rapid spread of religious settlements was fueled by the activism of Protestant ministers inspired by the Social Gospel, the self-help efforts of black urban churches, and the urban mission work of the Catholic Church. Despite their numbers, however, the church-based settlements never captured the leadership of the movement. The National Federation of Settlements, founded in 1911 by the early pioneers— all of whom, including Addams, shared Barnett's view on proselytizing—long resisted accepting as a member any settlement that served as a mission.

Settlements established by African Americans to serve their communities often were founded by churches, and some, like the Institutional Church and Social Settlement of Chicago, were churches and settlements at the same time. Others, like the Abraham Lincoln Centre, also in Chicago, were founded by blacks and whites together, to serve racially integrated communities.

Settlements shared an interest in forming personal relations with the poor with another new kind of organization imported from England, the Charity Organization Society (COS). By the 1890s, when American settlements first became numerous in major cities, COS efforts were well established in the United States. COS proponents typically viewed the poor as responsible for their poverty, crediting able-bodied men with moral decrepitude if they remained poor. COS workers saw themselves as "reformers." Their reform goals were to make the delivery of charity more scientific and to reform the individual poor person. These goals became those of the modern social work profession—a fact that is hardly surprising, given that profession's origins in the COS movement. By contrast, settlement leaders—or at least the most progressive ones—tended to see poverty as mainly caused by environmental conditions like low pay, poorly ventilated and unsafe housing, unsanitary streets, and unclean water.

Another difference, much discussed, lay in whom the two movements served. COS was concerned with efficiently providing the "worthy" poor with food, clothing, and shelter. Settlements mainly dealt with the working poor and avoided giving charity, except to neighbors in crisis. The distinction was important, although it was usually lost on visitors, newspaper reporters, and, later, some historians.

Although national COS and settlement leaders argued about theory, cooperation was extensive at the local level. Despite the fact that the COS and settlement philosophies and goals differed, many COS offices were housed in settlements, and some COS groups even founded settlements. COS volunteers, like those with ties to proselytizing churches, tended to have a conservative influence on settlements.

In keeping with the Toynbee Hall model, American universities were actively involved in settlements from the start. Those founded by professors or alumni were usually called "university" (for men) or "college" (for women) settlements. These groups often saw settlements as "laboratories" where college or seminary students could "study poverty." Several early male settlement leaders, such as Robert Woods and Charles Stover, with close ties to universities or seminaries, enthusiastically promoted the "settlement as laboratory" idea and the term "university settlement."

Jane Addams disagreed. As early as 1892, before a gathering of settlement leaders at a social ethics conference, she argued in favor of the idea of the "social settlement" and stressed the importance of knowing the neighbors as people, not as objects of study.[3] In 1899, in her lengthiest, most carefully crafted essay on settlements, "A Function of the Social Settlement" (strategically published in an academic journal), Addams took up the question again. The settlement, she argued, "stands for application, not for research; for universal interest, as opposed to specialization."[4]

Addams's reasons for rejecting the "settlement as laboratory" model went to the heart of her understanding of what a settlement was. In this essay she defined it as "an effort to apply knowledge to life, to express life itself in terms of life." Unlike the philanthropist, who seeks "to do good," or the sociologist, who "thirst[s] for data and analysis," the resident's "more . . . human desire" was for the workingman and workingwoman to have the opportunity to develop the "moral and intellectual qualities upon which depend the free aspects and values of living."[5] The settlement resident's purpose was life-transforming, both for herself or himself and for the neighbors. A desire for factual knowledge was too narrow and impersonal a motive for such work, Addams felt. Although Hull House residents did some studies of the neighborhood, and although Addams never argued against such work—indeed, she thought "investigations" valuable—she continued to point out the dangers of the "settlement as laboratory" model.

Addams's thoughtful speeches at the 1892 conference, published the following fall in the prestigious *The Forum* magazine, marked her emergence as a national leader of the fledgling American settlement movement. A year later she helped bring settlements to national and international prominence by organizing the first national and world conference on settlements, the Congress on Social Settlements, as part of the series of congresses held under the auspices of the Chicago World's Fair (the Columbian Exposition). Addams and Graham Taylor organized the first regional federation of settlements in Chicago in 1894, and she was one of the eleven founders of the National Federation of Settlements in 1911, of which she was promptly elected the first president.

The types of activities they undertook were another way to define settlements, yet even among the early settlements, patterns were difficult to discern. Kindergartens, children's clubs, and classes were the most widespread; but, as if to prove the point that no particular activity was defining, Denison House had neither a kindergarten nor children's clubs in its early years. Henry Street Settlement, initially called the Nurses' Settlement, had only one club and no kindergarten at first. Some—like South End House, Henry Street, Hull House, Chicago Commons, and University of Chicago Settlement—were particularly active in local politics and municipal reform; others were determinedly apolitical. Some settlements, most notably Hull House, had rich cultural offerings: drama clubs, literature classes, lectures, music classes, concerts. Others offered little beyond crafts. Some emphasized vocational education; others, literacy; still others, citizenship. Some worked closely with labor unions (Denison House, Hull House, South End House, University Settlement); others, fearing to alarm their communities, distanced themselves from the labor movement. (It should be noted that none of these activities was the sole purview of settlements. Missions, churches, temples, and other local organizations also undertook them.) In fact, a majority of settlements was always focused, some exclusively, on meeting the needs of the neighborhood through service. The average settlement house, as Ruth Crocker has persuasively argued, was no "spearhead" for reform, except at the neighborhood level.[6]

What made a settlement reform-minded (in the broader sense) was, of course, the outlook of its residents, which was influenced, at least in part, by the outlook of the head resident, particularly by his or her expectations of the residents. Consensus in the movement regarding the residents' role was absent from the beginning, although initially there was some agreement that the presence of residents was the most distinctive characteristic of settlements. In 1896 a survey of American settlements by the National Conference of Charities and Corrections found that the field considered the residents' presence essential to the settlement's "identity."[7]

Most of the early head residents were familiar with Barnett's belief that settlements were not to impose their solutions to neighborhood problems but to learn what the neighbors wanted changed. In one of her 1892 speeches, Addams echoed and elaborated on the point: "[The] residents must be emptied of all conceit of opinion and all self-assertion."[8] This belief, in turn, shaped Barnett's and Addams's method of leading their settlements. At Hull House, as at Toynbee Hall, the residents governed themselves through a committee of all residents that met weekly to set fees for room and board, vote on new residents after a trial period, decide what projects the House would undertake as a whole, and determine the House expectations of residents regarding shared tasks, such as answering the front door and tending the playground. Although Addams chaired the committee on most occasions, her power was limited by the parliamentary rules that governed the meetings, and her proposals were sometimes rejected.

Addams, like Barnett, gave Hull House residents the freedom to choose how to spend their time. She encouraged them to pursue their own interests. "Miss Addams," a volunteer recalled, "had a rare way of . . . letting [people] work out their own plans."[9] The freedom she gave residents was a policy that flowed directly out of her belief that a key purpose of the settlement was to teach the resident about life outside his or her own social class. Canon Barnett had first sounded the theme, but Addams was alone among the American settlement leaders in making a strong case for pursuing that goal. For her, the twin goals of social reform and self-reformation were inextricably intertwined. It was an old Protestant theme carried forward by Barnett and Addams into the settlement movement.

During the period before World War I, most settlements had no governing committee to which all residents belonged, although several (including Chicago Commons) had executive committees whose membership was elected by the residents.[10] Greenwich House in New York City did have a full residents' committee and in other ways was modeled closely on Hull House. Its founder, Mary Simkhovitch, was, along with Graham Taylor, one of the settlement founders (she was second generation) who caught the Toynbee Hall/Hull House spirit.

Residents at settlement houses were typically restricted in other ways as well. Like most head residents, Robert Woods viewed the volunteer residents as ''his'' staff, to be deployed as he saw fit after consulting them regarding their views. When residents at South End House departed, restless under his command, he decided the only solution was to change from residents to paid staff.

This attitude and the trend toward paid staff were repeated at most settlements during the 1890s. At the University Settlement in New York, for example, volunteer residents were expected to ''cooperate'' with the head worker and to ''offer suggestions'' for new policies.[11] At another settlement, volunteer residents were expected to ''contribute'' four hours a day. Probably as a result of the extensive demands placed on volunteer residents at most settlements, frequent turnover was also a problem. In response, as the twentieth century progressed, nearly all settlement houses converted to paid staff. By contrast, at Hull House, turnover was low and residents remained volunteers until after Addams's death in May 1935.

The degree of a resident's freedom to design his or her own settlement experience was hardly a minor detail. It affected the amount of creativity a resident could exercise and her or his freedom to undertake controversial work or make controversial public statements. In tight regimes, residents with new, or simply their own, ideas were seen as troublemakers. At Denison House, for a time, residents were forbidden to develop new projects on their own. Residents at such settlements were far less likely to originate fresh reform ideas. Although historians have rightly praised settlement workers for being, in Allen Davis's words, ''progressive with a vengeance,'' the movement as a whole was more conservative than the views of its most prominent leaders would suggest.[12] In that, the settlement movement was similar to most reform movements.

But the fact that the ideal resident—an open-minded learner exploring her or his own interests—was not perfectly or even widely realized should not obscure the ideal's power to transform a particular resident from a defender of the status quo to a campaigner for social and economic change. The experience of settlement residence was, when properly designed, the reason the settlement movement became, for a time, a reform-nurturing movement. When residents really learned from their neighbors, they arrived at a new understanding of the causes of social problems. The energy and ideas for state and national reforms came mostly from the leadership and the residents of the pioneer settlements. Jane Addams, Robert Woods, Charles Stover, Graham Taylor, Mary McDowell, and Lillian Wald had founded settlement houses by 1895. To their ranks were added residents of their settlements who became nationally known reformers in their own right: Julia Lathrop, Florence Kelley, Alice Hamilton, and Robert Hunter (all from Hull House); Albert Kennedy (South End House); and Raymond Robins (Chicago Commons). Many of these individuals, plus others who came later (Eleanor Roosevelt, Harold Ickes, Louise deKoven Bowen, Sophonisba Breckinridge, Edith and Grace Abbott), wrote movingly of the impact of their settlement experiences on their understanding of the obstacles facing the unemployed and the working poor.

The settlements were also the source of loyal networks for political mobilization that were part of what made these reformers so effective in their efforts. Addams worked closely with the individuals just named on one or more reforms at the state and national levels. Ideas first conceived at settlement dining room tables were sometimes transformed into national policy, after much letter writing and consulting, data gathering, speechmaking and testifying, and private sessions with elected officials. These reformers worked in tandem when they could, and agreed to disagree when they had to. The lines of cooperation remained strong in part because the settlement leaders did not demand consensus on every issue. Alliances emerged and fell apart amiably as the issues changed.

Community organizing, always an engine for reform, was also part of the original settlement vision and practiced by some houses. Experience had shown, Addams wrote in 1904, that the settlement's neighbors "have in themselves reservoirs of moral power and civic ability ... [and] that one can count upon tremendous aids from within the neighborhoods."[13] The residents' task was to arouse their neighbors to collective action and to "interpret the public opinion of their neighborhood" to those who lived outside it.[14]

Examples of what Addams meant stud the history of Hull House: its clubs for children and adults, which were self-governing organizations with constitutions and voting members; its cooperative coal society (headed by a neighbor with a neighborhood membership) was designed to keep fuel costs down by eliminating the middle man. Other community organizing included the campaigns to defeat the corrupt local alderman, the effort of the Hull House Women's Club to lobby city hall to improve garbage and sanitation services, and the settlement's support for the right of unions to organize and strike. As Addams said many times, she wished to work with others, not for others.[15] This was part of what she meant by "social democracy," a concept about which she wrote a great deal.

Very few settlements, however, embraced community organizing and democratic self-governance as part of their agenda. Instead, elements of the Hull House approach were borrowed piecemeal. Lillian Wald at Henry Street eventually established self-governing clubs. Robert Woods at South End House tried to encourage neighbors to lobby for better garbage services. Denison House welcomed union organizers to hold meetings there. It was not until the 1950s, however, that the approach became central to the methods of some settlements.

Racism, combined with classism, kept many settlement leaders from doing more to encourage community activism earlier. They feared an empowered community and thought the educated class better equipped than illiterate immigrants or African Americans to handle power. Despite their years of living in ethnically diverse communities, many residents and head residents felt themselves to be racially superior, particularly to southern European immigrants and African Americans, whose numbers were on the increase in major American cities between 1900 and 1920. Settlements located in areas where black people began to settle in increasing numbers often refused to serve them and even relocated to white neighborhoods, sometimes handing over the old settlement building to the African-American community to run—which, in the case of Christamore House in Indianapolis, it did with great success. Some white settlements, like Henry Street, founded separate branches in black neighborhoods.

Addams's deep convictions about democracy and the essential equality of human beings helped her to avoid practicing much of the racism prevalent in white society. She was, it appears, the first white head resident to invite a black resident to join a settlement serving a white community. Harriet Rice, a graduate of Wellesley College and a medical doctor by profession, was a resident of Hull House, with one or two breaks, from 1892 to at least 1904. Addams supported a prominent Chicago woman's effort to become the first black member of the Chicago Women's Club, supported African-American Chicagoans who sought to start a settlement house in a predominantly black neighborhood, and fought (but failed) to have the black delegates from the Southern states seated at the 1912 Bull Moose convention.

Addams's methods as head resident, her emphasis on "learning from life," and her respect for a community's knowledge and for the principles of democracy contributed to her distaste for what she called "professionalism"—a distaste she extended to the profession of social work, which began to be an influence in settlement houses and elsewhere after the turn of the century. Addams felt that those who sought to "do good" professionally were dangerous in their self-righteousness, in their disdain for the wisdom of the common people, and in their minute concern with method.[16] Although social workers, like everyone else, were welcome at Hull House, and although Addams had close friends involved in shaping the profession, she never considered herself a "social worker" (even though she was often introduced as one) or spoke on the need for training in the field of settlement work.

Addams's nephew chose to include only two accomplishments on the stone that marked her grave in the cemetery at Cedarville (she died 25 May 1935). It reads, "Jane Addams of Hull House and the Women's International League for Peace and Freedom." Her involvement in the peace movement began in 1898, triggered in part by the outbreak of the Spanish–American War, but was inspired, at a deeper level, by ideas on nonviolence she first absorbed from the Christian writings of Leo Tolstoy, which she read in the 1880s and 1890s. A visit to Tolstoy in Russia in 1896 moved her deeply, even as it raised questions in her mind about whether he was committed to nonviolence in all its forms. Eventually Addams opposed World War I at great personal cost. She founded the Women's International League for Peace and Freedom in 1919 and served as its president until 1929.

Despite the differences she had with social workers, and despite her expanding and controversial role in the international peace movement, Addams remained a prominent settlement leader until her death. She continued to be much sought-after as a speaker on the subject of settlements. Her famous and popular classic, *Twenty Years at Hull-House, with Autobiographical Notes*, published in 1910, made her name a household word and synonymous with the movement, but her most definitive writings on settlements remain her two 1892 speeches and her 1899 journal article.

Addams would not have labeled herself as a reformer either ("writer and lecturer" was how she chose to describe herself), but she wrote and thought a good deal about the subject of reform. Her views on the sources of the reform impulse were consistent with her desire to nurture residents' individuality. "The variation of the established type," she once wrote, "is at the root of all change."[17] Thus did she apply Darwin's theory of the evolution of species to explain social change. Although historians tend to call "reformers" those activists who promote a public policy reform agenda, Addams understood her greatest reform to be the creation of conditions at Hull House in which each resident could develop his or her individuality as a full human being, could become "a variation from established type" and therefore a source of social change. The record of the accomplishments of Hull House residents, unique among the residents of American settlements, testifies to her success.

In holding such views, Addams stood in opposition to strong trends within the settlement movement and wider society. By the 1910s, residents increasingly were trained social workers, although untrained paid and volunteer residents could be found at settlements in reduced numbers for many years. In time, resident programs disappeared altogether, replaced by paid, trained staff who went home every night.

The final trend, confirming the nonreform, conservative leanings of most settlements, was the increasing involvement of the business community, directly and indirectly, in settlement financing. Although businessmen had always supported settlements and served on their boards, the emergence after World War I of the federated charity fund-raising organizations—Community Chests—consolidated their influence. By the 1930s, if not before, many settlements were receiving the majority of their funding from these sources. Fearing such influences, Addams persuaded Hull House's board of directors to avoid such funding. The policy was changed only after her death.

Government funding, another trend that began in the 1930s, further inhibited settlements from seeking reforms. By the 1940s most settlements were community-based social service agencies, more often extensions of the government than critics of society—if they ever had been, which of course most had not.

Jane Addams and her colleagues in the settlement movement did not see eye to eye on many policy issues regarding settlement houses, but because of the decentralized nature of the movement (it was twenty-two years old before it felt the need for a national organization) and Addams's belief in individual freedom, these disagreements remained mostly uncontested. Despite Addams's enormous personal appeal as a much-loved public figure, her influence on the directions taken by the settlement movement was not great. Her greatest reform was Hull House. As its cofounder and head resident, she gave herself and others the opportunity to help to change America.

NOTES

1. Mary Sayles, "Settlement Workers and Their Work," *Outlook* 78 (1904): 311; Jane Addams to Alice Addams Haldeman, 23 February 1893, Jane Addams Papers, Jane Addams Peace Collection (Swarthmore College); Paul Kellogg, "Twice Twenty Years at Hull-House," *The Survey* 64 (1930): 266.

2. Jane Addams, *Twenty Years at Hull-House* (New York, 1910), 85.

3. This speech was later published as "The Objective Value of a Social Settlement," first in the *Forum* magazine (under a different title) and then in Henry C. Adams, ed., *Philanthropy and Social Progress* (New York, 1893).

4. Jane Addams, "A Function of the Social Settlement," *Annals of the American Academy of Political and Social Science* 13 (1899): 336.

5. Ibid., 50.

6. Ruth Hutchinson Crocker, *Social Work and Social Order: The Settlement Movement in Two Industrial Cities, 1889–1930* (Champaign-Urbana, Ill., 1992), 211, 222–225.

7. Harry P. Kraus, *The Settlement House Movement in New York City, 1886–1914* (New York, 1980), 31.

8. Jane Addams, "The Subjective Necessity for Social Settlements," in Adams, ed., *Philanthropy and Social Progress*, 24.

9. Louise deKoven Bowen, *Growing Up with a City* (New York, 1926), 88.

10. Louise C. Wade, *Graham Taylor: Pioneer for Social Justice, 1851–1938* (Chicago, 1964), 150.

11. Daniel Murphy, "Some Functions of a Settlement Resident," *Annual Report of University Settlement Society, 1912* (New York, 1912), 33.

12. Allen F. Davis, *Spearheads for Reform: The Social Settlements and the Progressive Movement, 1890–1914* (New York, 1967), x.

13. Jane Addams, "Neighborhood Improvement," in *Proceedings of the 31st National Conference of Charities and Corrections* (New York, 1904), 457.

14. Jane Addams, "Remarks," National Conference of Charities and Corrections, *Proceedings of the 23rd National Conference* (Boston, 1897), 136.

15. James Weber Linn, *Jane Addams: A Biography* (New York, 1936), 387.

16. Jane Addams, "A Modern Lear," repr. in Christopher Lasch, ed., *The Social*

Thought of Jane Addams (New York, 1965), 118; Jane Addams, "Presidential Address," in International Congress of Women at the Hague, April 28th–May 1st, 1915, *Report* (Chicago, 1915), 22.

17. Jane Addams, *The Spirit of Youth and the City Streets* (New York, 1909), 8.

BIBLIOGRAPHY

Addams, Jane. "Hull House, Chicago: An Effort toward Social Democracy." *The Forum* 14 (1892): 226–241.

———. "A New Impulse to an Old Gospel." *The Forum* 14 (1892): 345–358. [The *Forum* articles were reprinted with new titles, "The Objective Value of a Social Settlement," and "The Subjective Necessity for Social Settlements," in Henry C. Adams, ed. *Philanthropy and Social Progress*. New York, 1893.]

———. "A Function of the Social Settlement." *Annals of the American Academy of Political and Social Science* 13 (1899): 323–345.

———. *Twenty Years at Hull-House*. New York, 1910.

Barbuto, Domenica Maria. " 'The Matrix of Understanding': The Life and Work of Mary Kinsbury Simkovitch." Ph.D. diss., State University of New York at Stony Brook, 1992.

Bryan, Mary Lynn McCree, ed. *The Jane Addams Papers Microfilm*. Ann Arbor, Mich., 1985.

Carson, Mina. *Settlement Folk: Social Thought and the American Settlement Movement, 1885–1930*. Chicago, 1990.

Crocker, Ruth Hutchinson. *Social Work and Social Order: The Settlement Movement in Two Industrial Cities, 1889–1930*. Champaign-Urbana, Ill., 1992.

Davis, Allen F. *Spearheads for Reform: The Social Settlements and the Progressive Movement, 1890–1914*. New York, 1967.

———. *American Heroine: The Life and Legend of Jane Addams*. New York, 1973.

Doe, Seung Ja. "Christian Perspective on Poverty: An Ideological Foundation for Social Work, 1880–1920." Ph.D. diss., Washington University, 1990.

Knight, Louise W. "Jane Addams and Hull House: Historical Lessons on Nonprofit Leadership." *Nonprofit Management and Leadership* 2 (1992): 125–141.

Kraus, Harry P. *The Settlement House Movement in New York City, 1886–1914*. New York, 1980.

Lasch-Quinn, Elisabeth. *Black Neighbors: Race and the Limits of Reform in the American Settlement House Movement, 1890–1945*. Chapel Hill, N.C., 1993.

Staples, George Henry. "Stanley Coit and the Neighborhood Guild: Ethical Idealism and Social Reform in New York City." Ph.D. diss., City University of New York, 1991.

———. "Hull House and the Settlement Movement: A Centennial Reassessment." *Journal of Urban History* 17 (1991): 410–420.

Trolander, Judith Ann. *Settlement Houses and the Great Depression*. Detroit, 1975.

Wade, Louise C. "The Heritage from Chicago's Early Settlement Houses." *Journal of the Illinois State Historical Society* 60 (1967): 411–441.

Woods, Robert A., and Albert J. Kennedy, eds. *The Handbook of Settlements*. New York, 1911.

Ida Wells-Barnett
and the African-American
Anti-Lynching Campaign

LINDA O. McMURRY

The lynchings of Thomas Moss, Calvin McDowell, and Will Stewart in March 1892 were not significant for their rarity—that year at least 158 other African Americans were killed by angry mobs for alleged offenses against white society. The location of the lynchings in Memphis, Tennessee, was also not remarkable; seventeen other black Tennesseans were lynched that year and forty-six African Americans had been killed in an 1866 race riot in Memphis. The three deaths assumed a special importance mostly because of their impact on the young journalist, Ida B. Wells. She knew all three men and was godmother to Moss's daughter. Outraged by the murder of her friends, Wells mobilized her considerable talents and energies to battle the evil of mob violence. Thus began the perfect marriage of an individual and a cause.

Born to slave parents on 16 July 1862, in Holly Springs, Mississippi, Wells was the eldest of seven children. In 1878 her parents, James Wells and Lizzie Bell, and one sibling died in a yellow fever epidemic. Wells returned from Shaw (later Rust) University and rejected plans to divide the remaining children among friends and relatives. Instead, at the age of sixteen, she assumed responsibility for her brothers and sisters and became head of the household. She began teaching and eventually moved to Memphis, where she participated in the rich cultural life of the black elite. There she might have led a conventional life but for her temperament and a series of events.

The first event occurred on 4 May 1884, when a conductor asked Wells to leave the ladies' car of a train. She refused, then bit him on the hand when he sought to remove her forcibly, and finally sued the railroad. She won the suit, lost it on appeal, and launched her career as a journalist and a firebrand. Wells became a partner and editor of the Memphis *Free Speech and Headlight* in 1889. She also taught until 1891, when she was dismissed after criticizing the conditions of the local black schools in the newspaper. Becoming a full-time journalist, she continued to write militant articles, which were frequently reprinted in other black newspapers under her pen name, "Iola." By 1892 she had become known as a forceful, energetic, and uncompromising foe of discrimination.

The lynching of her three friends that year focused Wells's anger on the plague of mob violence. Lynching, however, was not a new issue to either her or the black community. The year before, she had written an editorial of praise for African Americans in Georgetown, Kentucky, who had set fire to the town after a lynching there. She could hardly be unaware of the growing menace of racial violence—too many black Southerners were being killed in the aftermath of Reconstruction. Murder by mobs had replaced the slave master's whip as an instrument to control recalcitrant blacks. The institution of slavery had served well to keep not merely slaves but all African Americans in various states of quasi-freedom. When slavery was destroyed in the course of the Civil War, white Southerners immediately sought to find other methods of racial domination.

The white South's desire for a new form of slavery was briefly thwarted by Republican rule in the region and the Thirteenth, Fourteenth, and Fifteenth amendments. In many areas, however, violence quickly became the remedy for emancipation and black political empowerment, as in the 1866 riot in Memphis. By the 1890s, white Southerners were freed of local Republican governments and had begun to craft a caste system based upon legalized repression. That system was like a three-legged stool with disfranchisement, segregation, and the threat of violence as its supports. The lynching of almost 2,000 African Americans between 1882 and 1902 bears witness to the whites' reliance on violence to overcome black resistance to segregation and disfranchisement.

White Southerners of that era, like the slave masters before them, were equipped with consciences. They not only wanted to dominate their black neighbors; they also wanted to feel their actions were justified. They had inherited a ready-made ideological basis for discrimination: the doctrine of black inferiority. Reinforced by arguments from Social Darwinists and American imperialists, the myths of white supremacy found fertile ground and became even more deeply rooted in the North as well as the South. Segregation and the denial of suffrage needed explanation in a democracy; denial of due process and murder demanded even more compelling arguments for justification. In an ironic distortion of facts, although white men had been raping black women with impunity for more than a century, the black man was depicted as a fiendish beast who could be restrained from ravishing white women only by extreme measures. The cry of "rape" excused torture, mutilation, and murder to both Northern and Southern whites. Few whites were outspoken critics of lynching in the 1890s.

African Americans were quicker to deplore lynch law. They understood that, whatever its cause, violence was the cement of the new caste system that replaced slavery as a source of cheap labor and exploitation. Most black leaders realized that just as the slave master's whip had prevented true freedom for any African American, the ability of whites to murder blacks with impunity limited all black freedom after emancipation. Thus lynching was one issue consistently recurring in the speeches and platforms of black leaders and organizations throughout the United States. Before the Civil War the Black Convention movement had emerged in the North to fight slavery and to advance the status of free blacks. After the war, conventions were held in both the South and the North, and racial violence was included on the agendas of all. Black newspapers and such organizations as the Afro-American League denounced lynching. Every major leader publicly deplored mob violence. The chorus of cries for justice was loud and long—but still ignored. Rape was seen as far more barbaric than lynching.

So pervasive was the myth that lynching resulted from rape that even black spokesmen often did not challenge it. Many included a denunciation of rape with appeals to let the justice system do its job; they merely asked that juries and judges, rather than mobs, decide guilt and mete out punishment. Wells later wrote that before the 1892 lynchings in Memphis, "Like many another person who had read of lynching in the South, I had accepted the idea meant to be conveyed—that although lynching was irregular and contrary to law and order, unreasoning anger over the terrible crime of rape led to the lynching; that perhaps the brute deserved death anyhow."[1]

The lynchings of Moss, McDowell, and Stewart opened her eyes and made her determined to open other eyes. None of the victims were even accused of rape. All were affiliated with the People's Grocery, which opened across the street from a store owned by a white merchant, W. H. Barret. Unhappy with his new competition, Barret was hostile and provoked a number of violent encounters. He then convinced a grand jury to indict the officials of the People's Grocery for operating a public nuisance. After some outraged blacks used violent rhetoric at a public meeting, Barret persuaded a criminal court judge to issue arrest warrants for two of his competitors, on the charge of conspiring against whites. When nine deputized white men in civilian clothes approached the store after dark, they were mistaken for a mob and fired upon. Three whites were wounded, and McDowell and Stewart were immediately arrested.

Chilling stories of race riot circulated in Memphis. As panic spread, black residents were disarmed by orders of the judge, and a small army of white men helped deputies arrest thirty more "rioters," including Thomas Moss. Four days after the incident, nine whites entered the jail at 3 A.M., dragged Moss, McDowell, and Stewart about nine miles out of town, and shot them. Sorrow at the loss of "three of the best specimens of young since-the-war Afro-American manhood" mingled in Wells's mind with the horror of knowing that no one would ever stand trial for the crime.[2]

Angry and discouraged, Wells wrote a number of editorials for the *Free Speech* and suggested that black citizens migrate west to find justice. When about 2,000 did leave, a number of white businesses felt the economic impact—

especially the streetcar company, which was being boycotted. Its owners asked the newspaper to tell blacks to return to the streetcars. Wells firmly refused their requests. She also began to investigate lynchings, and discovered that only about a fourth of lynching victims were even accused of rape. In addition, many times the charges of rape were unjustified. Merely speaking to a white woman in a suggestive way could be labeled "attempted rape." Wells also ascertained that far more voluntary sexual liaisons occurred between white women and black men than white men would acknowledge. The discovery of such relationships usually prompted cries of rape.

In a *Free Speech* editorial that appeared on 21 May 1892, Wells dared to say aloud what white men did not want to hear. She wrote, "Nobody in this section of the country believes the old thread bare lie that Negro men rape white women. If Southern white men are not careful, they will over-reach themselves and public sentiment will have a reaction; a conclusion will then be reached which will be very damaging to the moral reputation of their women."[3] Whites were outraged. One editorial suggested it was the duty of whites "to tie the wretch who utters these calumnies to a stake at the intersection of Main and Madison Sts., brand him in the forehead with a hot iron and perform upon him a surgical operation with a pair of tailor's shears."[4]

Even if she had been equipped with the requisite anatomy for such surgery, Wells was beyond the reach of a mob, attending a conference of the African Methodist Episcopal Church. Wrongly suspected of authorship, coeditor J. L. Fleming fled the city before a mob descended on the *Free Speech* office and vented its anger on the furnishings and machinery. Wells heeded the warnings not to return to Memphis and accepted an offer from T. Thomas Fortune of the *New York Age* to provide him with a list of her subscribers for a fourth interest in his paper. Her first assignment was to write a series of articles on lynching.

Calling herself "Exiled," Wells wrote an extensive article in June, describing the events in Memphis and recounting similar lynchings throughout the South. Ten thousand copies of that edition of the *Age* were distributed around the nation; a thousand copies were sold in Memphis. Wells's words created a sensation within the black community but were virtually ignored by the white press. Then black women in New York provided Wells with a platform from which to reach a larger audience. On 5 October 1892, at Lyric Hall, they organized and sponsored a testimonial meeting to raise funds to restart the *Free Speech*.

Hundreds of women attended, coming from Philadelphia and Boston as well as New York. Wells cried as she told of the murder of her friend Tom Moss. Dismayed by her uncharacteristic "weakness," she was delighted to be presented with a gold brooch and $500. She used the money not to restart her paper but to expand and publish her article as a pamphlet titled *Southern Horrors*. As usual she did not mince her words. After recounting a lynching that was thwarted by armed blacks, she wrote, "The lesson this teaches and which every Afro-American should ponder well, is that a Winchester rifle should have a place of honor in every black home, and it should be used for that protection which the law refuses to give.''[5]

Wells received numerous invitations to speak throughout the Northeast. By early 1893 her words had garnered enough attention to cause the white press of Memphis to seek to discredit her by defaming her character. She considered suing the *Memphis Commercial* for libel and consulted a number of attorneys, including Ferdinand L. Barnett. She and Frederick Douglass were working with Barnett to publish a pamphlet protesting the exclusion of African Americans at the Chicago World's Columbian Exposition in 1893. Wells was diverted from both projects by an invitation from the British reformer and editor of *Anti-Caste*, Catherine Impey, to come to England to help organize an ''Emancipation League.''

With her expenses paid, Wells left for England on 5 April 1893. She sought to play a role similar to that of Douglass prior to the Civil War in motivating the English people to join the abolitionist movement. Aware that white Americans were still sensitive to British criticism, she wrote: ''The moral agencies at work in Great Britain did much for the final overthrow of chattel slavery. They can in like manner pray, write, preach, talk and act against civil and industrial slavery; against the hanging, shooting and burning alive of a powerless race.''[6] Before she returned to America in June, her hosts founded the Society for the Recognition of the Brotherhood of Man, to combat all forms of discrimination, especially lynching.

Wells returned to Chicago instead of New York, arriving in time to aid in the publication of 20,000 copies of the pamphlet *The Reason Why the Colored American Is not in the World's Columbian Exposition*. It included her article ''Lynch Law'' as well as articles describing both the repression and the achievements of African Americans. Wells joined Douglass at the Haitian Pavilion to distribute the pamphlets to foreign visitors. While in Chicago, she also helped found a women's club that was later named after her. At the same time she increased her contact with Ferdinand Barnett by joining the staff of his newspaper, the *Chicago Conservator*. He had established the paper in 1878, the same year that he received his law degree from Northwestern University. Barnett and Wells were ideologically compatible; their relationship began to blossom but did not bear fruit immediately, because Wells was once again invited to England by the Society for the Brotherhood of Man.

On her second trip abroad, Wells agreed to write a column about her experiences for the white-owned *Chicago Inter-Ocean*. Her return journey received more press attention both in the United States and Great Britain—partly because it was riddled with controversies. Wells became embroiled in a split between two leaders of the Society for the Brotherhood of Man, which placed her in a precarious financial position. Isabelle Mayo was outraged by Catherine Impey's indiscreet behavior with a black man and insisted on a public denunciation of Impey. When Wells refused, Mayo withdrew her financial support for the tour. Wells therefore had to solicit funds, thereby provoking questions about her motives. Although she would not criticize her friend, Wells was not at all reluctant to criticize Frances Willard, the leader of the Woman's Christian Temperance Union (WCTU). Wells condemned Willard for comments in an 1890 speech in which Willard had said, "The colored race multiplies like the locusts of Egypt. The grog-shop is its center of power. 'The safety of woman, of childhood, of the home, is menaced in a thousand localities at this moment, so that the men dare not go beyond the sight of their own roof-tree.' "[7]

Wells did not single out Willard for condemnation; she also attacked evangelist Dwight Moody, American churches that remained silent on lynching, and Southern governors who tolerated mob murder in their states. The willingness of Wells to castigate respected institutions and individuals for their "moral cowardice" provoked negative press coverage and alienated some previous or potential supporters. For example, Lady Henry Somerset, the president of the British Women's Temperance Union, published an interview with Willard that implied Wells had intentionally distorted Willard's position on lynching. Nevertheless, even when Wells's words caused resentment, they often had a positive impact. In a speech at the November 1894 national convention of the WCTU in Cleveland, Willard refuted the statements by Wells and at the same time publicly announced the WCTU's opposition to lynching.

Southern governors also responded to Wells's charges. Missouri Governor W. J. Stone wrote to the *London News* in response to its editorial about a lecture by Wells. He and Governor W. J. Northern of Georgia used novel arguments to discredit Wells. They asserted that she was an agent for a group of investors who sought to lure immigrants away from the South to the West, for personal financial gain. The charges of the Southern white press tended to be more scurrilous. The *London Post* characterized two articles from the *Memphis Commercial* as "very coarse in tone, and some of the language is such as could not possibly be reproduced in an English journal."[8]

Undoubtedly, the favored tactic to discredit Wells was to report on black opposition to her activities. A number of African Americans did question the impact of the controversy that seemed to follow in her wake. Some moderated their support for her, for fear of alienating their white American allies, but few were willing to speak out against her publicly. Those who did were immediately proclaimed the "legitimate" spokespeople for their fellow African Americans by the white press in the United States. Memphis papers reported that a local black editor had proclaimed Wells's charges false and slanderous. The *New York Times* quoted a black Democratic politician who denounced Wells as a "fraud" and insisted, "A reputable or respectable negro has never been lynched, and never will be."[9] Although personal ambition likely influenced most such statements, Wells did alienate some black leaders by her willingness to criticize fellow African Americans for their timidity. Indeed, the list of leaders, black and white, whom Wells chastised grew over the course of her life to include U.S. presidents, Jane Addams, Susan B. Anthony, Frederick Douglass, Booker T. Washington, and W.E.B. Du Bois.

Her disdain of compromise and discreet language may have limited Wells's role as an organizational leader, but it made her written and oral rhetoric compelling. Both male colleagues and reporters were especially mesmerized by the contrast between her "feminine beauty" and her graphic descriptions of atrocities. Few reformers have provoked as many comments on their physical appearance. Reports of her English speeches indicate that audiences were often moved to tears as Wells recounted the grisly details of lynchings. In 102 lectures she constantly stressed that lynching was not about rape but about power. She also emphasized that most white American reformers were either silent on the issue or muffled their criticisms with disclaimers about the horrors of rape. Her arguments convinced numerous British leaders of the need to speak out against lynching in order to awaken and educate white Americans to its evils. During her second tour, supporters formed the Anti-Lynching Committee in London. The son-in-law of Queen Victoria headed the organization, and its membership included many distinguished persons.

Wells returned to New York in July 1894 to a mixed reception. Fellow African Americans welcomed her at a meeting in Fleet Street A.M.E. Church. The *New York Times* greeted her with a hostile editorial. It noted that the day after her arrival, a black man had assaulted a white woman in the city and declared, "The circumstances of his fiendish crime may serve to convince the mulatress missionary that the promulgation in New York just now of her theory of Negro outrages is, to say the least, inopportune."[10]

The editorial did not deter Wells from pledging to spend a year lecturing in the United States if she received financial support. Searching for funding, Wells called for the formation of a black anti-lynching organization. This was not a new idea; two previous groups had grown out of the desire to combat mob justice. T. Thomas Fortune had founded the Afro-American League in 1890, primarily as an anti-lynching vehicle; however, it lost that focus after the first convention and became increasingly inactive. In 1893 Henry McNeal Turner had issued a call for a convention that resulted in the formation of the Equal Rights Council. Both in his call and in his keynote address Turner highlighted lynching as the most critical issue facing African Americans. Nevertheless, both the Council and the League soon focused more on such issues as streetcar segregation—reflecting the priorities of the black elite that was far more likely to encounter discrimination than to be lynched. Anger over racial violence seemed to provoke conventions but not to sustain organizations.

Wells was not unusual for speaking out against lynching, but she was the only black leader to make it the focus of her efforts for an extended period of time. Perhaps lynching had touched her more personally than most middle- and upper-class African Americans. Thomas Moss had been a close friend, and his murder in Memphis brought home the fact that middle-class status did not immunize one from lynching. Probably her temperament and talents drew Wells to the issue. Her anger and fiery rhetoric were more appropriately applied to the hideous nature of lynching than to less graphic and concrete concerns.

Unable to get financial backing from any organization, Wells began to accept invitations from around the country and charge lecture fees to support her work. Her home base became Chicago, partly because that was where Ferdinand Barnett lived. As she traveled, his letters followed her. Almost a year after her return from England, they were married, on 27 June 1895. He was as militant as she was and fully supported her crusade. Four days after the wedding he gave her his newspaper, the *Chicago Conservator*, and centered his own efforts on the practice of law and politics. Even after their four children were born, Wells-Barnett returned to the lecture circuit, carrying nursing babies with her.

In addition to her newspaper work and lectures, Wells-Barnett continued her investigations of lynchings. She published her findings in periodicals and pamphlets. One such pamphlet, which appeared in 1895, was titled *A Red Record, Tabulated Statistics and Alleged Causes of Lynchings in the United States, 1892–1893–1894*. As usual, Wells-Barnett utilized the gruesome details of various lynchings to show the irrational barbarism of mob justice. She also stressed that white men continued to escape punishment for raping black women and girls. One case illustrates her tactics especially well. She described the murder of Eph. Grizzard for what she determined to be a voluntary liaison with a white woman in Tennessee. While the governor and state militia stood by, Grizzard was "dragged through the streets in broad daylight, knives plunged into him at every step, and with every fiendish cruelty that a frenzied mob could devise, he was at last swung out on a bridge with hands cut to pieces as he tried to climb up the stanchions." Wells-Barnett further noted that the mob left undisturbed in the same jail a white man who had raped an eight-year-old girl. "The outrage upon helpless childhood needed no avenging in this case; she was black."[11]

Such language in both her literature and her lectures continued to inspire white attacks on Wells-Barnett's character. In 1895 one Missouri journalist impugned not only her morality but also that of black women in general. The argument was a common one: black women did not need protecting because they had no morals to protect. Rooted in the justification for the sexual exploitation of slave women, the contention had become an integral part of the defense of the differential treatment of both black and white rape victims. The charge was particularly galling to women of the black elite, who probably valued respectability even more than their white counterparts. After the journalist mailed a copy of his letter to a black women's club journal in Boston, the club's leader decided the time had come for action. Josephine St. Pierre Ruffin, who had organized the club after she had heard Wells-Barnett speak in 1893, mailed copies of the letter to other black women's clubs and called a conference of clubwomen to meet in late July at Boston to refute his charges.

The women strongly protested the insults to Wells-Barnett and to black women in general. They also formed the National Association of Colored Women (NACW), the first permanent national organization to unite black clubwomen. Local women's groups had been instrumental in supporting Wells-Barnett from the beginning of her anti-lynching work, often sponsoring her visits to their cities. At the same time, her activities had spawned a number of those groups. Wells-Barnett hoped the NACW would become the national anti-lynching organization she had long sought. However, the women did not accept her as their leader or her cause as their issue.

Wells-Barnett was bitterly disappointed. She accused Mary Church Terrell, who had previously lectured against lynching, of purposefully ignoring the issue as NACW president, in order to reduce Wells-Barnett's influence. Actually, although the women believed in her work, Wells-Barnett was far too abrasive and controversial to be the leader of or the symbol for a group that prized respectability. Nevertheless, local women's groups continued to fight mob violence, especially the Ida B. Wells Club of Chicago. It wrote to both the president and Congress to protest lynching, and sent a delegation to visit Governor John P. Altgeld after an Illinois man was lynched.

Anger over particular lynchings and race riots continued to spark organizational efforts. The lynchings of two black postmasters in 1898 led to the revitalization and reorganization of the Afro-American League as the Afro-American Council. Wells-Barnett went with the group's delegation to ask President William McKinley for federal action on the murder of these federal officers. She also served as the Council's secretary in 1899 and later became the chair of its Anti-Lynching Bureau. Wells-Barnett used the organization as a pulpit from which she preached against the ideology of Booker T. Washington and the actions of President McKinley, until Washington and his supporters wrested control of the Council from the "militants."

Like most of the Southern-based opponents to lynching, Booker T. Washington made public denunciations of lynching that used relatively restrained rhetoric. The strength of his interest in lynching vacillated but later became more constant with the arrival of Monroe N. Work at Tuskegee. Work had long been compiling lynching statistics, and in 1912, he began issuing the annual Tuskegee Lynching Reports. Sent to Southern newspapers and leaders, the reports became widely accepted as accurate and provided ammunition to Southern-based, biracial anti-lynching organizations. First, however, a race riot in 1908 led to the formation of a Northern-based, biracial organization.

Every black leader was alarmed by the increasing number of race riots at the turn of the century. In riots the white mob did not murder an individual for a specific offense but instead turned its wrath on the black community as a whole, beating and killing African Americans randomly while destroying property. A serious riot in Wilmington, North Carolina, helped mobilize the newly formed Council in 1898. Over the years Wells-Barnett investigated several riots and published an account of one in *Mob Rule in New Orleans* (1900). Perhaps the most significant riot, however, occurred in 1908 in Springfield, Illinois.

The Springfield riot, like the Memphis lynchings, was not remarkable for its uniqueness. There had been many riots that were much more bloody. This type of violence, unlike lynching, had never been distinctly Southern. Indeed, black migration northward in the twentieth century increasingly made riots a national problem. The significance of the Springfield riot resides in its impact. Its location in Springfield had symbolic importance for white abolitionists and their descendants because of its ties to Abraham Lincoln. They were shocked into action.

White liberals had become somewhat complacent about race relations, perhaps in part due to the positive, conciliatory ideology of Booker T. Washington, who had become the recognized "race leader" after the death of Frederick Douglass. A number of African Americans, especially such intellectuals as W.E.B. Du Bois, had been insisting for years that things were worse than Washington painted them and that immediate militant action was needed. These beliefs were the basis for the formation in 1905 of the Niagara Movement, which emphasized lynching more than Washington had. However, the Niagara Movement attracted only a few dozen African Americans and no whites.

Other kinds of reforms had occupied most white reformers during the early years of the Progressive era. The Springfield riot, however, provided the final evidence that racial violence was becoming the same kind of blight on the nation's ideals and image that slavery had once been. The riot was the spark to action, but Wells-Barnett had supplied the kindling. The publicity her crusade received at home and abroad helped make lynching an issue that could no longer be rationalized or ignored. At the urging of fellow white Progressives, the grandson of abolitionist William Lloyd Garrison issued a call to action on Lincoln's birthday in 1909.

Oswald Garrison Villard's letter led to a conference in May and to the formation of the National Association for the Advancement of Colored People (NAACP) a year later. At the conference Wells-Barnett delivered one of the key addresses, calling for the end of "color line murder" through strong federal action. To answer the frequent assertion that the federal government did not have the power to stop lynching, she noted that it had stepped in on a number of occasions to protect foreign nationals in order to prevent international incidents. "If government has power to protect a foreigner from insult," she declared, "certainly it has power to save a citizen's life."[12]

Ironically, although lynching continued to be a major focus for the NAACP, Wells-Barnett did not remain an active participant. Once again, her uncompromising personality and militant reputation limited the organizational role she would play. At the conference a Committee of Forty was named to effect a permanent organization. Its composition was designed to attract a broadly based interracial following. Ardent "radicals" and "conservatives" were avoided, and only twelve members were black. Wells-Barnett was not among them. She was especially enraged when she learned that Du Bois had been responsible for her exclusion, over the objections of some white members. According to Wells-Barnett, Du Bois justified his action on the basis that she was already represented by the inclusion of a woman with whom she worked. His responses to other black leaders at various times suggest that he did not share the spotlight much better than Booker T. Washington. Perhaps Wells-Barnett was too bright a star for Du Bois willingly to share billing with her.

Wells-Barnett was not fully appeased by the white chairman's addition of her name and later wrote, "Of course, I did a foolish thing. My anger at having been treated in such fashion outweighed my judgment and I again left the building."[13] The incident reflects two qualities that limited her effectiveness within organizations: fierce pride and an unwillingness to compromise. She was easily hurt and angered when she did not receive the respect to which she felt entitled. Such feelings were constructive when dealing with railway conductors but sabotaged both friendships and working relationships. Even when she was due the center stage, her reluctance to yield it often hurt her more than it helped her. She frequently missed getting not only the leading role but also any role at all.

Another problem was perhaps Wells-Barnett's failure to play "appropriate" gender roles. Her assertiveness likely threatened both male and female colleagues. Her unusual status is apparent in I. Garland Penn's 1891 book *The Afro-American Press and Its Editors*. Of the eighteen women chronicled within it, Wells-Barnett is the only one to be compared with male journalists. Her designation by her male colleagues as "Princess of the Press" may mark their desire to remind her of her gender. Although Wells-Barnett attributed what she viewed as snubs by the women of NACW to jealousy, their desire for respectability probably played a major role in their rejection of her leadership. She did not reflect the image of "femininity" they wished to project. According to Susan B. Anthony, Wells-Barnett even refused to play the role of feminist properly by marrying and having children—leading to what Anthony called "divided duty." There seemed to be no niche into which Wells-Barnett could comfortably be fit.

The breach between Wells-Barnett and Du Bois never healed. They were both too proud and uncompromising to cooperate. She was further angered when Villard and Du Bois chose Jane Addams to head the Chicago chapter. The choice of Addams probably reflected the desire to recruit white moderates. At any rate, as director of publicity and research, Du Bois became the only black NAACP official, ensuring Wells-Barnett's participation would be perfunctory, given their strained relationship. In addition, as the editor of *Crisis*, the association's official organ, Du Bois gave scant attention to the activities of Wells-Barnett. Nevertheless, neither the NAACP nor Wells-Barnett deserted the crusade against lynching. From its beginning, through its transition to a predominantly black organization, the NAACP sought the key to end mob violence.

Until 1918 the NAACP relied mainly on educational projects and on pressuring local and state leaders to prevent lynchings or to punish lynchers in their communities. Lynching was one of several issues absorbing the organization's attention. In the wake of an outburst of racial violence following World War I, the NAACP dedicated the bulk of its efforts from 1919 to 1924 to finding a legal remedy for mob violence. NAACP leaders recognized that ending lynching would be difficult as long as lynchers went unpunished. By refusing to prosecute or convict lynchers, state and local law officials not only made the crime risk-free but also implicitly sanctioned it. The NAACP began lobbying for a national law that would remove lynching from local jurisdictions and try lynchers in federal courts, where there was at least a possibility of conviction.

After the Dyer Bill of 1918 encountered the roadblock of states' rights, the NAACP and its congressional allies tried various weaker formulations that punished not lynchers but local authorities who refused to prosecute them. Regardless of the wording, every federal anti-lynching bill from 1918 to 1950 stumbled somewhere along the road to enactment. Since the 1960s, however, the federal government has prosecuted acquitted lynchers for the violation of their victims' civil rights.

After the NAACP launched its anti-lynching crusade, Wells-Barnett continued her own, but at a slower pace. Her major activities were investigations of particular race riots and lynchings. These included a 1909 riot in Cairo, Illinois, and one in East Saint Louis, Illinois, in 1917. In 1919 she returned to the South for the first time since 1892, to investigate a riot in Elaine, Arkansas, during which twenty-five African Americans were killed and for which twelve more were sentenced to death. Wells-Barnett's efforts were instrumental in getting the twelve men released. She continued to denounce injustice in speeches and print.

Lynching had been Wells-Barnett's primary concern, but not her only one. Following the Springfield riot, she was able to raise funds to establish the Negro Fellowship League in 1910. It served the purposes of a settlement house for black men in Chicago. She also was active in the woman's suffrage movement and in 1913 founded the Alpha Suffrage Club in Chicago. That year she desegregated a suffrage march in Washington, D.C., by slipping into the Illinois delegation at the last moment. In addition, from 1913 to 1916 Wells-Barnett served as an adult probation officer in Chicago.

Always busy, Wells-Barnett participated in many organizations, including the Republican party. In the three years prior to her death, she began her autobiography and ran for the state senate. On 25 March 1931 death finally silenced her angry voice—a feat no other force could accomplish. That voice had forced white America to confront the myths that excused lynching. With the ugly realities of mob violence laid bare, white voices from all regions joined the black cries for justice. Less than five months before the death of Wells-Barnett, a group of white women met in Atlanta and listened to one of their own refute the link between rape and lynching. Almost four decades after Wells spoke out, Jessie Daniel Ames echoed her words and kept her message alive.

NOTES

1. Ida B. Wells, *Crusade for Justice*, edited by Alfreda M. Duster (Chicago, 1970), 64.

2. Ida B. Wells, *Southern Horrors*, repr. in Trudier Harris, ed., *Selected Works of Ida B. Wells-Barnett* (New York, 1991), 35.

3. Ibid., 17.

4. Ibid., 18.

5. Ibid., 42.
6. Wells, *Crusade*, 100.
7. Ida B. Wells, *A Red Record*, repr. in Harris, ed., *Selected Works of Ida B. Wells-Barnett*, 231.
8. Wells, *Crusade*, 183.
9. *New York Times*, 4 September 1894.
10. *New York Times*, 27 July 1894.
11. Wells-Barnett, *A Red Record*, 213–214.
12. Ida B. Wells, "Lynching: Our National Crime," repr. in Mildred I. Thompson, ed., *Ida B. Wells-Barnett: An Exploratory Study of an American Black Woman, 1893–1930* (New York, 1990), 264.
13. Wells, *Crusade*, 325–326.

BIBLIOGRAPHY

Aptheker, Bettina, ed. *Lynching and Rape: An Exchange of Views*. Occasional Paper no. 25. American Institute for Marxist Studies, New York, 1977.
Bederman, Gail. " 'Civilization,' the Decline of Middle-Class Manliness, and Ida B. Wells's Anti-Lynching Campaign (1892–94)." *Radical History Review* 52 (1992): 5–30.
Duster, Alfreda M., ed. *Crusade for Justice, the Autobiography of Ida B. Wells*. Chicago, 1970.
Grant, Donald L. "The Development of the Anti-Lynching Reform Movement in the United States: 1883–1932." Ph.D. diss., University of Missouri-Columbia, 1972.
Harris, Trudier ed. *Selected Works of Ida B. Wells-Barnett*. New York, 1991.
Hutton, Mary Magdeline Boone. "The Rhetoric of Ida B. Wells: The Genesis of the Anti-Lynching Movement." Ph.D. diss., Indiana University, 1976.
National Association for the Advancement of Colored People. *Thirty Years of Lynching in the United States, 1889–1918*. New York, 1919.
Thompson, Mildred I. *Ida B. Wells-Barnett: An Exploratory Study of an American Black Woman, 1893–1930*. New York, 1990.
Tucker, David M. "Miss Ida B. Wells and Memphis Lynching." *Phylon* 32 (1971): 112–122.
Zangrando, Robert L. *The NAACP Crusade Against Lynching, 1909–1950*. Philadelphia, 1980.

Jessie Daniel Ames and the White Women's Anti-Lynching Campaign

ROBERT F. MARTIN

In 1930 Coleman Livingston "Coley" Blease, campaigning in the Democratic primary for reelection to the U.S. Senate from South Carolina, declared to the voters of the Palmetto State, "Whenever the Constitution comes between me and the virtue of the white women of South Carolina, then I say 'to hell with the Constitution!' "[1] Blease was arguably as vacuous as he was flamboyant, but like many other Dixie demagogues in search of votes, he knew, almost instinctively, how to tap his region's deepest fears and most profound prejudices for the sake of political gain. His defiant justification of vigilante violence in retribution for the alleged rape of white women by black men was a simple but succinct expression of the volatile nexus of the South's complex and interrelated mythologies of race and gender. Yet even as Blease uttered his notorious words, a cadre of liberal white Southerners was already emerging to challenge lynching and the deadly and degrading patterns of belief that underlay the crime. Prominent among this band of dissenters was Jessie Daniel Ames, founder of the Association of Southern Women for the Prevention of Lynching (ASWPL). Throughout the 1930s the ASWPL mounted a narrowly focused but increasingly effective campaign against the most violent manifestation of Southern racism.

Although initially more a function of frontier social instability than of racial tension, by the late nineteenth and early twentieth centuries lynching had become an increasingly Southern and racist phenomenon. By 1909 the number of lynchings in the nation was approximately half what it had been in 1890. During this same period, the number of white victims declined from approximately 32.2 percent to about 11.4 percent, and the proportion of such crimes occurring in the South rose from roughly 82 to 92 percent of the total. Lynching, like other manifestations of de jure and de facto racism, was at least in part a legacy of attitudes informed by slavery and the turbulence of the Reconstruction era, and a corollary of the suppression of populism and the rise of Progressivism. Disfranchisement and segregation were often touted by Southern Progressives as reforms that would foster more stable race relations and remove the vexing issue of race from regional politics, thus enabling white Southerners to debate more freely the myriad social and economic problems confronting the South. And, if not touted, lynching was at least tolerated by many presumably enlightened Southerners as an unfortunate but sometimes necessary dimension of Southern race relations.

Racism and related violence surged in the immediate aftermath of World War I; however, Progressivism and the U.S. involvement in World War I had already begun to awaken some Southerners to the complexity and injustices inherent in their region's race relations. Although disheartened by the postwar situation, these fledgling liberals looked to the future with determination and optimism. During the 1920s young men and women of both races became involved in the nascent interracial work of such groups as the intercollegiate Young Women's and Young Men's Christian Associations, the women's missionary work of the Methodist Episcopal Church South, the Fellowship of Reconciliation, and, most notably, the Commission on Interracial Cooperation (CIC).

The CIC was a response to the violence and social turmoil that swept the nation immediately after the Great War. Longing for order and stability, those involved in the CIC sought peace through accommodation and reconciliation rather than repression. Funded largely by Northern philanthropy, this loose-knit association of black and white Southerners led by Will Alexander worked at the state and community levels to secure rudimentary justice, defuse tension, thwart violence, and promote contacts across racial lines. It soon became the most extensive force for interracial cooperation in the South during the interwar years.

The CIC initially was dominated by men. Many among the male leadership feared that women would be either too radical or too conservative, or they felt that issues such as lynching, linked in the popular mind with sexuality and race, were inappropriate for female consideration. Many Southern women activists were, however, increasingly interested in, and sometimes more enlightened on, questions of race than were some of their male counterparts. In time, both black and white women began to swell the ranks of the CIC and to demand a more prominent place in its activities. As a result, the Interracial Commission created a department of woman's work, and by 1924 eleven statewide women's groups were functioning across the South. The women attempted to facilitate interracial communication and to make health, educational, and recreational facilities more readily available to African Americans. It was through such work that Jessie Daniel Ames first became deeply involved in the fledgling interracial movement in the South.

Born on 2 November 1883, to James M. and Laura Leonard Daniel, in Palestine, Texas, Jessie Daniel spent her childhood and adolescence in the small towns of Overton and Georgetown in eastern Texas. The psychological roots of her activism, however, sprang less from her social environment than from her familial matrix. Daniel's childhood was marred by feelings of inadequacy and insecurity, stemming largely from the fact that she felt overshadowed by her older sister, Lulu, whose charm and intelligence made her their father's favorite.

Shortly after Jessie Daniel's graduation from Southwestern College in Georgetown, in 1902, her father moved the family to Laredo, Texas, where she met Roger Post Ames, a military surgeon thirteen years her senior; they were married in 1905. According to historian Jacquelyn Dowd Hall, the marriage was plagued by sexual incompatibility and by family tensions resulting from the Ames family's hostility toward Jessie. Although the marriage was characterized by prolonged separation and emotional strain, the Ameses had three children before Roger Ames's death in 1914. Hall suggests that Jessie Ames's unhappy and unfulfilling marriage compounded feelings of inadequacy and insecurity that resulted initially from an unsatisfying relationship with her father, who considered her less able and less feminine than her older sister. Consequently, Ames was never secure in her sexuality, and throughout her life had difficulty establishing and maintaining intimate relationships. As a defense mechanism, she developed a rather bold, aggressive, and somewhat domineering persona, which perhaps alleviated her insecurity but compounded her loneliness. Ames found in public life some of the satisfaction and fulfillment denied her in private relationships. Her insecurity bred in her a competitiveness and drive for success that served her well in the public sphere. It may also have intensified her sense of commitment to the powerless and victimized in society.

Following her father's death in 1911, Jessie joined her mother in the operation of the family-owned telephone company in Georgetown, Texas. Both women developed considerable business skill and earned the respect of the community. Her career in business enabled Ames to develop a measure of self-confidence and economic independence, both of which were assets when she became involved in public affairs. First as a local organizer for the Texas Equal Suffrage Association and then as its state treasurer, she began to emerge as an effective and formidable leader of the women of the Lone Star State.

When the Texas Equal Suffrage Association became the Texas League of Women Voters following the ratification of the Nineteenth Amendment, Ames was an active leader, agitating for educational, penal, and legal reforms that would benefit women, children, and the disadvantaged in her state. As she worked on behalf of a variety of progressive measures, Ames grew increasingly aware of the seamlessness of the social fabric and began to understand that injustice against one group was injurious to society as a whole. By the early 1920s, Ames's recognition of racial injustice, her awareness of the contradictions in a white-only reform movement, and her revulsion at the activities of the Ku Klux Klan precipitated her increased involvement in interracial work. An experienced public speaker, she worked first as a volunteer for the CIC, speaking out against racism, injustice, and the deleterious effects of both upon the South. Her volunteer work was so effective that she soon became a part-time field worker in Texas, and within less than a year was the first female executive director of a state interracial committee as well as field representative for the entire Southwest. Ames was experienced in both business and political activism, and thus brought to the cause of interracial work skills that were relatively rare among the women of her era. She was articulate, organized, efficient, and pragmatic in her approach to problems.

As southwestern field representative of the CIC, Ames's most extensive endeavor was an educational and legislative campaign against lynching. Although she called for anti-lynching laws, her primary objective was education. She doubted that statutes could end lynching unless white public opinion condemned it. Throughout the 1920s she investigated lynchings, called for more accurate and objective press coverage of mob violence, and sought to rally public opinion against the Klan.

Although often opposed by powerful political and social elements in Texas, Ames enjoyed her interracial work, regarding these turbulent years as some of the most satisfying of her public career. Combative by nature, she relished a fight, and rarely did she have more formidable foes than those in Texas in the 1920s. Under Ames's leadership the Texas CIC became one of the most successful state operations. It was therefore not surprising that in 1928, when the position of director of woman's work became vacant, a nominating committee representing the women of the CIC recommended Ames for the job. Although Will Alexander worried that her somewhat unconventional demeanor might alienate many Southerners, he acquiesced in the recommendation. Ames accepted, and assumed her responsibilities in the summer of 1929. Although her independence and assertive personality made her controversial, especially with some of the CIC's male leaders, who felt that she ''had a touch of the suffragette about her'' and ''was against men,'' Ames brought energy, ability, commitment, and efficiency to the job.[2] She did not, however, find her labors for the CIC wholly satisfying. She objected to the segregated nature of the women's work and felt that her role within the CIC limited her ability to have a significant impact upon the problems of her region. The resurgence of lynching in the early 1930s afforded her an opportunity for the kind of service she envisioned.

In spite of the popularity of the Klan, during the 1920s lynching was not only opposed by Southern liberals but also became increasingly unacceptable among many image- and dollar-conscious businessmen in the South's urban centers. There was a statistical decline in lynchings during the decade, but the practice remained viable in rural areas where the South's traditional cultural patterns remained intact. The economic distress and social instability of the Great Depression led to a resurgence of the practice in the early 1930s.

Will Alexander of the CIC responded to the renewed violence by organizing the Southern Commission for the Study of Lynching, which undertook to better understand both the socioeconomic and the legal dimensions of the crime. Women were largely excluded from its investigatory endeavors, and many were unhappy with this exclusion. Ames took advantage of this dissatisfaction to launch a new endeavor that rested solely on the white women of the South. She was never enthusiastic about the CIC's investigatory approach to lynching, believing prevention efforts at the local level were more efficacious and important than an understanding of the problem as a whole. Consequently, she persuaded Alexander to call a regional conference of women at which they could design their own agenda for dealing with racial violence. Out of a gathering in Atlanta, Georgia, in November 1930 and another in Dallas, Texas, a few days later emerged the Association of Southern Women for the Prevention of Lynching. The handful of charter members were women who were officers in their respective Protestant denominations, and the majority had been involved in church race relations programs as well as in the CIC women's work.

Despite Ames's protestations to the contrary, as it expanded, those participating in the ASWPL's campaign constituted something of an elite group among Southern women. The leadership clearly was not drawn from the broad spectrum of Southern white womanhood. Although the ASWPL aimed its anti-lynching program at the rural South, almost three-quarters of its leadership lived in the larger towns and cities of the region. Also, the average age of the leadership was forty-eight—many had been born before the turn of the century, and interpreted both social problems and their solutions in terms of a Victorian, evangelical frame of reference shaped in the nineteenth-century rural South. In time, the ASWPL's leadership expanded to include a larger number of women who resided in the countryside or small towns, but it retained its urban quality.

The leadership was atypical in other ways. A substantial number worked, at least for a time, outside the home. Most who had careers were engaged in clerical or professional occupations. Their educational level also was exceptional. Many had at least some college or university experience, and a few had graduate training. They were, however, typical in that most were married and had children. Their husbands were generally from the region's professional, business, or ministerial ranks. In other words, these couples were respected members of the community. Of those leaders whose religious affiliation is known, the majority came from the Methodist Episcopal Church South. Presbyterians, too, were disproportionately represented. Southern Baptists, the largest Protestant denomination in the South, accounted for only 11 percent of the leadership.

Although it is more difficult to determine the socioeconomic status of the rank and file of the ASWPL, they appear to have been less likely to have worked outside the home and to have had education beyond high school. Like their leaders, however, they were likely to be married with families, and they and their husbands in most cases were members of rural and small town economic and social elites.

Regardless of their social station, the women of the ASWPL thought of themselves as Southern ladies. Although they challenged some of the more restrictive features of their region's gender roles, they did not reject in its entirety the conception of ''Southern lady'' and in fact sought to use their image as ladies as an instrument in their war against lynching. They were not rebels challenging the fundamental racial and gender assumptions of their civilization, merely Southern ladies seeking to ameliorate some of the worst manifestations of their section's racism and the more demoralizing and degrading features of its notions about femininity. So conscious were they of their regional identity that they excluded women who were not from the South or who had not lived there sufficiently long to be legitimately identified with it.

The ASWPL also barred from membership many who had a legitimate claim to the designation "Southerner." It was not the first organized expression of Southern women's opposition to lynching. From Ida B. Wells in the late nineteenth and early twentieth centuries to the NAACP's Anti-lynching Crusaders in the 1920s, African-American women had struggled to stem the tide of extralegal violence against black men and had leveled criticism at the sexual and racial myths that underlay lynchings.

Although working in a common cause, Ames and the founders of the ASWPL chose to exclude their black sisters from the new organization. Black women who had solicited the support of white women in their anti-lynching endeavors often resented their exclusion. Ames and her associates, however, felt that it was essential for the ASWPL to be a white movement if it was to raise an effective voice against lynching and the racial and gender assumptions used to justify it.

Lynching was customarily justified as retribution for the rape of a white woman by a black man. This reflected cultural assumptions about the degradation of African-American men and the vulnerability of white women. In fact, alleged sexual assault precipitated lynching in less than a quarter of the documented cases between 1882 and 1946. Although little noted by the white South, the rape of black women by white men was a more common occurrence.

Ames was well aware of the contradiction between myth and reality with regard to lynching, and she sought to make this contradiction known as one means of undermining the crime. She and her associates, however, were not simply trying to end mob violence in Dixie. They were also challenging the myth of female inferiority, vulnerability, and dependence upon male protectors for their virtue and security. As the women of the ASWPL began questioning their region's assumptions about both race and gender, they found themselves confronting not only women who believed the myths, such as those who in 1932 founded The Women's National Association for the Preservation of the White Race, but also myriad men who professed to be the protectors of Southern womanhood. Their opponents sometimes condemned ASWPL women as misguided or reviled them as degraded betrayers of their race and region. The opposition was so virulent because for white men the issue was not merely protection but also, in a sense, possession. Black men were not to possess white women, who were the property of white men. To do so was to step across the bounds of caste, to challenge the superiority of whites. The ASWPL was, then, questioning not only racial but also caste and gender stereotypes and roles that were a sacred part of Southern culture.

ASWPL supporters believed that the white women of the South, in whose name the crime of lynching was often committed, were in a unique position to attack the practice and the assumptions that underlay it. To allow black women to join their campaign would diminish its effectiveness. Thus, to the chagrin of many black and some white opponents of lynching, the ASWPL remained lily white.

Throughout its existence the ASWPL operated on a shoestring. With a budget only a fraction as large as that of the CIC, Ames, the ASWPL's only salaried employee, managed to work effectively throughout the 1930s and early 1940s. The key to her success was her reliance upon volunteers and a preexisting network of religious and secular women's organizations to provide cohesiveness for the ASWPL.

The structure of the ASWPL was quite simple. A regional central committee met annually in Atlanta to issue resolutions, set policy, and provide moral support for the membership. Executive committees and small central councils in each state coordinated the ASWPL's investigatory, educational, and political activities at the state level and served as a link between the regional leadership and local membership. The association was actually rather loose-knit and had a relatively small membership, but it reached many people through its connections with the network of women's organizations across the South. Eventually, the ASWPL had councils in all eleven former Confederate states as well as in Oklahoma and Kentucky, with more than 40,000 active members at the local level engaging in activities ranging from education, to political action, to efforts to prevent imminent lynchings. Those states with the greatest extralegal violence against blacks, such as Mississippi, had the most active ASWPL organizations. Likewise, those areas where violence was minimal, such as Virginia and the southern Appalachians, received little or no attention.

Although only a small minority of Southern women were actively involved in the ASWPL, it secured a sufficiently broad base of support to enable it to make a credible claim to be speaking for the white women of the South. According to Jacquelyn Hall, by the early 1940s, 109 women's associations with a combined membership in excess of 4 million supported the ASWPL's work. These included the women's organizations of the major Protestant denominations, the national and regional federations of church women, the YWCA, and business and professional women's clubs. The mainstay of its support was the women's organizations of the major Protestant churches in the South, which both endorsed the ASWPL and included anti-lynching literature in their educational materials. The most important of these denominational groups was the Methodist Women's Missionary Council. No Catholic women were prominent in the ASWPL. Jewish women, although not in major leadership roles, gave both the ASWPL and the interracial movement in general strong support.

By working through existing religious and secular organizations, the ASWPL was able to reach into many of the rural and small town areas of the South while maintaining the all-important aura of an indigenous organization. The charge of outside agitation was fatal to any reform effort in Dixie, and its structure and manner of operation enabled the ASWPL legitimately to rebut such accusations and contend that it represented the women of the South.

The ASWPL was often criticized not only by conservative white Southerners, who opposed its philosophy and scorned its objectives, but also by some of the more radical younger activists in groups such as the Fellowship of Reconciliation, the Committee on Economic and Racial Justice, and the NAACP. The young radicals frequently criticized the CIC and the ASWPL for their caution and conservatism. It is true that the ASWPL was cautious and conservative, but they were a calculated caution and conservatism born of the conviction that to proceed too quickly or to adopt too radical a position might antagonize many individuals within the network of religious and secular women's groups upon whose cooperation it depended, and at the same time alienate the larger Southern audience whom the ASWPL hoped to convert. Much of the ASWPL's work, especially in the early years, was educational. Although it initially regarded lynching as a matter of social pathology, in time the ASWPL concluded that it was a product of the prejudice of society as a whole, and thus an act for which the white South in its entirety was responsible. The message of the ASWPL was threefold in its attacks on lynching. It contended that the practice dishonored Southern women, diminished respect for and undermined the effectiveness of law enforcement, and tarnished the reputation of the United States in the eyes of much of the rest of the world.

The ASWPL proceeded carefully when it came to the question of rape, which was a very real fear among many white women in the South. Members constantly reiterated that the actual incidence of rape of white women by black men was relatively low, but they could not deny that it sometimes occurred. They took the position that whenever sexual violence against white women by black men did occur, it should be addressed within the context of the law. With regard to the even more delicate matter of consensual relations between white women and black men, the ASWPL initially chose not to address the issue, but by the end of the 1930s it was quietly trying to deal with this question. Generally, the ASWPL condemned such relations, considering them a violation of decency and of the color line. Behind the scenes members sought to minimize such sexual contacts, recognizing their potentially volatile consequences for individuals and communities.

The ASWPL circulated thousands of pamphlets to church and secular women's organizations in an effort to disseminate the socioeconomic and cultural truth about lynching. Much of this material was designed to dispel the myth that lynching was customarily retribution for black men's rape of white women, and to suggest the destructive effects of mob violence. Generally, the literature was low key and informative, designed to appeal to reason rather than to the emotions. Perhaps more important than the literature circulated were the speeches that Ames and the other ASWPL women delivered. By the late 1930s, hundreds of Southern women were speaking publicly against lynching. When addressing audiences, they might sometimes be graphic and forthright in their appeal to the emotions, but rarely did they resort to the sensational.

Increasingly, the ASWPL, like the NAACP, CIC, and other groups, became actively involved in the investigation of lynchings. By 1941 it had undertaken forty-six such case studies. White women gathered information from the local white population and were sometimes surprisingly successful in gleaning facts from uneasy and suspicious black residents in the vicinity of a lynching, in order to construct a more accurate picture of the circumstances surrounding a particular act of violence. Once information had been collected, the ASWPL was able, through speeches or word of mouth, to disseminate the truth about lynchings, thus further helping to undermine the stereotypical picture of the crime.

During the 1930s Ames became more innovative in her attacks on lynching. Inspired by the popularity of folk drama, she sponsored a contest in search of plays that would sensitively and effectively portray the terrors of racial violence. The two winning entries were *Country Sunday* by Walter Spearman and *Lawd, Does you Undahstan?* by Ann Seymour. Usually presented in churches and colleges, these plays were sometimes controversial but often successful in bringing home to limited numbers of white Southerners the horrors of racial violence. To reach the wider audience of regional popular opinion, Ames relied largely upon the press. She stressed contradictions between condemnatory editorials and inflammatory reporting. She attacked the press for its portrayal of women as helpless and vulnerable, and its inherent assumptions about the bestiality and depravity of alleged black perpetrators of sexual crimes. Gradually, she gained the support of major newspapers, and by the late 1930s she professed to see a marked change in the policies of the press, in general, regarding lynching.

Beyond the level of moral suasion and education, the ASWPL attacked lynching more directly. Local law enforcement officers were frequently half-hearted in their opposition to lynch law. This failure was in part a product of fear, and in part a result of the fact that sheriffs and other law officers knew that powerful political elements sometimes condoned or even participated in the mobs (and opposing them would be an act of political suicide). The women of the ASWPL circulated anti-lynching petitions at the local level and presented them to authorities, in an effort to demonstrate that opposition to lynch mobs was a politically viable alternative to submission. They also tried to persuade law enforcement officials to sign pledges expressing their opposition to lynching. By 1941, 1,355 officers had complied, and the ASWPL could report that in a single year, police officers in forty cases had successfully opposed lynch mobs.

Conversely, the ASWPL increasingly exposed by name officers who failed to uphold the law. Sometimes the women themselves became directly involved in trying to thwart lynchings. Whenever local or regional ASWPL activists became aware of impending trouble, they pressured law enforcement officials and civic leaders to do their duty. At the same time, assuming that communities would be less likely to engage in vigilante violence if threatened with exposure, they kept in touch with the Associated Press and other sympathetic news media to assure that trouble would not go unpublicized. The women also worked quietly to persuade their husbands and sons that lynching was hardly the chivalric act portrayed in Southern mythology, and that to engage in such activity was to go against the wishes of those they professed to protect. Although such incidents were relatively rare, women, sometimes even those who were victims or whose families were victims of interracial sexual violence, occasionally confronted mobs in an effort to prevent lynching and uphold the legal process.

The impact of the ASWPL is difficult to assess. Various cultural, social, and economic factors were converging in the South by the late 1930s and early 1940s to reduce the incidence of lynching. There is, however, evidence suggesting that the ASWPL significantly reduced vigilante violence in those areas where it was active. At least one sociological survey found that during the twelve-year history of the ASWPL, the rate of decline in lynching was generally greater in counties in which it was active than in those in which it was not. The average county during the organization's history had 35 percent as many lynchings as it had had in the previous decade. Counties where the ASWPL was most active had only 26 percent as many. Furthermore, in the latter counties there was generally a dramatic decrease in the number of lynch victims surrendered to mobs by law officers.

Jessie Daniel Ames believed that the patient, persistent, persuasive course of the ASWPL was the key to the ultimate eradication of lynching in the South. She had little faith in federal anti-lynching statutes and refused to endorse the NAACP's efforts in the 1930s to secure passage of the Costigan-Wagner federal anti-lynching bill. Although such a refusal was contrary to the position taken by much of the liberal community in the South and the nation, Ames believed that publicly endorsing the bill would do little more than drive lynching underground and undermine the educational and local interventionist approach the ASWPL had built up over the years. She may also have feared that federal legislation would threaten her own hard-won role as a significant player on the stage of Southern social action. In any case, the sharp decline in reported lynchings by the early 1940s seemed to confirm for her the efficacy of the ASWPL's strategy.

By 1942 the apparent decrease in lynchings persuaded Ames that although interracial violence was not forever banished from the South, the socially sanctioned, institutionalized lawlessness that had plagued the region for decades was at an end. Furthermore, the practice of justifying lynching in the name of white Southern womanhood was, she believed, no longer viable. Consequently, in 1942, convinced that its goals were largely accomplished, she quietly dissolved the ASWPL.

After the Southern Regional Council superseded the Commission on Interracial Cooperation in the mid-1940s, Ames retired to Tryon, North Carolina. For a number of years she remained active in the cause of social justice, mobilizing and registering potential black voters and serving for a time as superintendent of Christian social relations for the Western North Carolina

Conference of the Methodist Church. In 1968 waning energy and crippling arthritis forced her to move to a nursing home in Texas, where she remained until her death on 21 February 1972.

Like a number of other liberal endeavors of its era, the contributions of the ASWPL were for a time overshadowed by the more ambitious, aggressive, and dramatic civil rights crusade of the 1950s and 1960s. Ultimately, however, as historians have sought to recover the work of earlier generations of socially conscious Southerners, they have recognized that although it was conservative, "paternalistic," and cautious by the standards of subsequent generations of activists, the work of Jessie Daniel Ames and her associates in the ASWPL was a significant part of the ferment of cultural and social change beginning to seethe beneath the surface of Southern life prior to World War II.

NOTES

1. George B. Tindall, *The Emergence of the New South, 1913–1945* (Baton Rouge, La., 1967), 171.
2. Wilma Dykeman and James Stokely, *Seeds of Southern Change: The Life of Will Alexander* (New York, 1962), 116.

BIBLIOGRAPHY

Ames, Jessie Daniel. *Southern Women and Lynching*. Rev. and repr. Atlanta, 1936.
———. *Toward Lynchless America*. Washington, D.C., [1939?].
———. *The Changing Character of Lynching*. Atlanta, 1942.
Ayers, Edward L. *The Promise of the New South: Life After Reconstruction*. New York, 1992.
Dudley, Julius Wayne. "A History of the Association of Southern Women for the Prevention of Lynching, 1930–1942." Ph.D. diss., University of Cincinnati, 1979.
Dykeman, Wilma, and James Stokely. *Seeds of Southern Change: The Life of Will Alexander*. New York, 1962.
Hall, Jacquelyn Dowd. *Revolt Against Chivalry: Jessie Daniel Ames and the Women's Campaign Against Lynching*. New York, 1979.
———. " 'A Truly Subversive Affair': Women Against Lynching in the Twentieth-Century South." In Carol Ruth Berkin and Mary Beth Norton, eds. *Women of America: A History*. Boston, 1979.
Raper, Arthur. *The Tragedy of Lynching*. 2nd ed. New York, 1970.
Tindall, George Brown. *The Emergence of the New South, 1913–1945*. Baton Rouge, La., 1967.
Woodward, C. Vann. *Origins of the New South, 1877–1913*. Baton Rouge, La., 1971.

Margaret Sanger
and the Birth Control Movement

ELLEN CHESLER

Margaret Sanger went to jail in 1917 for distributing contraceptives to immigrant women from a makeshift clinic in a tenement storefront in Brooklyn, New York. When she died fifty years later, the cause for which she defiantly broke the law had achieved international stature. Although still a magnet for controversy, she was widely eulogized as one of the great emancipators of her time.

For more than half a century, Sanger dedicated herself to the deceptively simple proposition that access to a safe and reliable means of preventing pregnancy is a necessary condition of women's liberation and, in turn, of human progress. Although she encountered enormous resistance in her own lifetime and still invites criticism, Sanger popularized ideas and built institutions that have widespread influence today. Her leadership, though often quixotic, helped create enduring changes in the beliefs and behavior of men and women who perceive themselves as modern, not only in America but throughout the world.

Birth control and the promise of reproductive autonomy for women have fundamentally altered private life and public policy in the twentieth century. As the late psychologist Erik Erikson once provocatively suggested, no idea of modern times, save perhaps for arms control, has more directly challenged human destiny than has birth control, which may account for the profound psychic dissonance and social conflict it tends to inspire.[1]

Margaret Sanger was an immensely attractive woman: small, lithe, and trim. Her green eyes were flecked with amber, her hair a shiny auburn, her smile warm and charming, her hands perpetually in motion, beckoning even to strangers. As H. G. Wells once described her, she had a quick Irish wit, high spirits, and radiant common sense. She married twice and enjoyed the affection and esteem of both men and women, who provided her a lifelong network of emotional, financial, and organizational support. At the same time, she could be impossibly difficult, and those who dared to disagree with her quickly discovered her explosive temper.

Sanger was born Margaret Louisa Higgins on 14 September 1879, in Corning, New York, the sixth of eleven surviving children of Irish-born Michael Hennessy Higgins, a stonemason who earned a meager living carving cemetery monuments, and his wife, Anna Purcell Higgins. Margaret learned to dream at an early age from her father, a freethinker and religious apostate who squandered his talents and humane social vision on too much talk and drink. From her devout and resourceful mother she absorbed a powerful motivation to improve her lot and the self-discipline that made it possible to do so. One parent taught her to defy; the other, to behave. She struggled between the two but took from both a distinctive resolve to gain a better life for herself and for others.

From 1896 to 1898, Margaret attended the Claverack College and Hudson River Institute, a preparatory school located across the state in Columbia County. Her older sisters paid her tuition, and she earned room and board by working in the school kitchen. Lacking the funds to complete her degree, she returned to Corning to nurse her mother through the final stages of chronic tuberculosis. After Anna's death, Margaret enrolled in a nurse's training program at the White Plains Hospital in Westchester County. After completing two years of practical training, she met and married William Sanger, a New York City architect. Forced to choose between marriage and work, she left school without obtaining the registered nursing degree then required for work in hospitals, a fact she never admitted but always regretted. Weakened by a tubercular infection that lingered until finally cured by surgery many years later, and soon pregnant with the first of three children, Sanger settled down to a quiet life in Hastings-on-Hudson, New York, a community of young professionals. Her contentment with domesticity and suburban complacency was short-lived.

Eager for wider horizons, and overextended financially after a fire damaged their new home, the Sangers moved back to New York City in 1910. There Margaret helped make ends meet by working part-time as a visiting nurse and midwife in the immigrant districts of the city's Lower East Side. What she came to think of as an "awakening" allegedly occurred while tending a young Jewish immigrant woman named Sadie Sachs, whom she assisted through the complications of a self-induced septic abortion. Countless times throughout her career, Margaret would repeat the saga of Mrs. Sachs's broken plea for reliable contraception and the doctor's callous rejoinder that she tell her husband, Jake, "to sleep on the roof." Returning several months later to find Mrs. Sachs dying of septicemia, Sanger resolved to abandon "the palliative career of nursing in pursuit of fundamental social change."[2]

Drugstore and mail-order remedies such as condoms, pessaries, and chemical douches had circulated widely in America in the nineteenth century, precipitating a dramatic decline in birthrates and a national preoccupation with moral and social purity. Ethnic and racial tensions in the wake of the Civil War helped fuel a conservative reaction to these developments, as well as to the changing dynamics of family life and the increasing independence of women in a rapidly modernizing society. During the 1870s, the federal government and almost every state adopted far-reaching obscenity statutes that criminalized contraception and abortion, and prohibited the distribution and sale of information or products intended to promote their use. Named after their principal architect and chief enforcer, Anthony Comstock, these laws did not succeed in suppressing the brisk traffic in contraception and abortion altogether, but they did push them farther underground, out of the jurisdiction of government bodies that might have regulated their price and quality. As a result, orthodox physicians, looking to consolidate their professional hegemony, defamed once common practices, and birth control became increasingly associated with medical charlatans. Despite these obstacles, middle-class birthrates continued to decline as the result of private arrangements. But the poor, especially the growing numbers of immigrant poor, could not afford contraception or understand the many popular subterfuges through which it was sold, such as feminine hygiene.

In New York, Sanger became active in local Socialist politics, first distinguishing herself as an organizer in the campaign for woman's suffrage and as the author of controversial columns on issues of health and sexuality for *The Call*, the Socialist party's daily newspaper. In 1912 she led an evacuation of the children of striking textile workers in Lawrence, Massachusetts. From her role she gained prominence as an organizer for the International Workers of the World (IWW) and as a romantic figure in the prewar cultural and political bohemia of Greenwich Village.

These were halcyon days before revolution, repression, and world war provided the century's more sober reality. The country seemed wide open with possibility. It was perhaps easier then than it has since become to believe in the potential of individual and social renewal—in the inevitability of human progress. Sanger teamed up with labor radicals and bohemians to organize strikes and pickets and pageants in the hope of achieving wholesale economic and social justice. "No Gods, No Masters," the IWW's rallying cry, became her personal and political manifesto.

Inspired by Emma Goldman's forceful anarchist and feminist doctrines, even as the two women jousted for celebrity and quarreled over personal differences, Sanger in 1914 published *The Woman Rebel*, a radical feminist journal that encouraged personal and sexual autonomy for women through the use of birth control. "Why the Woman Rebel?" Sanger asked in the inaugural issue. Her answer: "Because I believe that woman is enslaved by the world machine, by sex conventions, by motherhood and its present necessary childrearing, by wage-slavery, by middle-class morality, by customs, laws and superstitions."[3] The paper never published explicit information about contraception, but Sanger was soon indicted for inciting violence and promoting obscenity. Facing the likelihood of conviction and a prison sentence in line with the harsh punishments routinely being given to agitators on the left, she jumped bail and fled under an alias to Europe. Once outside U.S. jurisdiction, she ordered the release of the pamphlet *Family Limitation* (1914), which provided concrete instruction on a variety of chemical and barrier contraceptive methods and counseled women to use them as weapons in the struggle for their emancipation.

In Margaret's absence, William Sanger was framed by a government agent to whom he handed a copy of the pamphlet. His arraignment was attended by Anthony Comstock. The case gave the birth control movement its first clear-cut challenge to the constitutionality of the Comstock prohibitions on birth control and its first major publicity. Middle-class women rallied alongside radicals as Bill Sanger was convicted and chose to serve a thirty-day jail term rather than pay a $150 fine.

When Margaret Sanger learned of these events, she decided to return and stand trial herself. Upon leaving her ship in lower Manhattan in October 1915, she stopped at a newsstand. There, by her own account, the words "birth control," a phrase she had coined to give women a simple way of talking about the subject in public, now stared back at her from the headlines. Newspapers and magazines had quite suddenly turned their attention to the controversy. As Bill Sanger languished in a New York City jail, the prosecutors who had hoped to check birth control propaganda with his conviction achieved exactly the opposite effect. The tremendous public exposure given the issue substantially strengthened the rationale of Margaret Sanger's defense on free speech grounds. Who would be willing to punish her for initiating a debate that had since been conducted with impunity in major publications throughout the country? On 14 February 1915 all charges against Margaret Sanger were dropped, and the woman who had been a fugitive for more than a year was suddenly a celebrity.

The one casualty of these events was her marriage. When Sanger and her husband were finally reunited, he faced the reality of a callous and indifferent woman whose affections by then quite obviously lay elsewhere. He refused to grant her a divorce for several years, but she finally secured one in 1921, on grounds of desertion.

With her sophisticated understanding of the value of public relations over conventional political organization, Sanger devoted herself to gaining continued coverage of the birth control issue that helped destroy old taboos. She also took the opportunity to capitalize on her sudden fame by booking speaking engagements throughout the country; the fees helped support her children. Following her lectures she was often sought out in her hotel room by women eager to know of more effective birth control methods. Their intense hunger for personal communication and instruction convinced Sanger of the superiority of clinical distribution of contraception under scientific supervision, as she had seen demonstrated in Holland during her European sojourn. She was inspired to renewed militancy by the sudden and tragic death of her young daughter from pneumonia. Seeking to memorialize the child through a concrete achievement, she took a $50 contribution from a woman who had heard her speak in California and in 1916 opened the country's first birth control clinic behind the curtained windows of a tenement storefront on Amboy Street near the corner of Pitkin Avenue, in the Brownsville section of Brooklyn. Handbills advertising the location in English, Yiddish, and Italian promoted the benefits of contraception over abortion: "Mothers! Can you afford to have a large family? Do you want any more children? If not, why do you have them? DO NOT KILL, DO NOT TAKE LIFE, BUT PREVENT." The women of Brownsville patiently stood in line for the service—there were 464 recorded clients during the several weeks the facility remained open.

On the ninth day a modishly attired woman identifying herself as "Mrs. Whitehurst" arrived, and immediately aroused suspicion. The following day she returned with three plainclothesmen from the police department's vice squad, who arrested Sanger and her coworkers: her sister, Ethel Byrne, a nurse on the staff of Mt. Sinai Hospital in New York, and Fania Mindell, a social worker. Byrne was tried first and sentenced to one month in the workhouse on Blackwell's Island, where she made more headlines with a hunger strike she and Sanger had modeled on the attention-getting exploits of the British suffragists. The normally sensation-shy *New York Times* ran Byrne's story on the front page for four consecutive days. Mindell was fined $50 for handing out illegal information. Sanger was charged with the more serious crime of actually fitting as a birth control device a Mizpah pessary, then commonly sold in pharmacies as a support for a prolapsed or distended uterus. Swathed in a spermicidal solution, it prevented sperm from entering the cervix and replicated the more reliable and comfortable rubber-spring diaphragm and spermicidal jelly that Sanger had observed in Holland.

Found guilty on these charges, but aware that her story was being crowded out of the newspaper headlines by the escalation of World War I in Europe, Sanger quietly served a month's sentence in the women's penitentiary in Queens County. By her own account, she passed her time reading to the illiterate prostitutes and drug addicts on her corridor, and lecturing them on sex and birth control over the protest of a resident matron, who claimed "they knew bad enough already."[4]

Appeal of the conviction established a medical exception to the New York State law prohibiting birth control. Doctors (though not nurses, as Sanger had hoped) were granted the right to prescribe contraception for health reasons. That constraint determined the future course of the birth control movement in the United States. Independent, not-for-profit medical facilities became the model for the distribution of contraceptive services in the United States and throughout the world, a development that occurred largely in spite of leaders in American medicine, who remained shy of the subject for many years. The American Medical Association did not endorse birth control until 1937, well after Sanger's clinics had demonstrated the efficacy of the diaphragm-and-jelly regimen she endorsed.

During her year in Europe, Sanger had come under the influence of the renowned British physician and sexologist Havelock Ellis, who guided her conversion from conventional socialism to a Fabian faith in the ability of science and education to shape human conduct, and in the power of educated elites to

enforce meaningful social change. Sanger had grown weary of the violence that
had overtaken the labor movement in New York. She was ready to abandon the
left in favor of an alliance with progressives, confident that capitalism might
reform itself voluntarily and that bold public initiatives could be planned for
human betterment. This philosophical shift was reinforced by H. G. Wells, who,
like Ellis, became a lifelong mentor and intimate friend.

At the heart of this political transformation was the maturing of Sanger's
consciousness as a feminist. She decided to invest in the collective potential of
women. The victory for woman's suffrage had been achieved through the efforts
of middle-class women who were oriented to activism and looking for a new
cause. Sanger envisioned a united front of women who would claim the legalization of contraception, along with greater public candor about sexuality, as a
fundamental right. Birth control, she argued, would enhance the opportunities
of women beyond the promises of economic reformers, on the one hand, and
of suffragists, on the other. It would be a tool for redistributing power fundamentally—in the bedroom, the home, and the larger community. Women would
achieve personal freedom by experiencing their sexuality free of unwanted consequence. In taking control of the forces of reproduction, they also would lower
birthrates, alter the balance of supply and demand for labor, and thereby accomplish the revolutionary goals of workers without the social upheaval of class
warfare. Bonds of gender would transcend divisions of ethnicity, race, or class.
Not the dictates of Karl Marx but the refusal of women to bear children indis-
criminately would alter the course of history.

Through the 1920s and 1930s, Sanger divorced herself from her radical past,
bested her competitors for leadership, and made her name virtually synonymous
with the birth control cause. She had an uncanny feel for the power of a well-
communicated idea in a democracy. Sanger wrote widely read books, published
a journal, held conferences, gave lectures, and built a thriving voluntary social
organization. In 1920 she published *Woman and the New Race*, which emphasized the relationship between birth control and women's rights and sold more
than 250,000 copies. In 1921 Sanger incorporated and assumed the presidency
of the American Birth Control League, a voluntary organization of middle-class
women and male professionals whose objective was to educate public opinion
and lobby for reform of the Comstock laws. The following year a second best-
seller, *The Pivot of Civilization*, stressed birth control's economic, social, and
eugenic dimensions. In the face of Sanger's appeal, the former suffragist Mary
Ware Dennett, who was lobbying for total repeal of birth control prohibitions
rather than a medical exception, closed down her competing organization.

Booked by agents in New York as ''the international champion of birth control''—or on another occasion as ''the outstanding social warrior of the century''—Sanger crisscrossed the country numerous times, addressing civic
forums and women's groups and lending her support to the organization of local
birth control federations. No matter how much she toned herself down, however,
she remained a target of repression. A lecture at New York's Town Hall was

raided and closed down by police ostensibly acting on orders of political authorities under pressure from the powerful Patrick Cardinal Hayes of New York. Her appearances in the heavily Catholic cities of Albany, Syracuse, and Boston were either canceled or interrupted; these incidents sustained her image as a daring and controversial figure, always on the edge of respectability. In 1929, when civic authorities in Boston refused her the right to speak at Ford Hall, she dramatically stood silent, with a band of tape across her mouth. The image emblazoned the front pages of newspapers around the world.

In 1923 Sanger had established the Birth Control Clinical Research Bureau (later renamed the Margaret Sanger Bureau) in New York City; it became the prototype for a network of facilities that developed with local sponsorship in major cities around the country. These pioneering clinics provided a range of preventive health care services for women including contraception, gynecology, sex education, marriage counseling, and infertility services to poor women and to many who could afford private doctors but preferred a sympathetic female environment. Under the best circumstances they became laboratories for Sanger's idealism, but, as often as not, the experiment failed, and Sanger grew disillusioned.

The birth control movement stalled during the Great Depression and World War II, stymied by the cost and complexity of the task of reaching women most in need, engulfed by internal dissension, and overwhelmed by the barrage of opposition it provoked. Timid politicians shied away from sexual controversy and refused to reform anachronistic obscenity laws. Birthrates plummeted in the face of economic crisis, precipitating a backlash against women, much like what had happened years earlier. Physicians feared the specter of socialized medicine that birth control clinics came to represent as the complexity and cost of providing quality clinical instruction in contraception became apparent.

Moreover, in the social sciences, eugenic concerns for the promotion of physical and mental fitness that had once been highly regarded by progressive proponents of social reform quickly deteriorated into an excuse for the control of ''undesirables'' on the straightforward basis of race and class. Sanger, among others, was forced to condemn them.

Along with a great many Americans in the 1920s—from ordinary workers and farmers to university professors, Supreme Court justices, and many on the left (including her dear friend, the perennial Socialist party presidential candidate, Norman Thomas)—Sanger had argued that sensible programs of social reform ought to address the manner in which heredity and other biological factors, as well as environmental ones, affect human health, intelligence, and opportunity. The idea of intervening to improve the quality of the human race became nothing short of a popular craze. It was not viewed as an alternative to progressive social reform but as an enhancement to it.

Trained in medicine, Sanger saw new possibilities in the idea of helping those most in need through a comprehensive program of preventive social medicine. She envisioned public health clinics for women and young children in every urban neighborhood and traveling caravans of nurses in rural areas. In the same vein, she endorsed prevailing views about society's obligation to prevent the transmission of hereditary defects such as mental retardation. Although she focused her principal efforts on the organization of voluntary birth control programs, she also supported controversial state statutes then under consideration that called for the forced sterilization of individuals in institutions for the "feebleminded," a commonly used term identifying individuals suffering from a variety of mental and physical defects thought to be inherited. Despite a scientific foundation that has proved largely specious and insupportable on moral grounds as well, eugenic interventions of this nature gained a broad constituency during these years. By 1927 Virginia's eugenic law was upheld in a nearly unanimous decision of the U.S. Supreme Court, *Buck* v. *Bell*.

Sanger comfortably courted eugenicists, whose stature at the time often helped blunt the attacks of religious and social conservatives against the then far less respectable birth control movement. As a propagandist, she continued to stress the relationship of birth control to economic and gender equality and to the promotion of healthier, happier families, but she got caught up in the eugenic zeal as well and accepted the support of individuals whose motivations were far less laudable than her own. On a number of occasions, she bemoaned the burden of the "unfit" on the productive members of the community and once spoke of investing in a "race of thoroughbreds," phrases that, lifted out of context, have been used to seriously misrepresent her intentions. Most eugenicists of the 1920s actually opposed birth control on the grounds that middle-class women should have more babies, not fewer. Sanger always disdained the idea that a "cradle-competition" existed between rich and poor, native and immigrant, or black and white. The initiative for individual and racial regeneration must "come from within," she wrote, "it must be autonomous, self-directive and not imposed from without."[5]

To this end, Sanger distinguished between individual applications of eugenic principles and cultural ones. She advanced social policies fostering universal mental and physical fitness and spoke out against immigration prohibitions and other measures that promoted ethnic or racial stereotypes with a biological rationale. She argued instead that America's essential public health challenge was to eliminate the potential of inherited defects among all. Having worked as a maternity nurse, she was particularly sensitive to the individual and social costs of diseases transmitted from mother to child during pregnancy as the result of inadequate nutrition and prenatal care. Sanger worked throughout her career to provide reproductive health care to poor women, irrespective of ethnicity or race, because she saw it as an essential tool of individual liberation and social justice, not of social control.

Sanger envisioned a society where birth control would be universally available, but in failing to repudiate supporters and adversaries alike who promoted its use to advance the interests of one group or one social class over another, she left herself vulnerable to attacks of racism and bigotry. By the 1930s, moreover, the perverse application of all eugenic principles under Nazi Germany's racial and genocidal policies had virtually discredited the American eugenics movement on all grounds, and the reputation of anyone associated with it—however tenuously.

Defaming Sanger's character as a way of undermining her message has long been an effective political strategy. By the 1930s, the alliance she forged with the country's establishment had turned into a political liability. She became the target of vicious personal attacks just as the votes of socially conservative Catholics in the cities and fundamentalist Protestants in the rural South became critical to the coalition that secured the presidential ambitions of Franklin Roosevelt.

Armed with the testimony of the needy and the endorsement of the powerful, Sanger mounted a diligent congressional lobbying campaign each year from 1931 through 1936. She even abandoned the term "birth control" for "family planning," a friendlier concept, and urged that it be incorporated into government programs. She tied her cause to the New Deal's enthusiasm for social and economic reconstruction and built a nationwide grassroots movement that mobilized constituencies as far-ranging as the Federal Council of the Churches of Christ in America, the YMCA and YWCA, the Socialist party, and other unlikely allies. But opposition from an increasingly politically powerful Catholic Church held sway on Capitol Hill and at the White House. Bending to political considerations, the New Deal denied birth control a place in America's progressive social welfare and public health agenda.

The issue lost ground, moreover, as a burgeoning trade in commercial contraception began to overwhelm the government's meager regulatory and enforcement capacity, leaving little chance that licensed druggists and physicians would be harassed. Even the Sears Roebuck catalog had begun to advertise "preventives." By 1935 the journal *American Medicine* was claiming that the mailing of contraceptive supplies and instruction was "as firmly established as the use of a gummed postage stamp," and a long-anticipated report of the American Medical Association found no actual evidence of interference with private medical practice by state or federal laws.[6]

Sanger's rationale for lobbying as a tool to educate public opinion was also undermined by the publication of polls showing that 70 percent of Americans, comprising at least a clear majority in every state, supported the legalization of birth control. From an educational standpoint, her campaign had done its work, even if the Comstock laws remained technically in force. In 1936, with Hannah Stone, M.D., medical director of the Birth Control Clinical Research Bureau in New York, Sanger prevailed in a federal appellate court decision in the case of *U.S.* v. *One Package*, which actually licensed physicians to import contraception and to use the federal mails for its transport. Although the ruling did not override remaining state prohibitions in Connecticut and Massachusetts, the courts had come close to achieving the objectives of federal legislative reform.

Rebuked in Washington but unwilling to concede defeat, Sanger quietly advanced a partnership with public health officials in the South, a region less vulnerable to Catholic influence and one where the need for services was acute because black Americans had substantially been left out of New Deal health and welfare entitlements administered by the states. She worked with the full support of the established leaders of the national black community—W.E.B. DuBois and Mary McLeod Bethune—and with the help of Eleanor Roosevelt, who in 1939 finally broke free of political constraints that had silenced her on the birth control issue during most of her husband's years in the White House, in order to assist on this Negro Project, as it was then called. It was advertised as "a unique experiment in race-building and a humanitarian service to a race subjected to discrimination, hardship and segregation." "Birth control, per se, cannot correct economic conditions that result in bad housing, overcrowding, poor hygiene, malnutrition and neglected sanitation," the statement of mission reads, "but can reduce the attendant loss of life, health and happiness that spring [*sic*] from these conditions."[7]

After 1937 Sanger lived in partial retirement in Tucson, Arizona, with her second husband, J. Noah Slee, whom she had married shortly after her divorce. A self-made industrialist, Slee invented and marketed 3-in-1 Oil, a household lubricant, and after selling his company, he helped bankroll his wife's charitable interests. In a private arrangement unconventional for its day, he had agreed that she would keep her own name professionally and in all respects maintain her freedom. Although they argued frequently over her many absences and her fierce commitment to her work, he held, however grudgingly, to this contract until his death in 1943.

Embittered by her failure to win support at home, and disenchanted with the increasing pronatalism of Americans after years of deferred fertility during the Great Depression and World War II, Sanger turned her attentions abroad. She had long ago planted the seeds of foreign diplomacy. In 1922 she carried the birth control message to Japan and China, leaving several small indigenous organizations in her wake. In 1927 she sponsored a World Population Conference in Geneva, Switzerland, that brought together internationally prominent social scientists and demographers. The conference failed to secure the attention of the League of Nations, as Sanger had hoped, but the initiative did result in the staffing of a small, London-based international population committee. Under its auspices Sanger toured India in 1936, again leaving behind rudimentary voluntary family planning advocacy and services. In 1948 she founded the London-based International Planned Parenthood Federation, an umbrella for national affiliates, which remains today the largest nongovernmental organization providing contraceptive services in the world.

Sanger's most exquisite triumphs were her last. She was past seventy when the world finally began to heed her concern for unchecked population growth. She was past eighty when the team of doctors and scientists she had long encouraged first marketed the oral, anovulant birth control pill that was developed by Dr. Gregory Pincus at a private research laboratory in Worcester, Massachusetts, after Sanger introduced him to Katherine Dexter McCormick, heiress to an agricultural equipment fortune, who provided the research funds. Sanger lived to see the realization of her repeated efforts as a litigant and a lobbyist through the landmark 1965 ruling of the U.S. Supreme Court in *Griswold* v. *Connecticut* that guaranteed constitutional protection to the private use of contraceptives by married couples. Seven years later, in *Eisenstadt* v. *Baird,* the Court extended that privacy to the unmarried.

Sanger died on 6 September 1966 of arteriosclerosis and heart failure at a nursing home in Tucson, just as Lyndon Johnson incorporated family planning into America's public health and social welfare programs—and committed at least a fraction of the nation's foreign policy resources to it. Thus was fulfilled her singular vision of how best to achieve peace and prosperity at home and abroad.

Since Sanger's death the rebirth of a vigorous feminist movement has given new resonance to her original claim that women have a fundamental right to control their own bodies. Her direct legacy endures in the international Planned Parenthood movement.

Since 1965 the rate of population growth has unexpectedly slowed in almost all countries in the world outside of sub-Saharan Africa, although absolute numbers still continue to grow precipitously in many regions. Moreover, extreme variations in reproductive behavior from one culture to another have reawakened interest in the comparative quality and impact of organized family planning intervention, and in the relationship between declining fertility and the status of women. At the third U.N. Conference on Population and Development, held at Cairo in 1992, many premises that have guided international population policy in the generation since Sanger's death were altered. The phrase "population control" was abandoned in the official literature of the United Nations in favor of more client-sensitive approaches intended to locate family planning within a comprehensive package of services to promote women's overall reproductive health. Gone as well from U.N.-endorsed policy is support for programs that may be coercive to women because they rely on fixed targets or quotas for fertility reduction.

Instead, agreement was reached on the principle that giving women adequate information and access to a wide menu of contraceptive options is most important, that under these circumstances they will most often assume the responsibility of having fewer children voluntarily. To this end, investments in the overall health, education, and welfare of the world's women have been declared a priority. For the first time, principles of gender equity were endorsed by international development and population policymakers.

In so doing, they have accepted Sanger's insistent view that individual women can be motivated to limit their fertility, even in the absence of wholesale economic and social change. It is now officially agreed that organized intervention works best when contraception is offered as part of a larger package of maternal and infant health care reforms delivered under paraprofessional auspices, much as Sanger and others pioneered. Prodded by contemporary feminists in the field, the United Nations has finally committed to invest in Sanger's vision of comprehensive preventive health care for women.

In 1935 H. G. Wells raised his glass in an affectionate toast. "Alexander the Great changed a few boundaries and killed a certain number of men," Wells observed, "but he made no lasting change in civilization. Both he and Napoleon were forced into fame by circumstances outside themselves and by currents of the time, but Margaret Sanger made currents and circumstances. When the history of our civilization is written, it will be a biological history, and Margaret Sanger will be its heroine."[8] The words seem particularly well chosen in light of recent developments.

NOTES

1. Erik H. Erikson, "Once More the Inner Space: Letter to a Former Student," in Jean Strouse, ed., *Women & Analysis: Dialogues on Psychoanalytic Views of Femininity* (New York, 1974), 386.

2. Margaret Sanger, *An Autobiography* (New York, 1938), 89–92.

3. *The Woman Rebel* 1 (March 1914): 1, cited in Ellen Chesler, *Woman of Valor: Margaret Sanger and the Birth Control Movement in America* (New York, 1992), 98.

4. Sanger, *An Autobiography*, 243.

5. Margaret Sanger, *The Pivot of Civilization* (New York, 1922), 22–23.

6. *Journal of the American Medical Association* 106 (1936); and *American Medicine* 41 (1935). Both cited in Chesler, *Woman of Valor*, 371.

7. Birth Control Federation of America, "Birth Control and the Negro: An Analysis and Program" (1939), cited in Chesler, *Woman of Valor*, 388.

8. Birth Control Information Center, London, "Round the World for Birth Control," in Chesler, *Woman of Valor*, 361.

BIBLIOGRAPHY

Chesler, Ellen. *Woman of Valor: Margaret Sanger and the Birth Control Movement in America*. New York, 1992.

Cott, Nancy F. *The Grounding of Modern Feminism*. New Haven, 1987.

Degler, Carl N. *In Search of Human Nature: The Decline and Revival of Darwinism in American Social Thought*. New York, 1991.

Gordon, Linda. *Woman's Body, Woman's Right: A Social History of Birth Control in America*. New York, 1976.

Kennedy, David M. *Birth Control in America: The Career of Margaret Sanger*. New York, 1970.

Kevles, Daniel J. *In the Name of Eugenics: Genetics and the Uses of Human Heredity*. New York, 1985.

Moore, Gloria, and Ronald Moore. *Margaret Sanger and the Birth Control Movement: A Bibliography, 1911–1984*. Metuchen, N.J., 1986.

Piotrow, Phyllis Tilson. *World Population Policy: The United States Response*. New York, 1973.

Reed, James. *From Private Vice to Public Virtue: The Birth Control Movement and American Society Since 1830*. New York, 1978; rev. ed. Princeton, 1984.

Rosenberg, Rosalind. *Divided Lives: American Women in the Twentieth Century*. New York, 1992.

Sanger, Margaret. *Woman and the New Race*. New York, 1920.

———. *The Pivot of Civilization*. New York, 1922.

———. *An Autobiography*. New York, 1938.

Sen, Gita, Adrienne Germaine, and Lincoln C. Chen, eds. *Population Policies Reconsidered: Health, Empowerment and Rights*. Boston, 1994.

Ware, Susan. *Holding Their Own: American Women in the 1930s*. Boston, 1982.

Dorothy Day and the Catholic Worker Movement

ANNE KLEJMENT

"We were just sitting there talking and people moved in on us," explained Dorothy Day about the origins of the Catholic Worker movement, which was dedicated to caring for the poor and promoting nonviolent revolution.[1] Day's self-deprecating wit highlighted the role of ordinary people as agents of social change. By doing his or her small part, each person hastened the day of revolution. A traditional Catholic, devout and loyal to church authority, Day challenged the social and political orthodoxies of several generations of social activists, including New Dealers, Old Leftists, the New Left, charity volunteers, credentialed experts, and welfare bureaucrats.

The Catholic Worker movement began in 1933 with a monthly paper, the *Catholic Worker*, edited and published by Day, a Catholic journalist with ties to Greenwich Village radicals, anarchists, and Communists. Next came hospices for the homeless, begun on the initiative of a few enterprising people, guests and volunteers alike, who shared a pot of coffee, a kettle of soup, a few donated beds, and, all too often, vermin. Then came the farming communes, where the urban unemployed could adopt a self-sufficient and morally healthy way of life, independent of bosses, plutocrats, and unstable market forces.

The paper, the unique experience of community life, and informal programs on Catholic social thought educated people from all walks of life about the need for Gospel-based social justice and nonviolent revolution. In all of these endeavors, Dorothy Day and the Catholic Worker movement connected traditional Catholic spirituality (the mass, sacraments, prayer, fasting, works of mercy) to American radicalism. By taking the Gospel seriously, by loving even enemies, the Catholic Workers' revolution of the heart aimed to change society from the bottom up.

A winding path led Dorothy Day to Catholic social radicalism and nonviolent revolution. Born on 8 November 1897 in Brooklyn, New York, she was the third of five children of John and Grace Satterlee Day. The comfort and security of her birth into the middle class proved illusory. Before her nineteenth birthday, she and her family had crisscrossed the United States, following the lofty ambitions of her newpaperman father and escaping from downward plunges that were the result of natural and economic disasters.

The protective parents attempted the impossible task of shielding their children from the harshness of life. While living in Oakland, California, the Days survived the 1906 San Francisco earthquake but suffered an enormous financial reverse, losing both home and income. Starting anew in Chicago, they slowly recovered, only to fail again through no fault of their own.

"First in violence, deepest in dirt," according to reformer Lincoln Steffens, Chicago left a lasting imprint on young Dorothy. The precocious and introspective child related the sights, sounds, and smells near the family's tenement to her reading. The social realism of socialist novelists Upton Sinclair and Jack London, whom she surreptitiously read, graphically portrayed the abuses of capitalism suffered by the working class. These favorite authors advocated systemic change coming not from the tinkering of Progressive reformers but through socialism, through a redistribution of power and wealth. Day's brother Donald was employed by the *Day Book*, a Socialist paper unencumbered by capitalistic advertisements. Copies of the paper that he brought home reinforced the radical message of the novels his sister read. Dissatisfied with the nominal Christianity of her parents at about the same time she was forming her social conscience, Day joined the Episcopal Church.

At the age of sixteen, Day entered the University of Illinois on scholarship. She became disillusioned with the failure of Christians to challenge social injustice, and on campus she joined a club for aspiring writers and briefly attached herself to a campus Socialist forum, where she heard provocative speakers like Rose Pastor Stokes and Scott Nearing. Finding all but her literature courses dull, Day left after two years without a degree and rejoined her family in New York City.

Armed with a few published articles, she sought employment in journalism against the wishes of her conservative father, who opposed careers for women. An editor at the *New York Call*, a Socialist daily, was beguiled into hiring Day. Working for a pittance, she launched her career in journalism with a colorful human interest series on working women that was based on her own experiences. Within a few months, she was promoted to covering a wide variety of causes dear to Socialist hearts: poverty, labor protests, peace activism, bread riots, and birth control. Often, while researching her articles, which reflected the Socialist creed of her editors, she joined in the protests that she was covering.

Two events of 1917, the Russian Revolution and the American entry into World War I, informed Day's consciousness for a lifetime. At a rally in Madison Square Garden, Day celebrated the power of common people to shape a socialist future. Soon war clouds overshadowed the joyous event. The United States entered World War I, and Day and a handful of radicals and pacifists refused to cooperate. Day objected to the war's benefits to capitalist arms merchants and its division of the international working class into soldiers who fought each other. Watching helplessly as the suppression of dissent resulted in the arrests of friends and the closing down of the radical press, she opposed the draft and wartime government censorship.

Day spent her first night in jail in 1917, but not for antiwar activity. Having traveled to Washington with militant women's suffragists, she and her companions were charged with blocking traffic near the White House. At the notorious Occoquan Workhouse in Virginia, Day scuffled with her jailers over their denial of her basic human rights. Conservative critics, horrified by the prospect of an increase in women's political activity, noticed the antiwar attitudes of the militant suffragists, some of whose signs referred to "Kaiser Wilson." Day later wrote that she had intended to support political prisoners in Washington. Although she was leading the life of a new woman, independent in spirit, career-oriented, and open to free love, she was no suffragist. Impatient with politics, the young revolutionary Socialist preferred mass action to balloting and compromise.

Upon her return to New York, Day found herself unable to earn a living as a radical journalist. Recently an assistant editor at the chic and naughty *Masses*, the "awkward and charming young enthusiast, with beautiful slanting eyes," as her boss Floyd Dell described her, had remained at that radical magazine long enough to edit a couple of issues that attracted the attention of postal censors.[2] The senior editors of the *Masses* twice faced sedition charges and twice won acquittal. But the magazine was dead, one of the many literary casualties of the war, replaced by a tame (and to Day unappealing) pretender, the *Liberator*.

From 1918 through 1923, Day lived a life that evoked an embarrassed silence in her autobiography. Weary of overbearing editors and government repression of writers and activists, she studied nursing and worked at menial jobs while continuing to write. A tempestuous love affair, an abortion, a failed marriage, and an apparent suicide attempt suggest her faltering sense of purpose and disenchantment with radical activism.

By 1924 Day had managed to turn her life around. Publication of *The Eleventh Virgin*, a heavily autobiographical novel of disillusionment, and its sale to Hollywood brought Day modest financial security. Shortly thereafter, she settled contentedly into a domestic partnership with Forster Batterham, brother of a friend. The birth of a daughter, Tamar, in March 1926, sparked a crisis. Since childhood Day had from time to time yearned for a rich spiritual life. Now she could no longer suppress the desire. The birth of her daughter, her blissful partnership, and Batterham's infectious appreciation of nature focused her thoughts on God. Drawn to Catholicism, she was forced to choose between Batterham, an adamant nonbeliever, and the church, which could not bless their irregular union. After hesitating, Day was baptized a Catholic in December 1927.

Conversion addressed complex needs in Day's life. Tired of her moral drift, Day was still attracted to the cause of industrial workers although her activism had diminished. She naturally turned to the church of workers and immigrants. The conversion, however, did not bring instant comfort. Anguished by the loss of her partner, Day was also troubled by the social conservatism of church leadership, the smug self-satisfaction of bourgeois Christians, and their practice of charity without social justice. "I loved the church," she admitted, "for Christ made visible. Not for itself, because it was so often a scandal to me."[3]

Finding a career suited to a radical Catholic single mother took time. During the winter of 1932–1933, five years after her conversion, Day was beginning to grasp her new calling. Using her radical connections, she gained entry to a protest in Washington organized by the Communist-influenced Unemployed Councils, then reported about the concerns of workers and farmers for readers of two Catholic magazines.

At least one reader, fifty-five-year-old Peter Maurin, an immigrant from rural France, was captivated by the accounts of the demonstrations. Rooted in European Catholic culture, the Gospel, and agricultural life, Maurin could often be found proclaiming his message of social change and spiritual renewal from a soapbox in Union Square or handing out mimeographed copies of his free verse social thought. Like Day, he took Christ's teaching of love for one's neighbor seriously.

In contrast to Day, the quintessential urbanite, Maurin gloried in the rural ethos, which he had experienced as a child in southern France. He called for a green revolution, a return to the soil minus high technology and a marketplace mind-set. In place of city life and capitalism, he imagined a simple Christian cooperative society. Skilled craftsmen—he did not advance the cause of women workers—would create useful items. Each craft would be regulated by its own guild. Farmers, formed into communes, need not fear the perils of profit and loss. Shared surpluses would eliminate want. Maurin's utopia meant an escape from such evils as worker alienation, low industrial wages, the impersonality and corruption of cities, rugged individualism, secularism, dependency, class warfare, and the extremes of capitalism and state communism. Work, Maurin taught, should support basic human needs rather than create profits for the few and poverty for the masses. Hospitality would be the work of every individual, following the Christian code of love. Those in need would be cared for by their neighbors, not by an impersonal bureaucracy.

To encourage people to organize themselves to effect a nonviolent social revolution, Maurin wanted to implant his ideas in enthusiastic followers. He could reach a few people from his soapbox and with his leaflets, but in the midst of the Great Depression, Maurin imagined that more people than he could personally reach would be interested in the green revolution. Having sensed a kindred spirit in Day's writing, he sought out the author.

Under his tutelage in Catholic social thought, Day became cofounder of a new radical Catholic movement and editor and publisher of its newspaper. She was a perfect complement to Maurin. Deeply religious and committed to revolution, Day wrote powerful articles about social issues. Native-born and respectable, but with a dash of bohemianism from her Greenwich Village past, she could reach a larger group of potential disciples than Maurin. Never before a leader in the radical movement or in the church, Day already displayed great energy and enthusiasm, self-discipline, deep spirituality, and can-do optimism. With Maurin's encouragement, she would shape the Catholic Worker movement.

In order to hear Maurin's message, Day ignored his eccentricities of demeanor, dress, and personal hygiene. Her new platonic friend convinced her of the urgency of meeting human needs and the ability of lay Catholics to undertake programs without special permission from the church hierarchy. Day moved forthrightly to promote the works of mercy, nonviolent revolution, and spiritual renewal. Since the idea of editing her own paper was so appealing, the Catholic Worker movement started with the distribution of an eight-page, tabloid-style penny paper.

At the same time the New Deal was attempting to restore public confidence in government and in the economy, Day launched the *Catholic Worker* with small donations, including $2 from a nun, and small loans. Religious faith reinforced her radical values. She expected capitalism to be crushed by the depression. Its failure, she believed, would hasten a nonviolent revolution leading to a cooperative Christian society. Mistrustful of centralized power, Day was still grounded in the experience of wartime repression in 1917–1918 and the excesses of the Red Scare. Still influenced by her youthful radicalism, she thought that the state, its laws, and its enforcement agencies were unnecessary. In decentralized Christian communities the Gospel spirit of love would be supreme, not the letter of the law. Surveying the lives of ordinary folk around her, Day found abundant evidence of human need: evictions, hunger, and joblessness were among the most obvious problems. Rather than treating symptoms without eradicating the causes, or working for revolution while ignoring present human needs, Day believed that a program founded on the daily practice of works of mercy, such as feeding the hungry and sheltering the homeless, combined with nonviolent direct action—Maurin's program met the test—was the surest path to social change and the most direct route to social revolution.

The paper made an unforgettable impression. Priced at a penny a copy, the *Catholic Worker* advocated Gospel values over profit. Volunteers wrote stories; helped to edit, address, bundle, mail, and hawk the paper; and cared for the poor. The paper and the movement survived on small donations, which, Day pointed out, kept the movement humble and its following large. At a modest twenty-five cents a year for a subscription, most readers could afford an offering above the cost of the paper. By operating without corporate sponsors (the paper was advertisement-free) or grants from foundations, and by deliberately avoiding legal incorporation as a charity, Day kept her editorial and investigative freedom without fear of offending a corporate sponsor or the government.

Peter Maurin had anticipated a paper devoted solely to his writings and ideas, but Day prevailed, producing a high-quality paper of wider interest. Besides Maurin's didactic verses and her appealing column, eyewitness accounts of injustice; major theological treatises; lively essays on labor, farming, race relations, liturgy, calligraphy, and other subjects; and letters from Catholic Workers throughout the country attracted a remarkably diverse readership. Day wrote most of the unsigned copy in the early years and invited articles from great minds. Social critics Eric Gill and Lewis Mumford, liturgist Virgil Michel, philosopher Jacques Maritain, and sociologist Paul Hanly Furfey shared their thoughts in the early years. Later the paper published the poetry of Claude McKay and William Everson (Brother Antoninus), and the writings of social justice advocates Michael Harrington, Thomas Merton, and Daniel and Philip Berrigan. Belgian-born Ade Bethune, who depicted saints as workers, was the first of many exceptional artists to offer her work to the paper. Others were Fritz Eichenberg, Rita Corbin, and Robert McGovern.

Measured by any standards, the paper was a success. Low in cost, high in quality, original in viewpoint, and aesthetically pleasing, it attracted a large readership. Volunteers hawked the paper on New York streets, sometimes calling out "Read the *Catholic Worker* daily!" in good natured verbal competition with Communists selling copies of the *Daily Worker* nearby. Day herself urged readers to "[p]ass your copy of THE CATHOLIC WORKER *[sic]* on to a friend—that's how our circulation has grown from 2,500 to 20,000 in six months!"[4] By 1938 circulation peaked with 190,000 copies, many of which were sent in bulk orders to parish priests. Day's insistent pacifism during World War II led to a slump in subscriptions. At the war's end, slightly more than 50,000 copies of each issue were circulated. But Day's reputation, the movement's unflagging advocacy of the poor, and its consistent Christian ethic led to a rebirth of the movement and the paper by the 1950s. During the 1980s and early 1990s circulation of the *Catholic Worker* usually hovered between 90,000 and 100,000 copies per issue.

Volunteers and supporters were attracted to the movement largely by its principles and work, the *Catholic Worker* paper, and Day's charismatic personality. Art student Ade Bethune helped out after hearing from a classmate about two women (Day and volunteer Dorothy Weston) sleeping on the floor, whenever necessary, to shelter the poor. Joseph Zarrella, recalling that at the time he "wasn't particularly a good Catholic," volunteered after encountering Catholic Workers selling the paper in Union Square. He was "captured" by the "excit[ement]" generated by the movement.[5]

As critical as ideas and leadership were, Day knew that action was essential. "We start to write about justice, about changing the social order," she stated, "and we are overwhelmed by those coming to claim our pity and our sharing."[6] Following the example that Day set throughout her life, *Catholic Worker* editors engaged in direct action; picketed for organized labor; attended meetings and marches in support of housing, labor, peace, and other causes; educated themselves and others about social issues; committed civil disobedience; and shared their lives and goods with the poor.

Voluntary poverty was a cornerstone of the movement's nonviolent revolution. As Day explained in one of her columns, "Love of [others] means voluntary poverty, stripping one's self . . . denying one's self. . . . It also means non-participation in those comforts and luxuries which have been manufactured by the exploitation of others."[7] If everyone took less, she calculated, then fewer would be in need.

In her writing, on the picket line, in court, and in jail, Day supported the right of laborers to unionize, to be paid decently, and to work in conditions that protected their health and safety. The immigrant Catholic Church of the late nineteenth and early twentieth centuries was a church of manual laborers. First a few Catholic leaders, then the collective voice of the Catholic hierarchy, supported workers' rights. Day built on their efforts.

More than a generation before Day joined the church, Catholics like Terence Powderly of the Knights of Labor and James Cardinal Gibbons supported organized labor at a time when many Catholics, including members of the hierarchy, feared that the Vatican had targeted them when it denounced secret and anti-Catholic groups. Gibbons defended the Knights of Labor, convinced Rome to tolerate labor organization, and reassured American Catholics that blanket condemnation of unions had been based on an erroneous view of these groups. After World War I, the most visible Catholic guardian of labor was John A. Ryan, a priest who advised both the bishops and New Dealers. A committed reformer, Ryan used orthodox theological method to sanctify Progressive reform and workers' rights.

Day founded the Catholic Worker movement to address the immediate concerns of workers. A cooperative apartment kept low-paid women workers off the streets. From the 1930s, the movement sided with union militants, sharecroppers, and migrant farm workers. Its breadline fed the unemployed and unemployable. Dedicated to unionism, the movement nonetheless challenged the materialist ethos of workers and even suggested during World War II that defense industry jobs compromised Gospel pacifism.

The meager resources of the Catholic Worker movement were generously expended on workers attempting to unionize. In 1936–1937, when seamen decided to organize the National Maritime Union in New York, Day responded with publicity and material aid. Throughout the strike period, the paper ran articles sympathetic to the unionists. The Catholic Worker movement even added a branch near the docks so that the seamen would have a place to eat and relax. When the victorious strikers shipped out, Day was left with a sizable debt for their food and rent. The movement typically supported labor with boycotts and picketing. For Day, picketing was a spiritual discipline, "a form of supplicatory procession such as the Church has always through the ages upheld."[8] At the age of seventy-five she was arrested for the final time, picketing with César Chávez's United Farm Workers in California's vineyards. Given the limited resources of the movement, the aid rendered to labor activism was significant. Such help made a difference—for example, when the *Catholic Worker,* writing of the low wages earned by workers at the National Biscuit Company during the 1930s, convinced readers to sell their shares of Nabisco in protest.

On labor issues, Day sometimes asserted her independence from the bishops and Peter Maurin. During the 1930s she supported a proposed child labor amendment, whereas the Catholic bishops, anxious about government intrusion into family issues, opposed it. A defender of strikes, Day early on found herself in opposition to Maurin, who hoped workers would exchange their machines for plowshares. Both Maurin and Day, however, agreed to support sitdown strikes, which were emblematic of a radical restructuring of the workplace.

Day's antistatist tendencies (she preferred self-organization at the community level to a strong nation-state) made her suspicious of government initiatives. Critical of liberal reform for its failure to get to the root of social problems, Day nonetheless believed that in an emergency, government should provide economic assistance to the needy. Thus, she praised some New Deal programs while criticizing others.

The new cooperative Christian social order advocated by Day and the Catholic Worker movement would come about through a nonviolent personalist revolution. Borrowing from French philosopher Emmanuel Mounier, Day advocated personalism, an individual's free initiative to take responsibility for others, to change the world by the cumulative effect of the humble efforts of serious Christians. In this way, nonviolent revolution could come one day, and the profit motive would no longer drive the economy, create class divisions, fuel racism, or dominate politics.

The Catholic Worker movement was an intentional community in which activists who shared a hunger for spiritual growth, service to the poor, and social revolution could support each other. Members took no vows. Some, like seventeen-year-old Stanley Vishnewski, who came to help, stayed for a lifetime. Many of the young remained until marriage. Several married couples persisted in the work. Dorothy and Bill Gauchat of Avon, Ohio, for example, cared for handicapped children. Others, perhaps repelled by the literal truth in Day's view that "poverty is lice," left quickly.

To end her "long loneliness" outside the Catholic Church, Day had desired spiritual community as a convert. But even as a Catholic, she found that few of her coreligionists totally shared her emerging vision of love, peace, revolution, and voluntary poverty. Thus, Day created her own community within the church. The paper, the intellectual ferment, the house of hospitality, and the farming communes drew like-minded people into the movement. Communal life also resolved, albeit somewhat inadequately from Day's point of view, one of her major difficulties. Ever anxious about her parenting, Day was helped by members of the movement as she juggled her conflicting roles as single parent and activist journalist.

When she was not at boarding school, Day's daughter lived at the Catholic

Worker hospice or farm and enjoyed the company of the young volunteers and neighbors, who shared responsibility for her care. But a childhood spent in a hospice was hardly carefree. The shy little girl had to deal with the odd and aggressive behaviors of unbalanced guests, some of whom could not be restrained from destroying her toys. The uneasy mother entrusted her daughter to a spiritual parent—Mary, the mother of Christ—to compensate for her maternal deficiencies. As Tamar neared adulthood and an early marriage, Day took her only sabbatical from the movement, in part so she could spend more time with her daughter.

Before the first Catholic Worker hospice opened, poor folks depended on a network of kin, friends, churches, charities, shelters, and public relief, all of which were stretched to their limits by the magnitude of need during hard times. Catholics had begun to coordinate charitable efforts by 1910 with the National Conference of Catholic Charities, which worked with the dioceses to provide regulated and professional charity as well as to unite against conservative and anti-Catholic opposition. Catholic charitable work, however, was largely directed by religious orders, leaving the laity with the task of funding these efforts.

For Dorothy Day, the New Testament command to love one's neighbor suggested a personal responsibility for others. Christ's commandment was unburdened by restrictive clauses; the law of love applied to all. To do the church's social work, Day tapped the talents of the underutilized laity. She reminded Catholics that they are the church, layperson and religious, male and female, rich and poor, educated and unschooled alike. Eager volunteers crossed gender, class, and race lines as they pitched in to provide relief and to agitate for social revolution. Women's domestic work was elevated to a high spiritual value and, in response to the Gospel, men and women cooked, cleaned, and cared for others. Women could escape domestic work at the soup kitchen to edit the paper, write, speak in public, and picket. Finally, the spiritual leadership of the Catholic Worker movement fell to Dorothy Day, despite her occasional disclaimers.

Catholic Worker hospitality was influenced by contemporary theology. Day popularized a papal theme of the 1930s, the unity of the Mystical Body of Christ and the dignity of each individual member of that body. Each person had a unique place and duty. Because Christ was within all people, the ''ambassadors of Christ,'' as the poor were known in the Catholic Worker movement, were all deserving of help.

Catholic Worker hospitality offered an alternative to the rigidity of the detested ''turnstile charity.'' To maintain the human dignity of those receiving aid, Catholic Workers provided necessities with no questions asked and with no red tape. Guests and volunteers ate the same food, slept in the same dormitory, and wore the same donated clothing. Unlike the situation in public shelters and private charities, where professionals ministered to their charges, Day's movement blurred social distinctions. Guests sometimes became volunteers. And, as Day realized, guests were not the only ones who benefited from association with the movement. Volunteers shared in the largesse that fed, clothed, and sheltered the homeless and reaped spiritual gain.

What began as a small local effort rapidly matured into a loose national (and later international) network of houses and farms influenced by the New Testament. By the end of the 1930s, this community included hospices and agrarian communes stretching from Boston to Houma, Louisiana, and from the District of Columbia to Seattle.

If the Catholic Worker movement in the city meant hospices, in the country it meant a farming commune. Advocated by Peter Maurin, the farming commune idea came to life with the publicity, initiative, and gifts generated by Day. A small plot of land and a house on Staten Island became the first garden commune. By 1936 a more spacious farm was purchased near Easton, Pennsylvania.

These agrarian communities proved taxing to operate. Poorly capitalized, the farms were sometimes no better than rural slums. Resistance to the use of technology and untrained farmhands hindered efficiency and kept production low. Innocent of farming, the New York Catholic Workers purchased the Easton property before anyone noticed the lack of water. One of the more serious tests of Day's leadership and the movement's principles was a dispute during the 1940s involving a group of disgruntled rural Catholic Worker families with their own alternative understanding of farming communes and spirituality; it was resolved by Day's decision to cede land to the dissenters, sell the remainder of the Easton farm, and buy new land elsewhere. Problems aside, the farming communes were an integral part of the Catholic Worker movement. Besides feeding Catholic Workers in the cities, the rural communities provided opportunities for work and functioned as spas for tired volunteers, sanatariums for the ill or unbalanced, and conference centers for spiritual renewal and intellectual growth. By promoting harmony with nature, the Catholic Worker movement appreciated divine creation and foreshadowed the environmentalism of more recent times.

Harmony with creation was also expressed in the Catholic Workers' pacifism. As a Catholic, Day's absolute pacifism was rooted in the gospel of love. Again relying on contemporary themes in theology and philosophy, Day synthesized personalism and Mystical Body theology with an unusual thought for Catholics at that time: biblical pacifism. In so doing, she reached the conclusion that all war was evil. "As long as [people] trust to the use of force," she wrote, "only a superior, a more savage and brutal force will overcome the enemy."[9]

Once a Socialist opponent of war, as a Catholic pacifist, Day no longer approved of class warfare. But she sprinkled some of the antiwar ideas of her radical youth into her Christian writings. Her criticism of war profiteering, whether by arms merchants or imperialistic governments, was evidence of the lingering influence of her radical past.

By the 1930s, Day advocated absolute nonviolence, recommending prayer and reception of the sacraments to spiritually overpower armies. Once an opponent of war on political and social grounds, she believed that to follow in

Jesus' footsteps, one must love one's enemy. The same Gospel command that had led to the founding of houses of hospitality and to advocacy of the poor and workers lent authority to Day's controversial religious pacifism. For Day, "a disarmament of the heart" meant active resistance to war and injustice by using spiritual weapons such as prayer, fasting, and love.

Catholic Workers did not invent pacifism. Until the Christianization of the Roman Empire under Constantine, early Christians had refused to engage in war. To defend the Christian state, the teachings of Augustine and Thomas Aquinas set conditions under which war was morally defensible. Pacifism entered into the modern era from a few smaller Protestant sects. In the United States, the Catholic Church normally found its country's wars to be just. But after World War I, when public opinion reflected revulsion with war and disillusionment, elite Catholics sought peaceful alternatives to armed conflict.

The Catholic Association for International Peace (CAIP), founded in 1927, supported international organization and collective security. Adhering to a just war rationale rather than to Gospel pacifism, the CAIP concluded that the United States fought just wars. Unlike the Catholic Worker movement, the CAIP exercised its muscle through its high-level lobbying and educational efforts, avoiding the visible antiwar activism of Dorothy Day and Catholic Worker pacifists.

By the late 1930s, Catholic Workers promoted pacifism in editorials and articles, and established the peace group PAX. Catholic Worker representatives, including Day, testified vigorously but unsuccessfully against a peacetime draft measure before Congress in 1940. When war came, Day remained firmly pacifist, although the movement was divided by the issue of war.

Day tolerated supporters of World War II in the movement so long as they did not block open discussion of pacifism. She lent crucial emotional and financial support to Catholic conscientious objectors in the Civilian Public Service camps. But Day's preferred response to war was complete noncooperation or radical pacifism. She took the precaution of signing a petition against extending the draft to women, refused to pay war taxes, and advocated refusal to register for the draft or to work in war industry.

The Catholic Worker movement was one of the pacifist groups that built the foundation for the antinuclear movement. Day condemned the annihilation of the civilian populations of Hiroshima and Nagasaki with atomic bombs as a "colossal slaughter of innocents," reminding all that " '[t]he Son of Man [Christ] came not to destroy souls but to save.' He said also, 'What you do unto the least of these my brethren, you do unto me.' "[10] The enormous power of governments in the nuclear age reconfirmed Day's mistrust of the state.

Neither domestic political witch-hunting nor fear of international communism during the 1950s curtailed Catholic Worker antinuclear activism. Joining with other radical pacifists, Day and several Catholic Workers were repeatedly arrested and jailed for violating mandatory Civil Defense air-raid drills. By the early 1960s the drills were discontinued, and the federal government urged citizens to construct home bomb shelters.

As a pacifist group, the Catholic Workers were early critics of the Vietnam War. In 1954, when French forces were on the brink of defeat, Day rejected the need for American military involvement in Southeast Asia. And Catholic Workers were burning their draft cards before the Gulf of Tonkin Resolution of 1964 guaranteed extraordinary powers to the president in order to repel any threat to the U.S. military overseas. Slowed down by a heart condition, Day still supported young pacifist noncooperators and lent her name to the newly organized Catholic Peace Fellowship, which provided draft counseling for young men, used the spiritual weapons of prayer and fasting for peace, and gave thoughtful consideration to the merits of the draft board raid movement led by the priests Daniel and Philip Berrigan.

Day's pacifism was premised upon nonviolent resistance to state authority and economic hegemony, and on obedience to the laws of God over human decrees. Rejecting the standard view of "rendering to Caesar the things that are Caesar's," Day argued that God's claims to human obedience superseded those of the state when in conflict with the Gospel.

Although the Catholic bishops moved slowly in condemning the Vietnam War and guaranteeing the right of conscience to oppose war during the 1960s, by the 1980s they denounced the stockpiling of arms and celebrated Day's nonviolence. Some of them, including Maurice Dingman of Des Moines and Raymond Hunthausen of Seattle, advocated noncooperation and engaged in acts of resistance on their own.

Day died in New York City on 29 November 1980, at the age of eighty-three. Although a few critics question whether the movement still lives up to her ideals, Day's influence is strongly felt both inside and outside of the Catholic Worker movement. Her writings awaken consciences, keeping her revolutionary spirit alive in a conservative age. Catholic Worker hospices and farms throughout the United States, Canada, Europe, and Australia provide relief.

Some supporters of Dorothy Day have launched a campaign for her canonization as a saint. However, many of her closest followers refuse to support her formal canonization, honoring instead Day's belief that "[a]ll are called to be saints. Not to do the extraordinary—if sanctity depended on doing the extraordinary, there would be few saints."[11] Day wanted to set an example requiring no heroic feats, only simple acts of feeding, sheltering, and clothing those in need; a spiritual life drawing from the rich Christian heritage; and a willingness to live nonviolence.

The Catholic Worker spirit of personalism, or individual responsibility for one's community, has countered an emphasis in the modern American reform tradition to seek redress for economic, social, and political inequality from the federal government. "We are not denying the obligations of the State," Day explained. "But . . . we must never cease to emphasize personal responsibility."[12]

The Catholic Worker principles anticipated Catholic renewal during the Second Vatican Council of the 1960s. A pilgrim in Rome during part of the council,

Day used spiritual tools—prayer, fasting, and education—to reassert what she believed was the early church's pacifist ethic. Although the bishops fell short of condemning the possession of nuclear weapons and continued to rely on "just war" theology over absolute pacifism, they did uphold the right of conscientious objection and endorsed economic and social justice throughout the world.

Catholic Worker stands on economic justice, social equality, the rights of political prisoners, and peace seemed similar to the positions of the Left. Admirers of the movement, such as the Communist Elizabeth Gurley Flynn, who bequeathed her modest estate to the movement, and Yippie leader Abbie Hoffman, who viewed Day as the first hippie, understood the utter authenticity of Day's radicalism. Unlike these sympathetic radicals, Day insisted on an explicit spiritual grounding for the movement, an appreciation of the Catholic heritage. When a few young Catholic Workers of the early 1960s whose beer blasts, free sexuality, and uninhibited expression (they printed the magazine *Fuck You!* on the *Catholic Worker*'s press) displayed their preference for a bohemian lifestyle over service to the poor, Day demanded that they leave, an incident known humorously as the "Dorothy Day Stomp."

Both a traditional Catholic and a dedicated lifelong radical, Day possessed a genius for synthesis. Without compromising her social radicalism, she joined the Catholic Church. By fortifying herself with a spiritual shield, Day built a nonviolent revolution from daily service to the poor and agitation for change. Dedicated to building a new heaven on earth, she understood that the poor "are not put in our way to be judged, only that we may purchase heaven from them." Love, prayer, and works of mercy were for Day the "holy force" leading to revolution and salvation.[13]

NOTES

1. Dorothy Day, *The Long Loneliness* (New York, 1952), 285.

2. Floyd Dell, *Homecoming: An Autobiography* (New York, 1933), 296.

3. Day, *Long Loneliness*, 149–150.

4. *Catholic Worker* 1 (November 1933): 2.

5. Rosalie Troester, ed., *Voices from the Catholic Worker* (Philadelphia, 1993), 5–6.

6. Dorothy Day, "Here and Now" (1949), in Robert Ellsberg, ed., *By Little and by Little: Selected Writings of Dorothy Day* (New York, 1983), 101.

7. Dorothy Day, quoted in Stanley Vishnewski, ed., *Meditations: Dorothy Day* (New York, 1970), 48.

8. An anonymous author covered the spirituality of picketing in "Orbach and Klein Violate NRA Codes and Jail Pickets," *Catholic Worker* 2 (February 1935): 1, 6.

9. Dorothy Day, "Editorial—CW Stand on the Use of Force" (September 1938), quoted in Thomas C. Cornell and James H. Forest, eds., *A Penny a Copy: Readings from the Catholic Worker* (New York, 1968), 36.

10. Day's much-quoted jeremiad first appeared in the *Catholic Worker* in September 1945, and is reprinted in Ellsberg, ed., *By Little*, 266–269.

11. Dorothy Day, quoted in William D. Miller, comp., *All Is Grace: The Spirituality of Dorothy Day* (Garden City, N.Y., 1987), 102.

12. Dorothy Day, *House of Hospitality* (New York, 1939), 258.
13. Dorothy Day, quoted in Miller, comp., *All Is Grace*, 134, 93.

BIBLIOGRAPHY

Catholic Worker. 1933–.

Coles, Robert. *Dorothy Day: A Radical Devotion*. Boston, 1987.

Cornell, Tom. "Dorothy Day Remembered." *Sign* 60 (June 1981): 5–11, 54.

Coy, Patrick, ed., *A Revolution of the Heart: Essays on the Catholic Worker*. Philadelphia, 1988.

Day, Dorothy. *The Eleventh Virgin*. New York, 1924.

———. *From Union Square to Rome*. Silver Spring, Md., 1938.

———. *House of Hospitality*. New York, 1939.

———. *The Long Loneliness*. New York, 1952.

———. *Loaves and Fishes*. New York, 1963.

Ellsberg, Robert, ed., *By Little and by Little: The Selected Writings of Dorothy Day*. New York, 1983.

Klejment, Anne, and Alice Klejment. *Dorothy Day and "The Catholic Worker": A Bibliography and Index*. New York, 1986.

Klejment, Anne, and Nancy L. Roberts, eds. *American Catholic Pacifism: The Influence of Dorothy Day and the Catholic Worker Movement*. Westport, Conn., 1996.

McNeal, Patricia. *Harder Than War: Catholic Peacemaking in Twentieth-Century America*. New Brunswick, N.J., 1992.

Merriman, Brigid O'Shea. *Reaching for Christ: The Spirituality of Dorothy Day*. Notre Dame, Ind., 1994.

Miller, William D. *A Harsh and Dreadful Love: Dorothy Day and the Catholic Worker Movement*. New York, 1973.

———. *Dorothy Day: A Biography*. San Francisco, 1982.

———, comp. *All Is Grace: The Spirituality of Dorothy Day*. Garden City, N.Y., 1987.

Murray, Harry. *Do Not Neglect Hospitality: The Catholic Worker and the Homeless*. Philadelphia, 1990.

O'Brien, David J. *Public Catholicism*. New York, 1989.

Piehl, Mel. *Breaking Bread: The Catholic Worker and the Origin of Catholic Radicalism in America*. Philadelphia, 1982.

Roberts, Nancy L. *Dorothy Day and the "Catholic Worker."* Albany, N.Y., 1984.

Troester, Rosalie, ed., *Voices from the Catholic Worker*. Philadelphia, 1993.

Betty Friedan and the National Organization for Women

BARBARA McGOWAN

Feminism and concern for the rights of women have been a continuing but not always particularly strong theme in American history since the founding of the Republic. The first visible women's rights movement, associated with the fervor of reform in antebellum America, was symbolized by the Seneca Falls convention and declaration of 1848. The second push for women's equality coincided with the Progressive era and resulted in ratification of the Nineteenth Amendment in 1920. What can be described as the third identifiable wave of American feminism emerged in the early 1960s.

One of the signal events in the third wave of American Feminism was the publication in 1963 of *The Feminine Mystique* by Betty Friedan. Friedan—born Betty Naomi Goldstein on 4 February 1921 in Peoria, Illinois, the third child of Harry and Miriam Goldstein—was a Westchester County, New York, housewife with an impressive educational background (Smith College summa cum laude, 1942, followed by a year of graduate work in psychology at the University of California at Berkeley) and some journalistic experience. The book, which drew on findings from a survey of Smith alumnae in the late 1950s, described "the problem that has no name," Friedan's term for the discontent experienced by millions of American women who wanted roles beyond the socially prescribed ones of wife, mother, and homemaker.

Friedan's book traced the roots and dimensions of the domestic role, blaming its limits and frustrations on such factors as Freudian psychology, functionalist sociology, and media images of acceptable female roles. She demonstrated how Freudian psychology hurt women by convincing them and their spouses that female fulfillment could be achieved only through deep personal acceptance of the culture's definitions of wife and mother roles. Functionalist theories on social organization harmed women by suggesting that society worked most efficiently when men exercised public, political, and economic power, and women restricted themselves to domestic concerns. Friedan condemned advertisers for encouraging American women to be housewife consumers. The book sold three million copies. In addition, excerpts ran in both *Good Housekeeping* and the *Ladies Home Journal*, magazines which normally celebrated and promoted the feminine mystique that Friedan criticized. The book and its reception made Friedan a visible and controversial figure, and provided her with a career as a lecturer, a writer, and eventually an organizer for feminist causes.

At the same time that Friedan's book was prompting intense reaction from the American public, more traditional and institutionalized supporters of women's rights were benefiting from the policies of a new administration in Washington. In 1960 John F. Kennedy was elected president with the active support of women like Esther Peterson, longtime activist in trade union movements, educational organizations, and the Democratic party. Peterson, who was appointed head of the Women's Bureau at the Department of Labor, suggested to the new president that he consolidate his position with her branch of the party by naming a National Commission on the Status of Women.

The resulting reports from the National Commission and various similar state commissions documented widespread discrimination against women and made specific recommendations, most having to do with federal action on equal pay and job equity. Service on the commissions brought together many skilled and determined women who were willing to go beyond traditional women's organizational tactics to bring about change. In 1964 the oldest surviving branch of the suffragist movement, the National Women's party, was instrumental in obtaining an ambiguous but welcome victory when the 1964 Civil Rights Act was amended to bar employment discrimination against women as well as racial minorities. Eventually this amendment, and the federal government's reluctance to enforce it, served as the catalyst that caused Friedan and a group of "middle-aged, middle-class women" to found the National Organization for Women (NOW) in 1966.[1]

But Friedan and NOW would never have had the opportunity to change the lives of American women if they had not been the beneficiary of larger demographic and economic changes. By the mid-1960s, a number of social trends were altering the lives of American women and challenging traditional sex roles, no matter what the ideological inclinations of individual women and men. Increased numbers of women were in the work force, including women with young children. American women, especially middle-class women, were increasingly well educated but still faced persistent discrimination in the workplace and especially in admission to professional schools and training programs. Middle-class women, because of their high levels of education but low chances for high-paying, professional careers, felt the relative deprivation that can be a powerful base for reform movements. In addition, longer female life spans, better contraceptive technology, and more household conveniences were making motherhood and homemaking both less of a full-time job and less of a lifetime occupation. Another source of strength for the burgeoning women's movement was the New Left activism that had its roots in the civil rights and anti-Vietnam War movements. Many younger women, most of them students at elite colleges and universities, had become disillusioned with the demeaning attitudes toward women expressed by male movement leaders and were more than willing to transfer their organizing skills and revolutionary fervor to a renascent feminist movement.

The NOW organization actually emerged in October 1966, when longtime activists within the government and their sympathizers, many of them members of state Commissions on the Status for Women, failed to persuade the Equal Employment Opportunity Commission to take job discrimination against women seriously. Frustrated, these "very reluctant women," in Friedan's words, organized the National Organization for Women, "to take the actions needed to bring women into the mainstream of American society, now, full equality for women, in fully equal partnership with men."[2] Friedan drafted the statement of purpose, and it was accepted as she wrote it with one interesting exception. Friedan wrote that women had the right to choose—to control her own childbearing—meaning access to birth control and abortion. Her fellow founders deemed this stand too controversial.

The statement is an important document because it shows that Friedan was well within the American liberal tradition calling for equality of opportunity and freedom of choice for women on the basis of their rights as individual Americans and as human beings. As was subsequently noted by many of her more radical critics, Friedan criticized the American educational and employment systems only for their discrimination against women; otherwise, she seemed fully to support their social and economic aims. Although Friedan and NOW later were also taken to task for ignoring the needs of working mothers, the original statement averred: "We do not accept the traditional assumption that a woman has to choose between marriage and motherhood, on the one hand, and serious participation in industry or the professions on the other. . . . True equality of opportunity and freedom of choice for women requires such practical and possible innovations as a nationwide network of childcare centers." Nor did Friedan's statement ignore the role of men within the family, unwittingly laying the groundwork for the "superwoman" charge that was later made against the liberal, "individualistic" founders of NOW. (When men took on more duties in the home, thus freeing women *to pursue careers*, women often felt they had to overachieve in both career and home to justify their place in each.) She wrote: "We believe that a true partnership between the sexes demands a different concept of marriage, an equitable sharing of the responsibilities of home and children and of the economic burdens of their support."[3]

From the beginning, NOW, with Friedan as its founder and first president, relied heavily on media publicity to communicate its message and achieve specific objectives. At first, the organization reflected the relative sophistication and professionalism of its charter members and concentrated on approaches and goals that fit their generally middle-class orientation. One of NOW's first actions was to fight sex-segregated help wanted ads and age discrimination against airline stewardesses. Their tactic was to hold small demonstrations against the Equal Employment Opportunity Commission (EEOC) and invite the national television networks to cover them. The ploy worked, and in both cases the commission was forced to change its rulings in favor of nondiscrimination. NOW also sent a strongly worded and lengthy letter to President Lyndon Johnson, one tangible result of which was an executive order barring discrimination against women by federal contractors.

Looking back on this period of NOW's existence, Jo Freeman, an activist coming out of the student-oriented New Left, claimed that the organization was too elitist and inaccessible: "I first read of the National Organization for Women—with feelings of delight and relief—early in 1967 in a newspaper interview. My letter to the interviewee was never answered. Nor were any of the other five letters I wrote during the next year. . . . Clearly something was happening, but I couldn't find it."[4] Friedan's perception, reflecting her own temperamental distaste for prolonged meetings and procedural disputes, was that "all we wanted was enough organization to keep women in touch with one another."[5] Being at the center of the organization, Friedan obviously felt "in touch," and she was clearly bored by organizational issues relating to the development, leadership, and autonomy of local branches and chapters of NOW.

Soon NOW was both bolstered and challenged by women from Freeman's generation and sharing her perspective. Ironically, though, the first dissent within the organization came from moderates rather than radicals. The United Auto Workers (UAW) women were forced, temporarily, to withdraw their support from NOW because their union would not allow them to work for an organization that supported the Equal Rights Amendment (ERA). (The union still subscribed to the idea that women workers benefited more from protective legislation based on gender difference than from full legal equality.) In the second year, a small group of women, concerned by NOW's decision to support abortion rights and wary of Friedan's controversial public image, broke off to found the Women's Equity Action League (WEAL), an organization that concentrated on legal approaches to gender equality in education and employment.

From that point on, the conflicts within NOW and the women's movement, and the criticism directed at Friedan, came much more from the left than the right. NOW was not a monolithic organization and was becoming, by the late 1960s, a complex structure with a national board but also with local branches that exercised considerable autonomy. There were numerous board members, local chapter heads, and task force members.

NOW welcomed younger, often more radical women but also encountered problems with them. For example, Ti-Grace Atkinson, president of the New York chapter of NOW, began to advocate separatism from men, told a joint NOW-National Conference of Christians and Jews meeting that the only honest woman was a prostitute, and smuggled the SCUM (Society for Cutting Up Men) manifesto out of Valerie Solanis's hospital room (Solanis was confined in a mental hospital after she shot pop artist Andy Warhol in the stomach). On a less dramatic level, Atkinson denounced the NOW leadership structure as hierarchical and called for rotation of decision-making positions by lottery. Her proposals were rejected, and Atkinson left to found an extremely radical group called The Feminists. Friedan described this controversy as "short-lived." She later lamented, however, that "the media continued to treat Ti-Grace as a leader of the women's movement, despite its repudiation of her. And her kind of thinking has from time to time crept up again to disrupt the women's movement in the years that followed."[6]

Whereas the Atkinson incident clearly demonstrated the potential for conflict between the liberal mainstream feminist movement (organizations like NOW were characterized by sociologists as women's rights organizations or bureaucratic organizations) and more radical feminists (these were described by the same sociologists as women's liberationist organizations or collectivist rather than bureaucratic), the strong stance taken by NOW on the abortion issue brought temporary unity to the movement. Friedan was extremely active in the fight for abortion rights, and in 1970 the movement won a key victory when New York State made abortion available on demand.

In 1970, according to Friedan, NOW had about 3,000 members in 30 cities. At that time, for political and personal reasons, she decided to step down as president of NOW. As a farewell gesture, she proposed a strike for 26 August 1970, to commemorate the fiftieth anniversary of the Nineteenth Amendment and to call attention to "the unfinished business of women's equality."[7] The NOW convention supported the idea, but incoming president Aileen Hernandez, who was afraid the strike would fail, joined with other board members to insist Friedan take full responsibility for the strike.

The Strike for Equality was the largest demonstration ever held for women's rights. It marked the beginning of the women's movement as a mass movement, because after the strike, polls showed 80 percent of American adults were aware of the women's movement. The strike made women and the public conscious of the tremendous potential for power inherent in an organized women's movement. The strike also created a false sense of unity, for by the summer of 1970, the women's movement was deeply divided and NOW was obviously implicated in those divisions.

Friedan's own assessment of the period is pessimistic. Looking back on events in 1976, Friedan wrote: "It has been said that the women's movement had three golden years, in which we discovered ourselves, that 'sisterhood is powerful.' But after August 26th 1970, the day that made the power visible to the world, the women's movement became the target—the vulnerable, even willing victim—of others' political and economic ripoffs and of women's own hunger (greed or desperate need) for a personal taste of that power and its economic payoffs." In her statement Friedan alluded to her feeling that many people in the movement, particularly in NOW, felt hostile toward her because of the success of the strike. But they also felt hostile toward her because she used the strike's success to urge NOW to take the leadership "in organizing a permanent, ongoing political coalition of women based on the diverse elements we had brought together." Friedan wanted to draw on the support of women who were probably not theoretical feminists but supporters of the practical benefits offered by the expansion of work and educational opportunities for women, equal pay for equal work, and better child-care options.[8]

NOW's reaction to Friedan's proposal revealed further the growing rift between the organization and its founder and most prominent member. Discussing why she stepped down from leadership of NOW in 1970, Friedan gave a variety of reasons: "I'd been spending virtually full time as an activist. Divorced myself now, I had to go back to my writing and otherwise pay the rent." Friedan also mentioned the availability of Aileen Hernandez, a former EEOC commissioner and minority group member, to serve as president and conceded that "a black woman—and a good administrator—could be right for NOW at this time." In addition to these reasons, Friedan also confessed that she "didn't want to be a 'straight woman' fronting for a lesbian cabal.'"[9]

Although Friedan clearly overstated the presence, if not the influence, of lesbians in NOW in 1970, most observers seem to agree that the issue of sexual preference was a real and divisive one. By December 1970 it threatened to split the movement apart. Kate Millet, author of *Sexual Politics*, publicly declared her bisexuality, thereby winning the enthusiastic support of feminists like Gloria Steinem and Flo Kennedy and the extreme disapproval of Friedan, who feared the public discussion of lesbianism would cause a backlash against the women's movement. While conceding that Friedan was correct in seeing the lesbian issue as causing conflict, Friedan's critics, then and now, argue that by denigrating lesbianism and denying its connection to feminism, Friedan cut herself off from the women's movement, lost all right to leadership in the movement, and became increasingly irrelevant to many feminists. This is an arguable point, but it is certainly true that Friedan's influence within NOW declined after the summer of 1970.

In the 1970s, Friedan's relationship with NOW was a troubled one. In many ways, Friedan became a critic, as well as a supporter, of the women's movement. Organizationally, she concentrated her energies on the National Women's Political Caucus (NWPC), which was founded to increase women's participation in conventional politics. The NWPC won an early and lasting victory when it convinced the Democratic National Committee to mandate basically equal representation for women at Democratic party conventions. The NWPC also played an instrumental role in winning Senate ratification of the ERA in March 1972. It proved particularly effective during the Nixon, Ford, and Carter administrations in identifying possible female candidates for federal positions and ensuring their appointment.

But from the outset the NWPC was divided by disputes between Friedan and more radical members led by New York Democratic Congresswoman Bella

Abzug and *Ms.* magazine founder Gloria Steinem. The conflict was between Friedan's vision of the organization as bipartisan, broadly based, and essentially interested in women's issues, and, in Friedan's words, "attempts to narrow the appeal, to take positions and stands couched in radical jargon that was okay for the East Village in New York or counterculture San Francisco, but not for the breadth of women throughout America wanting their own political voice. It wasn't the same voice. (Women from Middle America were not that interested in lesbianism, for instance.)"[10] The infighting within the NWPC became so bitter that after Friedan lost a disputed, possibly fraudulent election for a seat on its board in 1974, she withdrew from the organization.

Friedan once described her life in the 1970s as a retreat undertaken "to try to come to new terms with the political as personal, in my own life." For a while in the early 1970s, she wrote for *McCall's*, a mass-circulation women's magazine, and in her columns expressed her doubts about the direction of the women's movement. She attacked the belief that "the conditions we are trying to change are caused by a conspiracy for the social and economic profit of men." She reassured her middle-American readers that feminism "does not mean class warfare against men, which denies our sexual and human bonds with men, nor does it mean the elimination of children, which denies our human future."[11]

In 1973 Friedan attended the NOW national convention in Washington, D.C. She gave a speech that she believed warded off moves to "disavow equality with men and partnership with men as purposes of NOW—and even to eliminate men as members of NOW." Still, she came away from the meeting concerned that the "organized women's movement was caught up in the rage and exhilaration, of uncovering, defining, confronting all the ways women had been oppressed and exploited in every profession and local community across the country." Friedan was also upset that "the major pre-occupation of the media, and many of the delegates, seemed to be lesbianism."[12]

One of Friedan's few positive contacts with NOW in the 1970s involved her addressing a conference called by the NOW Task Force on Marriage and Family. In that speech, Friedan combined the appealing, common-sense descriptions of reality with prescriptions for action that had made her so effective a decade earlier. She noted that "divorce has increased 1,000 per cent in the last few years" but cautioned, "Don't blame the women's movement for that—blame the obsolete sex roles on which our marriages were based." She called for immediate televised hearings by state legislatures nationwide to discuss basic reforms of marriage and divorce laws. Among the reforms she suggested were payroll deductions for child support, marriage and divorce insurance, and financial compensation to divorcing wives who had put their husbands through college and professional schools.[13]

The occasion was also noteworthy because it was one of the few times in the 1970s that Friedan referred to her 1969 divorce from Carl Friedan, an advertising executive whom she had married in 1947 and with whom she had three children. Obtaining a divorce was a wrenching experience for Friedan, raising fears that it would hurt both her personal career and the women's movement. As she put it: "I was warned by my publisher, editor, agent, and my dear husband that I would be ruined, I would be destroyed, if I got divorced—that my whole credibility, my ability to write in the future about women and the credibility of the movement would be destroyed—and I didn't dare say boo. At the time I did not know personally a single woman who had gone through the experience. . . . And then somehow the women's movement began to give me the strength. . . . And I said, I don't care, I have to do something about my own life."[14]

While Friedan was alternately retreating and speaking out through a variety of public forums, NOW in the 1970s was experiencing bitter internal struggles interspersed with some very real accomplishments in the public arena. The problems within NOW were as much structural as ideological. By 1973 NOW had over 600 chapters, 27 national task forces, and countless ad hoc committees and continuing committees at the national, state, and local levels. Communication between the national board and the state and local branches was imperfect, a situation constantly exacerbated by personal and philosophical differences at each level of the organization.

In 1974 the differences became more visible to the public when there was an open contest for the presidency of NOW. The winner, Karen DeCrow, characterized herself as a radical, but by 1975 her successful reelection bid was marked more by dubious tactics than by radical actions. The organization did not regain its focus until 1977 with the election of Eleanor Smeal and the embracing of ERA ratification as the primary goal of NOW. Although the ERA campaign ultimately failed, the organized efforts for its ratification brought NOW new membership, favorable media coverage, and some unity for the first time since the Women's Strike for Equality in 1970.

Despite these problems, NOW, in concert with other organizations, especially NWPC and WEAL, continued to achieve breakthroughs at the national level. Acting as an interest group directly lobbying Congress, by the mid-1970s they managed to obtain minimum wage for domestic workers, educational equity, access to credit, female admission to military academies, job protection for pregnant workers, and funds for the observance of the International Women's Year. Lawyers working for the organized women's movement brought *Roe v. Wade* to the Supreme Court, winning a landmark decision establishing basic abortion rights.

In assessing the relationship between Betty Friedan and NOW throughout the 1970s, a number of points can be made. Perhaps the primary consideration explaining the relationship was the personality, temperament, background, and ambitions of Friedan herself. Unlike many of the other founding NOW members, she was not a lawyer, nor had she worked for the government or a lobbying group. She had no experience with any of the other older-line feminist groups or much political experience beyond voting. Her original ambitions, which had been thwarted after college graduation when she left Berkeley to pursue a romantic relationship, centered on research psychology. Friedan was an extremely well-educated woman with some journalism experience who had written a best-selling book describing a problem. Only after its publication was she drawn into political and social activism.

From the beginning, Friedan was intolerant of organizational detail and planning. Ideologically, she was a liberal pragmatist who had arrived at her controversial conclusions about women's lives through analysis of her own life and the lives of similarly placed women as revealed by a survey of fellow Smith College alumnae. What Friedan wanted for herself and other women was full participation in the American public arena. As long as NOW remained focused on goals related to fuller participation for women in the political and economic system, she was satisfied. But when the infusion of younger, more radical women into the organization in the late 1960s brought with it a tendency to dwell on male oppression and female self-expression, particularly lesbian sexuality, combined with a basic questioning of the existing social system, Friedan grew uneasy.

Actually, for most of the 1970s NOW was an umbrella organization able to contain within its ranks radical and liberal members, younger and older women. Although its rhetoric was sometimes heated—in the late 1970s NOW declared itself to be out of the mainstream and into the "Revolution"—most of its policies and strategies remained compatible with the original aims of liberal feminism.

This perspective on NOW and Friedan is much more easily arrived at from a distance. It also fails to take into account the possibility that Friedan was at least partially correct in her opinion that NOW, by openly discussing and dwelling on issues like lesbianism, did hurt the women's movement in the 1970s, narrowing its appeal and opening it to media ridicule and criticism. Although NOW did increase its membership in the 1970s and did win some significant victories, the organization and the women's movement as a whole suffered some real setbacks. The most notable defeat was the failure to secure ratification of the ERA. In assessing that defeat, it is very possible to accept an analysis that lends credence to Friedan's fears about the impact of feminists' attack on such institutions as the family. In many ways, campaigners for the ERA were not able to separate support of the amendment from the rhetoric of the women's movement nor to differentiate it from such controversial issues as lesbianism. Thus, negative public images of feminists and their attacks on traditional family life and conventional sexual arrangements and morality in the end helped defeat the ERA. Friedan made much the same observation when she stated: "The sexual politics that distorted the sense of priorities of the women's movement during the 1970s made it easy for the so-called Moral Majority to lump ERA with homosexual rights and abortion into one explosive package of licentious family threatening sex."[15]

The beginning of the 1980s presented a confused picture of progress and retreat. On the one hand, female participation in the workforce reached 51.5 percent of all adult women working, including 45 percent of women with children under the age of six. Twenty-five percent of medical school graduates were female, as were 30 percent of law graduates. The percentage of women office-holders on both the national and local level had more than doubled, and in 1984 the Democratic party nominated a woman for the vice presidency. On the other hand, Ronald Reagan had been easily elected president on an antiabortion, anti-ERA platform, and the organized antifeminist movements were attracting millions. For example, the antiabortion National Right to Life Committee claimed 11 million members. (NOW, at its height in the early 1980s, had 220,000 members.) One possible interpretation of these realities was that American women wanted to work outside the home or were forced to do so for economic reasons, but outside employment, even in a professional career, did not necessarily mean a commitment to a feminist agenda. Another possibility was that employment was creating, as well as solving, problems for American women.

Friedan, who now criticized feminists for creating a new "feminist mystique" just as damaging as the old "feminine mystique," responded to these changing realities in her book *The Second Stage* (1981). First, she described what she saw as the problem: "What worries me is 'choices' women supposedly have, which are not real. How can a woman 'choose' to have a child when her paycheck is needed for the rent or mortgage, when her job isn't geared to taking care of a child, when there is no national policy for parental leave, and no assurance that her job will be waiting for her if she takes off to have a child?" Then she stated her belief that solutions to these problems could come only when feminists and all women admit that they have dual needs: the first, a need for "power, identity, status and security" through work, and the second, a need "for love and identity, status, security and generation through marriage, children, home, the family." Friedan labeled as reactionary those feminists who denied the female need to love and nurture, which she viewed as usually expressed through family life. She saw a need for personal accommodations and national policies that acknowledged the realities of motherhood.[16] Although Friedan's concerns distanced her still further from NOW, they were reflected in the works of other respected commentators such as economist Sylvia Hewlett (*A Lesser Life*), sociologist Arlie Hochschild (*Second Shift*), and philosopher Jean Bethke Elshtain (*Public Man, Private Woman*).

NOW's reluctance to accept this new family-oriented definition of feminism was symbolized by its position on *California Federal Savings and Loan Ass'n. v. Guerra* in 1986. In this case NOW, sticking to its position of gender-blind equality, argued against maternity leave on the grounds that such benefits should be extended to all workers and that limiting maternity leave to women unfairly favored women over men. Friedan disagreed, pointing out that "there has to be a concept of equality that takes into account that women are the ones who have the babies."[17]

Another point of friction between Friedan and the organized women's movement in the 1980s was the fight against pornography. Whereas many feminist groups, including NOW, supported legislation prohibiting pornography as a form of sex discrimination and a violation of civil rights, Friedan saw the concern as irrelevant to most women and expressed the civil libertarian view that laws prohibiting explicitly sexual material were, in the words of a former NOW leader and lawyer, "far more dangerous to women than the most obscene pornography."[18]

Aside from such criticisms and comments, Friedan shifted direction in the 1980s to concentrate on the research and writing of a new book on aging. Meanwhile, NOW struggled throughout the decade to find effective leadership, defining issues, and attractive strategies. Judy Goldsmith succeeded the charismatic Eleanor Smeal in 1982 and was blamed for the fact that during her term of office membership fell to 185,000 and debt exceeded $1 million. Smeal returned to head NOW in the mid 1980s and promptly became involved in a very public fight with the Catholic Church (Smeal was a Catholic) over birth control, abortion, and women in the priesthood. Her successor, Molly Yard, angered many feminist groups by calling for a third political party devoted to feminist issues. Members of the NWPC and the National Abortion Rights Action League were quoted as calling the idea "silly" and "narrowing."[19]

In the 1990s, Betty Friedan and NOW are no longer connected, except, perhaps, in the public mind. Friedan immersed herself in a new role as an advocate for innovative approaches to aging. Her book *The Fountain of Age* (1993) was a conscious effort to transfer her basic insight about the lives of women in the 1960s—that the culture was not describing or confronting women's problems and potentialities with any degree of accuracy—to a discussion of old age in late twentieth-century America. In much the same way that she searched for new roles and patterns for women, Friedan now looked for creative possibilities in love, work, and play for older Americans.

Meanwhile, NOW continued its tradition of public controversy accompanied by assiduous lobbying for particular pieces of legislation, such as public funding of abortions. Both Friedan and NOW members still viewed themselves as feminists, and in their similarities and differences demonstrated the depth and diversity of the movement. But in the mid-1990s their contributions and activities were being supplemented and occasionally challenged by an inchoate movement labeled Feminism's Daughters. These women, mostly under thirty years of age and many literally the daughters of 1960s activists, were introducing new issues and new perceptions. They appeared to be interested in causes ranging from eliminating harassment in the workplace to ending women's poverty. Although she disagreed with some of their specific approaches, Friedan realized the historical import of the continuing movement, saying in 1993 that "Young Women are true daughters of feminism; they take nothing for granted and are advancing the cause with marvelous verve. If they keep doing what they're doing, 30 years from today we may not need a feminist movement. We may have achieved real equality."[20]

Future historians, assessing the significance of Betty Friedan, NOW, and the many changes that took place in women's lives between the early 1960s and the 1990s, will have to consider some provocative questions. First, how important was the organized women's movement in enabling women to break down barriers to their educational and occupational advancement? Was the women's movement really "responsible" for later age at marriage, increased female participation in the workforce, and a declining birth rate—or did those developments cause the women's movement? Were the disputes between Friedan and NOW basically the result of personal animosities, or did they reveal deep, continuing fissures within the feminist movement? Also, how does one define and describe a "movement" that at certain times and on various issues involved literally millions of women and at other points attracted the support of only a handful of activists? These are all important questions that should be explored and answered. Yet there is a certain simplicity and truth in Friedan's statement that for her, and countless other women, "it [the movement] changed my life."

NOTES

1. Betty Friedan, *It Changed My Life* (New York, 1976), 75–91.
2. Ibid., 87.
3. Ibid., 90.
4. Jo Freeman, *The Politics of Women's Liberation* (New York, 1975), xi.
5. Friedan, *It Changed My Life*, 106.
6. Ibid., 109.
7. Ibid., 142.
8. Ibid., 155.
9. Ibid., 140–141.
10. Ibid., 175.
11. Ibid., 245.
12. Ibid., 258.
13. Ibid., 325.
14. Ibid., 324.
15. Friedan, quoted in *Current Biography Yearbook* (New York, 1989), 190.
16. Betty Friedan, *The Second Stage* (New York, 1981), 23, 95.
17. Friedan, quoted in *Current Biography Yearbook*, 191.
18. Betty Friedan, "How to Get the Women's Movement Moving Again," *New York Times Magazine*, 3 November 1985, p. 28.
19. "Taking Issue with NOW," *Newsweek* 114 (14 August 1989): 21.
20. "Feminism's Daughters," *U.S. News and World Report* 115 (27 September 1993): 71.

BIBLIOGRAPHY

Atkinson, Ti-Grace. *Amazon Odyssey*. New York, 1974.
"Betty Friedan." In *Current Biography Yearbook*, 188–192. New York, 1989.
Blow, Richard. "Don't Look NOW," *New Republic*, 11 April 1988, pp. 11–12.
Bunch, Charlotte. *Passionate Politics*. New York, 1986.
Carden, Maron Lockwood. *The New Feminist Movement*. New York, 1974.

Cassell, Joan. *A Group Called Women: Sisterhood and Symbolism in the Feminist Movement.* New York, 1977.

Elshtain, Jean Bethke. *Public Man, Private Woman.* Princeton, 1981.

Evans, Sara. *Personal Politics: The Role of Women's Liberation in the Civil Rights Movement and the New Left.* New York, 1979.

———. *Born for Liberty: A History of Women in America.* New York, 1989.

"Feminism's Daughters." *U.S. News and World Report* 115 (27 September 1993): 68–71.

Ferree, Myra, and Beth Hess. *Controversy and Coalition: The New Feminist Movement.* Boston, 1985.

Filene, Peter G. *Him/Her Self: Sex Roles in Modern America.* Baltimore, 1974.

Freeman, Jo. *The Politics of Women's Liberation.* New York, 1975.

Friedan, Betty. *The Feminine Mystique.* New York, 1963.

———. *It Changed My Life.* New York, 1976.

———. *The Second Stage.* New York, 1981.

———. "How to Get the Women's Movement Moving Again." *New York Times Magazine,* 3 November 1985, pp. 26–28, 66–67, 84–89, 98 106, 108.

———. *The Fountain of Age.* New York, 1993.

Gelb, Jean, and Marion Lief. *Women and Public Policy.* Princeton, 1982.

Hewlett, Sylvia. *A Lesser Life.* New York, 1986.

Hochschild, Arlie. *The Second Shift.* New York, 1989.

Hoff-Wilson, Joan, ed. *Rights of Passage: The Past and Future of the ERA.* Bloomington, Ind., 1986.

Klein, Ethel. *Gender Politics.* Cambridge, Mass., 1984.

Kopkind, Andrew. "NOW Redux." *Nation* 245 (August 1987): 76–77.

Mansbridge, Jane. *Why We Lost the ERA.* Chicago, 1986.

Rosenberg, Rosalind. *Divided Lives: American Women in the Twentieth Century.* New York, 1992.

Rupp, Leila J., and Verta Taylor. *Survival in the Doldrums: The American Women's Rights Movement, 1945 to the 1960's.* New York, 1987.

"Taking Issue with NOW." *Newsweek* 114 (14 August 1989): 21.

Wandersee, Winifred D. *On the Move: American Women in the 1970's.* Boston, 1988.

Wickenden, Dorothy. "What NOW?" *New Republic* 194 (5 May 1986): 19–25.

Index

Abolitionism, 33, 34, 35, 37; African Americans and, 19–20, 22–25, 28–30; Mary Ann Shadd Cary and, 19–20, 28–30, 33, 34–35; women's rights and, 12, 15, 25–27, 31–33, 37, 43, 46–48, 51. *See also* Antislavery movement

Abortion: NOW and, 155, 156–57, 160; opposition to, 126–27, 161–62

Abzug, Bella, 158–59

Addams, Jane, 104, 109; concept of the settlement house, 86, 91–92, 94–95, 96; life, 86–87, 95; the peace movement and, 95–96; role in the settlement house movement, 85, 88, 91, 94, 96–97

African Americans: reforms to benefit, 22–24, 29–33, 37, 114; the birth control movement and, 134; educational reformers and, 24–25, 27, 30–31; Ida Wells-Barnett and, 99–110, 118; Jessie Daniel Ames and, 114, 115–18, 121–22; Mary Ann Shadd Cary and, 19, 24–25, 29–33, 36; the NAACP and, 108, 109, 118; Reconstruction, 36–38, 48–50, 100; settlement houses and, 88, 89, 90, 95, 110. *See also* Abolitionism; Antislavery movement; Racial justice; *and names of specific reformers*

African Methodist Episcopal Church, 27, 30, 102, 105

American Colonization Society, 24, 29, 35

Ames, Jessie Daniel, the anti-lynching campaign and, 110, 113, 115–18, 121–22; life, 114–15, 123

Anthony, Susan B., 42, 45, 48, 104, 109

Anti-lynching campaign. *See* Lynching

Antinuclear activism, 149

Antislavery movement, 11, 12–13, 20; women's rights and, 11–13, 15, 25–27, 31–32, 43–44, 46–48. *See also* Abolitionism

Antiwar activism: during the Vietnam era, 150, 155; during World War I, 96, 141. *See also* Pacifism; Peace movement

Association of Southern Women for the Prevention of Lynching, 113, 117–22

Atkinson, Ti-Grace, 156

Baptists, 117

Barrett, Janie Porter, 88

Beecher, Catharine: educational reform and, 1–11, 14–15; ideology of domesticity, 1–4, 9–10, 12–13, 16, 61; life, 1–2, 4–7, 10–11, 14, 16

Stanton and, 43, 48–51; Ida Wells-
Barnett and, 110; Mary Ann Shadd
Cary and, 37–38; the temperance
movement and, 50, 75–76
Women's International League for Peace
and Freedom, 95–96
Women's rights, 41, 45; African Ameri-
cans and, 25–28, 32, 109; the antislav-
ery movement and, 11–13, 15, 25–27,
31–32, 43–44, 46–48; Catharine
Beecher and, 1–3, 9–10, 12–14, 16;
Dorothea Dix and, 61–62; Elizabeth

Cady Stanton and, 15, 41–49; Mary
Ann Shadd Cary and, 25–27, 31–33,
37–38; post-1960, 154, 157–58; school
reform and, 2–3, 6–8; temperance reform and, 74, 78. *See also* Feminism;
NOW; Woman suffrage
Workers, reforms to benefit: Dorothy Day
and, 140–42, 144–46; Frances Willard
and, 76–77; Margaret Sanger and, 127,
130; the settlement house movement
and, 91, 92, 94–95; women and, 154,
155–56, 158, 160

About the Editors and Contributors

EDITORS

PAUL A. CIMBALA is Associate Professor of History at Fordham University in New York City. He has published several articles on slavery and Reconstruction and was an editor of *The Black Abolitionist Papers: Canada, 1830–1865* (1986). He is also the author of the forthcoming book, *The Freedmen's Bureau and the Reconstruction of Georgia*.

RANDALL M. MILLER is Professor of History and Director of American Studies at Saint Joseph's University, Philadelphia. He has published sixteen books, including the award-winning *"Dear Master": Letters of a Slave Family* (1978; rev. and enl. 1990) and (with John David Smith) the award-winning *Dictionary of Afro-American Slavery* (Greenwood, 1988; enl. 1997). His latest book (with Linda Patterson Miller) is *The Book of American Diaries* (1995).

CONTRIBUTORS

KATHLEEN C. BERKELEY is Professor of History at the University of North Carolina at Wilmington.

ELLEN CHESLER is a fellow at the Twentieth Century Fund in New York City.

ANN D. GORDON is Editor of the Elizabeth Cady Stanton and Susan B. Anthony Papers project at Rutgers University.

ANNE KLEJMENT is Associate Professor of History at the University of St. Thomas, Minnesota.

LOUISE W. KNIGHT is an independent researcher and biographer of Jane Addams who also teaches at Spertus College.

ELISABETH LASCH-QUINN is Assistant Professor of History at Syracuse University.

BARBARA MCGOWAN is Professor of History at Ripon College.

LINDA O. MCMURRY is Professor of History at North Carolina State University.

ROBERT F. MARTIN is Professor of History at the University of Northern Iowa.

IAN R. TYRRELL is Senior Lecturer in History at the University of New South Wales, Sydney, Australia.